The Economics of Water Scarcity in the Middle East and North Africa

The Economics of Water Scarcity in the Middle East and North Africa

Institutional Solutions

Dominick de Waal, Stuti Khemani,
Andrea Barone, Edoardo Borgomeo

Contents

PART I THE STATUS QUO INSTITUTIONS THAT ALLOCATE WATER

MAPS

TABLES

Foreword

The long-standing challenge of water in the Middle East and North Africa (MENA) has become even more urgent as the wide-ranging impacts of climate change unfold. With current water management strategies across MENA, a conservative estimate of water demand in 2050 points to the need for an additional 25 billion cubic meters a year. Satisfying this demand would equate to building another 65 desalination plants the size of the Ras Al Khair plant in Saudi Arabia—currently the largest in the world.

To meet that twenty-first century challenge, this bold report goes where we have rarely gone before by explicitly acknowledging the politics that make it difficult for leaders to pursue policies to sustainably manage scarce water resources. What's clear from this report is that the region can no longer rely on a strategy of investing in water infrastructure to increase its supply for agriculture and cities, without also making systematic institutional reforms to finance and maintain that infrastructure and regulate the demand side. Across all MENA countries only two water utilities were able to cover their expenditure on operation and maintenance, let alone their capital costs.

The Economics of Water Scarcity in MENA: Institutional Solutions identifies promising institutional reforms to tackle the political challenges of pricing water, improving the performance of water utilities, and allocating water between agriculture and cities. These reforms involve delegation of greater autonomy and policy powers to manage different aspects of water services and allocation: to professional utilities and national-level technical agencies on the one hand and to local governments on the other hand. Together, these reforms are envisioned to *build legitimacy* for pricing and regulating water, so that citizens start owning these policies, thus making them sustainable and durable. The reforms hold potential to *build trust* in government agencies to deliver reliable water services, reduce waste and leakages, and generate sufficient revenues to attract long-term financing for long-lived water infrastructure.

Managing the existential issue of water in MENA is not only about the political will of a few leaders at the top of the hierarchy. It is also about changing the beliefs and expectations of people down the chain of authority in myriad government agencies that manage water services and allocation, all the way to the citizens living in rural and urban communities. To change these beliefs and expectations, we need to understand them, and design institutional reforms accordingly. Thus, outreach campaigns, transparent decision-making, and civic education become a significant part of the reforms program.

For example, outreach with citizens will uncover which types of water tariff structures may resonate with ideas of fairness, such as by ensuring affordability of a minimum basic amount needed for life. Data on incentives and norms among utility managers and staff will help utilities design contracts that improve performance by building trust that each person is working to improve utility performance. Strengthening the capacity of local government leaders will help them work with and support citizens through the difficult challenges of managing water allocation between agriculture and cities.

Using rigorous data-driven evidence, different countries can tailor institutional reforms to their own socio-political contexts. These reforms would seek to empower utility staff and local government leaders to manage different aspects of water by building trust with the citizens they serve. Institutional reforms in the critical sector of water can be potentially transformative, not only by shifting how the state functions in devising and implementing water policies but also, more broadly, by changing the social contract in MENA.

Ferid Belhaj
Vice President for the Middle East and North Africa
The World Bank

Main Messages

- The Middle East and North Africa (MENA) region faces *unprecedented water scarcity,* both for life and to sustain livelihoods. *Farmers and cities* are competing for water, which is stretching water systems to the brink of collapse.
  - By 2030, the water available per capita annually in MENA *will fall below the absolute water scarcity threshold* of 500 cubic meters per person per year.[1]
  - Water scarcity will become even more acute as the population grows. The region's population grew from just over 100 million people in 1960 to more than 450 million in 2018. It is estimated to reach more than 720 million by 2050.
  - With current water management strategies, a conservative estimate of water demand in 2050 is that an additional 25 billion cubic meters a year will be needed, equivalent to building 65 desalination plants the size of the Ras Al Khair plant in Saudi Arabia—currently the largest in the world.
  - Without action, water shortages will have *a detrimental impact on livelihoods and agricultural output* and may *raise tensions among users*.
- MENA has tackled water scarcity by exploiting multiple ways to increase water supply (building more dams, tapping into groundwater, and increasing desalination) without adequately addressing critical efficiency and governance issues. This is *fiscally and environmentally unsustainable*.
  - There has been *little focus on reducing water losses* and introducing efficiency measures that would conserve water. For example, half of the utility service providers reported that more than 30 percent of the water they produce is not billed to customers due to a combination of leaky pipes, inaccurate water meters, and illegal connections.
  - Unsustainable withdrawal of groundwater has enabled policy makers to *delay tackling water management and services reforms*. Unsustainable withdrawals of water and increasing brine discharges from desalination are degrading marine ecosystems.
  - MENA has relied increasingly on *imports of virtual water*—water used to produce commodities such as cereals—which doubled between 1998 and 2010. Reliance on virtual water imports exposes countries to supply shocks, such as the recent war in Ukraine.
  - Existing *institutions* that manage the allocation of water across competing needs—particularly between agriculture and cities—are *highly centralized and technocratic*—which limits their ability to resolve trade-offs in water use at the local level.
  - Reforms are needed to *increase autonomy and decentralize decisions* about water management and service delivery.
- The report identifies a series of *institutional policy reforms* for national water agencies and utilities and proposes *delegating decision making over water allocations* to locally representative governments, which would help the region tackle and overcome water distress.
  - The report addresses two crucial challenges: *lack of legitimacy* and *trust*. Evidence from the World Values Survey shows that people in the region believe that a key role of government is to keep prices down and that governments are reluctant to raise tariffs due to the risk of widespread protests.

- *Devolving greater powers over water allocation decisions* to locally representative governments, within a national water strategy, could *lend legitimacy* to difficult trade-offs in the use of water, compared to top-down directives from central ministries.
- Giving greater autonomy to utilities to reach out to customers on tariff changes could also win greater compliance with tariff structures, *lowering the risk of protests and public unrest*.
- Management reforms in utilities could help to *build trust* in government agencies to manage long-term financing for water infrastructure, by delivering reliable services, reducing waste and leakages, and generating revenues to service long-term debt.
- For institutional reforms to succeed, there must be *better communications* around water scarcity and national water strategies. In countries such as Brazil and South Africa, strategic communication efforts complemented reforms to reduce water use. For example, in Cape Town, the city shared a "water dashboard," which gave weekly updates on total water usage in the city as it approached "Day Zero" (when water was set to run out). Such transparency by a locally elected representative city government persuaded residents of the urgency and made them more likely to comply with restrictions.
- In sum, these *institutional reforms* could help governments to *renegotiate the social contract* with the people of MENA. Instead of "top-down" directives to price and regulate water use, greater delegation to technical water resource management agencies, utilities, and local governments could build the legitimacy of and trust in the state to manage water scarcity.

NOTE

1. As defined by Falkenmark, Lundqvist, and Widstrand (1989).

REFERENCE

Falkenmark, M., J. Lundqvist, and C. Widstrand. 1989. "Macro-Scale Water Scarcity Requires Micro-Scale Approaches." *Natural Resources Forum* 13: 258–67. https://doi.org/10.1111/j.1477-8947.1989.tb00348.x.

Acknowledgments

The authors are grateful for contributions from Rajesh Advani, Elvira Broeks Motta, Luke Gates, Mohamad Mahgoub Hamid, Amal Talbi, Mili Varughese, and Sally Zgheib (World Bank), as well as for background inputs from Sophie Erfurth, Dustin Garrick, Hussam Hussein, and Isabel Jorgensen (University of Oxford), and Adrian Cabas and Ricardo Garcia Leandro (International Technical Assistance Consultants).

We would also like to thank the peer reviewers at the concept stage, Richard Damania, Quy-Toan Do, and Irina Klytchnikova (World Bank), and the peer reviewers at the decision stage, Quy-Toan Do, Irina Klytchnikova, Fan Zhang (World Bank), and Shanta Devarajan (Georgetown University).

Additional advice and guidance were provided by Richard Abdulnour, Amat Ali, Mohamed Al-Soswa, Oliver Braedt, Eileen Burke, Nabil Chaherli, Roberta Gatti, Nancy Gracia, Michael Haney, Daniel Lederman, Lamia Mansour, Carmen Nonay, Gustavo Saltiel, Jenifer Sara, Ayat Soliman, Pieter Waalewijn, and Sally Zgheib (World Bank), Hassan Benabderrazik (Economist, Former General Secretary of the Moroccan Ministry of Agriculture and the Ministry of Economic Affairs), Namrata Kala (MIT Sloan School of Management), Hamid Mohtadi (University of Wisconsin/Minnesota), Will Rafey (UCLA), and Rajiv Sethi (Barnard College and Columbia University).

This publication received the support of the Global Water Security & Sanitation Partnership (GWSP). GWSP is a multidonor trust fund administered by the World Bank's Water Global Practice and supported by Australia's Department of Foreign Affairs and Trade, Austria's Federal Ministry of Finance, the Bill & Melinda Gates Foundation, Denmark's Ministry of Foreign Affairs, the Netherlands' Ministry of Foreign Affairs, Spain's Ministry of Economic Affairs and Digital Transformation, the Swedish International Development Cooperation Agency, Switzerland's State Secretariat for Economic Affairs, the Swiss Agency for Development and Cooperation, and the U.S. Agency for International Development.

About the Authors

Andrea Barone is a senior economist in the World Bank's Digital Development Global Practice. He is an industrial economist with nearly 20 years of experience in applying economic tools to gain insights on market dynamics and outcomes. Previously, he was a senior consultant in the Chief Economist's Office of the World Bank's Middle East and North Africa (MENA) region, where he advised on infrastructure regulatory reform, competition policy, and promotion of the digital economy. Earlier in his career, he was an economist at the Italian Competition Authority, where he carried out antitrust investigations, merger control analyses, and market studies in various sectors. His research focuses on applied industrial organization, competition policy, regulation, and microeconometrics. He holds an MSc in Economics from the London School of Economics and Political Science and a PhD in Economics from the European University Institute.

Edoardo Borgomeo is a water resources management specialist in the World Bank's Water Global Practice. His work focuses on water resources management, climate change adaptation, and infrastructure planning. In his current assignment, he leads analytical and advisory activities on water security and transboundary water management and works on water sector projects in Africa and Central Asia. Prior to joining the World Bank, he worked at the Food and Agriculture Organization of the United Nations in Rome and at the International Water Management Institute in Sri Lanka. He has held research appointments at the European University Institute, University of Oxford, International Institute for Applied System Analysis, and Imaflora. In 2018, he was awarded the Prince Sultan bin Abdulaziz International Prize for Water for his research work on water resources planning in times of climate change. He holds an undergraduate degree from Imperial College London and a PhD on climate change adaptation in the water sector from the University of Oxford.

Dominick de Waal is a senior economist working with the World Bank's Water Global Practice. He has worked in the Africa and MENA regions leading country and regional reports on water sector financing and performance, including financial modeling of the Jordanian water sector, a regional report for the African Ministers' Council on Water, and this report on the economics of water scarcity in MENA. He has managed lending operations for water sector infrastructure and reform, spearheading an expansion of World Bank water sector lending in fragile states across Africa and the Middle East. Most recently he has been working on Country Climate and Development Reports, helping countries better align their development visions with climate action. He holds an MSc in Public Policy and Management, University of London, SOAS; an MSc in Tropical Horticulture and Crop Science, University of London, Wye College; and an MSc in Microbiology from the University of Warwick.

Stuti Khemani is a senior economist in the World Bank's Development Research Group. Her research on the political economy of public policy choices and the role of institutions in economic development has been published in leading economics and political science journals. She is the lead author of *Making Politics Work for Development: Harnessing Transparency and Citizen Engagement* in the Policy Research Report Series. She is currently examining how the role of government has resurged in the

21st century to address problems such as climate change, water scarcity, public health, conflict, and (lack of) fairness in economic systems, which fuels social unrest. She applies economic theory to develop innovative policy ideas for how to strengthen state capacity to address these problems and build trust and legitimacy in society. Her research and advisory work span a diverse range of countries, including Benin, China, India, Nigeria, the Philippines, Tanzania, and Uganda. She holds a BA in economics and mathematics from Mount Holyoke College and a PhD in economics from the Massachusetts Institute of Technology.

Executive Summary

The Middle East and North Africa (MENA) region is facing an acute lack of water for life and livelihoods. Despite significant infrastructure investments over the past decades, countries in the region are grappling with unprecedented, ever-worsening water scarcity due to population growth, climate change, and socioeconomic development. The region has seen its population grow from just over 100 million people in 1960 to more than 450 million in 2018, with the medium forecasts of population in 2050 estimated at more than 720 million. By 2030, average annual per capita water resource availability across MENA will fall below the absolute water scarcity threshold of 500 cubic meters per person per year.[1] Underlying this average, the MENA region is made up of a highly diverse range of countries in terms of both economic and hydrological contexts. Economic circumstances have shaped water use, and water availability has shaped economies.

The old water scarce countries—those below the absolute water scarcity threshold—are the more urbanized countries in the region, with lower per capita water withdrawals as they are less reliant on water intensive rural livelihoods. However, as a result, most are heavily reliant on cereal imports for over 80 percent of their needs. The *high-income countries* in this group have spent heavily on nonconventional water (desalination and wastewater reuse), with the aim of "decoupling" their water needs from the ecological limits of renewable water resource endowments. The *middle-income countries* in this group have started to invest in nonconventional water and are beginning to see the fiscal implications of desalinating water, transferring it to demand centers, and then treating wastewater for agricultural use. The *fragile countries* in this group rely heavily on aid for supply-side infrastructure and for operation and maintenance of water and sewer systems.

The new water scarce countries in the region—those above the absolute water scarcity threshold of 500 cubic meters per person per year—are middle-income countries. Five countries in this group—Iraq, the Syrian Arab Republic, the Arab Republic of Egypt, the Islamic Republic of Iran, and Morocco—have sizable agrarian populations and are home to over 70 percent of the region's rural population. They grow over half the amount of cereal they need and are self-sufficient in fruits and vegetables. However, their populations are growing rapidly, and increasing the supply of nonconventional water is an emerging area of policy debate and investment.

A common long-term trend across the diversity of countries in the region is that greater emphasis has been put on increasing the supply of water rather than managing demand. This established the widespread belief in societies across the region that the problem of water scarcity is driven by supply-side constraints. Increasing the supply of water, without equal emphasis on demand-side measures, has led both water utilities and irrigated agriculture across MENA to undervalue water and thus underinvest in reducing water losses and other efficiency measures. Half of the utility service providers for which data were collected reported that more than 30 percent of the water they produce is not billed to customers due to a combination of physical and other losses.[2]

Countries have also relied on rising levels of virtual water imports, including imports of cereals, and are resorting to unsustainable water withdrawals. Virtual water imports across MENA—the water embodied in the production of agricultural commodities—doubled between 1998 and 2010. Relying on these rising levels of virtual water imports along with unsustainable withdrawals of groundwater has enabled policy makers in the region to delay tackling water management and water services reforms.

Whole communities of farmers are seeing water sources, on which they have relied for their livelihoods for generations, rapidly deteriorating or disappearing. From time to time, urban residents have turned to the streets to demand basic services, while water utilities are unable to cover the costs of operations and raise the financing needed to improve water and sanitation services.

Policy regimes for managing water allocation across competing needs are entirely determined by state ownership of large water infrastructure. Despite the water scarcity faced in the region, water markets have not emerged.[3] Agriculture, industry (oil in particular), and water supply and sanitation (WSS) compete for access to water controlled by the state in the absence of market mechanisms. The current policy regimes for managing the allocation of water both within agriculture as well as across sectors are unsustainable because the availability of water as a resource is being outstripped by its consumption.

This report confronts the persistence and severity of the problem of water in MENA and calls for new thinking and insights into resolving the institutional challenges faced by applying the tools of public economics—going beyond the standard economic tools of market-based competition. The state, and its institutions of government, has a key role to play in the allocation of water across agriculture and cities, regulation of utilities, and management of water as a scarce resource. The report provides policy ideas for how to organize and manage a variety of government agencies that are tasked with playing these inescapable roles of the state in managing and allocating water. These policy ideas address two crucial challenges facing states in MENA: lack of *legitimacy* and *trust*. The report shows how the economics of government (the public sector) can be used to clarify what legitimacy and trust are in the context of the problem of water in MENA, and how policies can be designed to bolster legitimacy and build trust not only to tackle immediate issues in the water sector, but also for broader economic transformation.[4]

Legitimacy, as used in economic theory and in this report, is the ability of the state, or its leaders, to win voluntary compliance with laws or public orders, such as restrictions on the quantity of water that can be used, or the tariff that needs to be paid to cover the costs of delivering water services.[5] States across MENA have tried to manage scarce water resources by regulating the amount of water that can be abstracted, for example in agriculture, but these regulations are difficult to enforce. Case studies of groundwater use in Morocco, for example, describe how farmers regularly disregard public regulations because they do not believe the state should restrict their use of water, and they believe none of their neighbors in the community are following the rules. In Jordan, there are examples of water regulation officials being driven out of villages when they tried to close illegal wells.[6] Even if governments can enforce compliance by using the coercive power of the state, widespread lack of legitimacy is a threat to stability and can inhibit government policy makers from taking necessary but difficult (because they imply loss of livelihoods for farmers, for example) decisions over the management of water.

Trust consists of beliefs or expectations among people about whether others are behaving in cooperative ways for mutually beneficial outcomes, versus the opposite—noncooperative ways where each person's actions result in losses on all sides. For example, corruption is a manifestation of lack of trust. If people believe that others are likely to be extracting rents in the public sector (low trust that others are behaving honestly), they may be more likely to behave in the same way, although most people know that corruption is bad for society. Trust can be examined in the water sector as the core of why utility reforms are so difficult—whether it is reforming tariffs to cover utility operating costs, reducing water leakages and wastage (nonrevenue water), or attracting long-term financing to build infrastructure. If utility staff do not trust that their peers are performing their tasks professionally, such as by holding up decisions or not completing their assigned tasks on time or effectively, then they are arguably more likely to behave the same way, yielding outcomes of poor utility performance. For example, in Jordan, citizens do not trust that increasing tariffs will lead to improvements in service delivery. In Jordan and many other countries, citizens protest proposed tariff increases, and in areas where services are unreliable, people do not to pay their bills, contributing to the vicious cycle of low-performing, financially stressed utilities.

These seemingly abstract concepts of legitimacy and trust have real implications for the most pressing economic questions facing not only MENA's leaders, but also global financial markets. For example, why is global capital "frozen" and not flowing to finance much-needed, long-lived infrastructure for water in MENA? Global capital is not flowing sufficiently to finance water infrastructure in MENA because investors are not assured of recouping steady returns. Returns to capital are risky because available evidence suggests that the infrastructure that would be financed is not well managed for cost efficiency and revenue-raising potential. Attracting private investment, while representing citizens' interests in the face of monopoly power, requires a legitimate or credible policy environment and trusted and creditworthy state agencies. But political conditions in the region are such that global markets worry about policy legitimacy, lack of transparency, and creditworthiness. Of the 45 WSS utilities for which data were collected for this report, only five published their audited financial statements online and only two had credit ratings with the global agencies.

Evidence from the World Values Survey shows that people in MENA believe that a key role of government should be to keep prices down. There is widespread concern about governments "raising prices" and states in MENA facing protests following tariff increases.[7] This explains why governments are reluctant to raise tariffs because of the risk of widespread protests and political instability. Instead of avoiding this problem as "politically sensitive," this report argues that reform leaders and their external partners can tackle the problem through a combination of policy instruments that takes seriously the role of the beliefs and expectations that underpin the concepts of legitimacy and trust. The report tackles the policy question of what can be done to transition from a situation where lack of legitimacy and trust is preventing the state from effectively managing problems of water, and connected issues of economic transformation, to better outcomes. The following broad contours of policy ideas are sketched and may be applied and developed in specific country contexts:

- Trusted and creditworthy WSS utilities may be built through complementary reforms of incentives and management. Growing evidence suggests that giving greater autonomy to staff managing complex organizations, for example, to frontline teams reducing water losses, can improve organizational outcomes. Communication is a key complement to strengthen professional norms and peer pressure for better performance within organizations. For example, at the opening stage of Uganda's National Water and Sewer Company reforms in 2000, the chief executive officer actively encouraged staff to decide themselves what needed to be done and be accountable for whatever they agreed to do. This set the scene for reforms in which teams planned and competed for internally delegated area management contracts.[8]
- The revenue-raising potential of the state can be strengthened through communication and outreach to citizens. For example, in Cambodia, the water supply authority undertook a survey of customers to understand their willingness to pay for improved water services. It used the information from these surveys to increase tariffs successfully without public protest. The economic insights in this report suggest that there is considerable scope for public consultation if redesigned tariff structures address equity and justice considerations, with a special role for local leaders in this process. Available survey evidence from MENA suggests that citizens may have greater willingness to finance utilities through general taxation.
- An especially difficult area is trade-offs in the allocation of scarce water across the needs of agriculture and cities. Even the most advanced market economies of the world are grappling with this, with no clear blueprint or off-the-shelf solutions. The reason this is such a difficult problem is

because market-based solutions do not readily apply. The world lacks sufficient understanding of how to design nonmarket institutions so that water use can be appropriately regulated and shared fairly across its competing needs. The report provides a way of thinking about this problem using the tools of public economics, recommending which "tasks" to assign to different types of government agents. This approach simultaneously yields ideas for strong central institutions to manage water as a resource and a role for greater decentralization and empowerment of local elected leaders. The general principles of a "cap-and-trade" policy regime are laid out for consideration, where the "property rights" over local water are assigned to local governments, and gains are envisioned as emerging from both reallocations within and trade among local government jurisdictions. These economic gains are envisioned to result from local information and trust in and legitimacy of local leaders to identify these opportunities for the reallocation of water. Once again, communication is a key complement to enable existing forms of local political contestation to move away from patronage, tribalism, or vote buying and toward issues of the public good. Growing evidence from across the world shows that the combination of local elections and local media for communication has significant potential to strengthen the performance of local government in delivering on public good policies.[9]

All the above ideas for policy reform are thus in the direction of giving greater autonomy and power over water management and allocation decisions to professionals staffing utilities or the leaders selected by communities to head local governments, accompanied by strategic communication to strengthen the incentives and performance norms of these agents.

The report anticipates that policy makers may question these ideas because they do not trust utility staff, local leaders, or the local political process through which communities select these leaders. That is, there is lack of trust in citizens and society among leaders. This is where the report draws on economic analysis of political institutions and what this analysis shows about the key role of local political contestation in the process of building legitimacy and trust. The report calls for using these ideas to embrace policy experimentation, impact evaluation, and learning from both success and failure. The region needs new ideas to address the persistently difficult problems of water that are growing more urgent.

The report is structured as follows.

Part I sets the stage by laying out the economics of water and describing the status quo institutions that allocate water and the overall outcomes in terms of sector financing, service delivery, and environmental stress. This part of the report builds on important prior work showing how water is becoming increasingly scarce in the MENA region and how current demand trajectories are outstripping supply. Available renewable water resources are overallocated across consumptive uses (agriculture, cities, and industry). While the key drivers of water scarcity are related to demographics and economic growth, the cost of climate-related inaction is much higher in MENA than in other regions of the world. Continuing along the current path of water management and allocation could cost the region between 6 and 14 percent of gross domestic product (GDP) by 2050—compared to a global average reduction of GDP of less than 1 percent by 2050.

The data point to difficult socioeconomic trade-offs. Water withdrawals for agriculture in MENA (83 percent) are higher than the world average (70 percent), reflecting the critical role of irrigation in such an arid region. The large share of water for agriculture contrasts with agriculture's falling contribution to GDP but significant contribution to employment. Sector institutions have struggled to win the compliance of irrigators to keep water withdrawals within sustainable limits (that is, their legitimacy to do so has been challenged). Instead, faced with the ecological limits of available renewable water resources, there has been significant growth of desalination and wastewater reuse. Countries across the MENA region account for 50 percent of global desalination and 40 percent of reuse capacity.

On average, desalinated water produced with current technologies costs four to five times more than treated surface water, using 23 times as much energy.[10] Desalinated water for agricultural production is currently only possible for the high end of use cases, such as soft fruits for export; it cannot be used for the bulk of agricultural water use cases, such as staple grain production, which have low economic water productivity.[11]

In middle-income countries, nonconventional water supply-side strategies weigh heavily on public finances. These strategies are driving up the recurrent deficits of WSS utilities, as tariffs have not kept up with the higher incremental costs associated with desalination and wastewater treatment for reuse in agriculture. Creating greater synergies between water for agriculture and water for cities relies on the WSS business model for long-term sustainable financing of the water sector.[12]

In countries across the region, government leaders are worried about increasing urban water tariffs while inefficiencies in water management by utilities remain high. Despite the high level of subsidy to cover the difference between utility costs and revenue from customers, the relatively poor quality of public WSS services experienced by households drives them to supplement these with more expensive alternative sources of water, such as bottled water and tanker trucks.

Thus, although financially viable WSS business models present opportunities to develop circular uses of water, they rely on the willingness of citizens to trust that increased tariffs will translate into improved services and the benefits of locally produced food will materialize.

This part of the report also details the uniquely high level of water control infrastructure in MENA. This water control infrastructure is both from past investments—such as in dams and canals—as well as more recent investments in desalination, wastewater treatment, and bulk water transport infrastructure. Saudi Arabia has 8,400 kilometers of bulk water pipelines. Bulk water pipelines in the United Arab Emirates transport more than 4 billion cubic meters of water a year, with more than half from desalination plants and the rest from groundwater. Even middle-income countries such as Iraq, Jordan, and Morocco have multiple inter-basin transfer mechanisms and pipelines moving water from sources to demand centers. This highly "networked" nature of bulk water management may offer opportunities for *MENA-specific* ways of managing water—developed in parts II and III of the report—such as moving water around countries, and is increasingly detached from traditional river basin management models.

Part II provides an economic framework to examine the institutions and political economy of water in MENA. This part of the report provides answers to the following questions. *Why* have governments relied excessively on supply-side investments and not addressed the negative externality in the demand for water through price and quantity regulations in MENA? *Why* are utilities unable to raise the financing needed to cover their operations and investments for reliable water services in MENA? *Why* are utilities suffering from large leakages and losses of water in MENA, and why are they so difficult to address? The answers to these questions are found in an economic framework of complex organizations of the state in which strategic interactions between thousands and millions of actors, with differing powers and authority over water allocation, aggregate into outcomes or equilibria. In the economic theory of "principal-agent relationships," one type of actor, the agent, takes actions on behalf of another, the principal. This part of the report uses this theory to show how the lack of legitimacy and trust can be used to summarize the variety of water problems experienced in the region. Public policies, including for water, are selected and implemented by the state through a series of principal-agent relationships: (1) between citizens and political leaders, (2) between political leaders and public officials who lead government agencies, and (3) between public officials and frontline providers.

The strong, centralized leadership (principals at the highest levels of government) that characterizes political institutions in MENA has succeeded in getting capital expenditure–driven engineering projects done, such as: expanding dam storage capacity and irrigation infrastructure, building piped water networks, and using desalination plants and wastewater treatment plants for water reuse in agriculture. However, these centralized institutions are failing to resolve the competing demands for water within available limits, as they are not suited to addressing the task of building trust among the large variety of actors whose beliefs and behaviors affect how water is allocated and used.

Key reasons for the institutional failures covered in this report include (1) the allocation of water is not only decided by the ministries responsible for water, but also shaped by the uses and demands of many other ministries and sectors (agriculture, energy, environment, urban, and so forth); (2) within irrigated agriculture, the largest user, the tendency has been to focus on water conservation technologies, with much less emphasis on water conservation polices; (3) legal pluralism and assumed water rights related to historical use patterns challenge top-down quantity regulation; (4) the long-term financing needed to escape ecological water limits has been undermined by weak regulation of urban WSS services; and (5) the autonomy of service delivery institutions to improve performance has been constrained.

Ministries that perform the function of regulation are often reluctant to increase the price of water for household consumers or farmers, out of concern about possible protest reactions. The mere mention of water tariff increases can stir public anger.[13] In the rare instances where tariffs are increased, they are increased for industry or noncitizens or under the guise of technical modifications such as tariff unification. Line ministries are similarly reluctant to restrict the quantity of water used in agriculture due to concern about farmer unrest. Events such as the protest march by farmers in response to limited well closures by the river basin office in Souss-Massa, Morocco, in 2005, or farmers in the Abu Simbel region of Egypt holding 200 tourists hostage to protest inadequate levels of irrigation water in 2012, ring loud in the minds of policy makers.[14]

In the face of public protest, political leaders have strong incentives to back down from demand-side interventions and default to tackling the problems of water by building new supply-side infrastructure. Government leaders, from the highest levels to mid-tier and frontline officials, lack *legitimacy*, in the sense that they struggle to win citizens' compliance with increased tariffs and/or restrictions on the quantity of water consumed on the demand side.

In the MENA context of overallocation and legal plurality—customary, Islamic, and statutory law over both land and water (ground and surface) often coexist—the setting of water use limits (quantity restrictions) forces users into those who are considered legal and those who are not. Not recognizing assumed water rights makes implementation of quantity restrictions difficult for public officials and their frontline staff. Without renegotiating this aspect of the social contract, which is foundational to the citizen-state relationship, the legitimacy of imposed limits will be contested by users. Being closely linked to complex land reforms, the pathway to reforming individual water rights calls for intermediate steps that bring legitimacy to water allocation decisions through collective action mechanisms. These collective action mechanisms need to span all water users, not just agriculture, and draw on other available means of resolving trade-offs (for example, safety nets and livelihoods support) that are beyond the water sector.

The centralizing nature of the water policy framework across MENA has also constrained the regulation, financing, and autonomy of service delivery institutions. As set out in part I, the core problem across the vast majority of WSS utilities in MENA is that they are unable to cover even operation and maintenance costs, so they defer maintenance, resulting in low service quality.

Regulation has been focused on utility performance without sufficient attention paid to the capture and commitment problems of regulation. There are WSS utility regulatory agencies in only four countries across the region, and these are mainly focused on monitoring key performance indicators. In only one country is the regulatory agency in a position to regulate contracts with private service providers—to avert the regulatory "capture" problem. Most public-private partnerships (PPPs) in the water sector in MENA are regulated by contracts, the terms of which are not public. Without the contracts being in the public domain, there is potential for both regulatory capture and that the PPPs are profitable enclaves in a loss-making system and quite possibly on more favorable terms than the remaining public sector elements of the system. The regulators are also not in a position to make independent tariff determinations to resolve the regulatory "commitment" problem; it is the state's responsibility to ensure that the institutional mechanisms to recover its long-run capital costs are in place.

The autonomy of management within utilities is also constrained. Utility staff are not empowered or encouraged to explore ways of reducing losses, such as nonrevenue water, through better management of frontline staff within the organization. Recognizing that staff motivation and customers' payment morale play a key role in organizational performance, innovative projects have begun to complement infrastructure investment in building intrinsic motivation among the ranks of water sector organizations.[15,16,17] These recent interventions are based on both economic theory and empirical evidence from other sectors, which show that organization-wide performance depends on levels of *trust* that others in the system are trying to exert effort to improve performance.[18] If there are widespread beliefs that little effort is being exerted, this can lead to "bandwagon" behavior (of also engaging in rent-seeking, because everyone is doing it anyway) or demoralization and resignation (why try to improve if no one else is).

In sum, the problems of water allocation can be explained by the economic theory of principal-agent relationships as arising from the beliefs, expectations, and incentives of a large number of actors—within utilities and ministries and in society (citizens and farmers). These beliefs, expectations, and incentives can be summarized as:

- Lack of legitimacy for winning compliance with price and quantity regulations to address the negative externality in water consumption
- Lack of trust within public sector agencies that peers/others are motivated to find innovative ways of improving outcomes even within existing constraints
- Lack of trust among millions of water users (domestic or agricultural water users) that there is compliance with rules (payment for water and/or sticking to quotas).

Part III uses the framework to highlight policy principles and illuminate ways to build the legitimacy and trust needed to address the problem of water scarcity and service delivery. It offers ideas to reform leaders on how they can build trust and legitimacy through a three-pronged approach—greater delegation and autonomy to utilities and their managers, empowerment of locally elected government leaders, and strategic communication.

This part of the report argues that formal institutional reforms, such as, for example, PPPs, will not work without addressing the *informal institutions* of legitimacy and trust. Formal institutional reforms, copied from other places, can be ineffective because informal institutions have not changed. Independent of any formal reform, policy efforts to build legitimacy and trust are essential for MENA. They are the route through which societies can transition to better outcomes and attract long-term financing to invest in sustainable infrastructure for water security.

Building and maintaining water infrastructure ultimately relies on financing. In turn, whether from the internal budget, external partners, or the private sector, financing relies on the state's ability to cover costs through water tariffs plus other government revenues—addressing the regulatory "commitment" problem. Where countries cannot attract private sector financing, without substantial increases in water tariffs, they need to persuade citizens and society to contribute to state revenues through tariffs, other fiscal instruments, or a combination of the two.

Policy principles span both public and private sector solutions. Policy actions to build legitimacy and trust are foundational regardless of whether public or private solutions are pursued. Even when partnerships with the private sector are likely to yield benefits, the success of these PPPs will depend on legitimacy to reform tariffs and quotas. Reflecting the challenge for any agency—private or public—to raise sufficient revenues to cover the costs of supplying water services, Guasch et al. (2014) find that

87 percent of PPP contracts in water are renegotiated within a year, a higher rate than for other types of infrastructure (78 percent for transport contracts and 41 percent for electricity contracts).

In the absence of interest from the private sector, or when governments prefer to keep water utilities public (as Joskow (2007) and Lyon, Montgomery, and Zhao (2017) find even in the United States, an advanced market economy), management reforms can be pursued within public sector agencies to promote cost efficiency and improved service delivery. There is no evidence from rigorous research that privatization per se is necessary for these efficiency and performance gains. For example, Bel and Fageda (2009) find no robust evidence in their meta-analysis of the water and solid waste sectors in Organisation for Economic Co-operation and Development countries that privatization leads to cost efficiencies.

Furthermore, the success of a PPP depends on the government representing the interests of its citizens. One of the most celebrated cases of a PPP that improved water access, and consequently health indicators, is that of Argentina. Galiani, Gertler, and Schargrodsky (2005) find that moving from federal government–owned water utilities in Argentina to long-term concessions to private companies to operate the utilities led to lower child mortality because water service provision improved and decreased water-borne diseases. Their case study of Buenos Aires suggests that the good outcomes may have had a lot to do with good regulation—the terms of the concession stipulated that 100 percent of the households had to be connected to water service and 95 percent to sewerage service by the end of the 35-year period. It also established service quality and waste treatment standards. Getting these results was a bumpy process. The Buenos Aires water concession was subject to prompt and frequent renegotiations (Gerchunoff, Greco, and Bondorevsky 2003; Clarke, Kosec, and Wallsten 2004).

Building trust in creditworthy utilities. When reform leaders face the problem of badly performing utilities—high rates of losses, high costs, little customer outreach to improve revenues, and so forth— turning around the utility involves transforming complex organizations, often with multiple tiers of management, thousands of frontline workers, and an interface to millions of customers. For the majority of utilities that are managed in the public sector, reform options involve building professional norms and intrinsic motivation for efficient public service delivery of quality water and sanitation. It is worth experimenting with these reforms, in learning-by-doing partnerships between reformist government agencies and researchers who can help evaluate and inform the design of reforms. Options include providing greater autonomy to utility managers, to restructure incentives in ways that shift professional norms and intrinsic motivation through addressing deficits in trust among workers and legitimacy between utilities and customers. The "key performance indicators" that are typically part of the hierarchical monitoring toolkit of ministries of water can be used more innovatively for potentially transformative impact. Key performance indicators can be used to feed communication among the professionals staffing a utility, to build peer-to-peer pressure and new norms and motivation for service delivery.

Decentralizing accountability for marginal water reallocations to local political institutions under a national "cap-and-trade" regime. In the case of water, where the institution of private property rights is so fraught, due to the nature of the resource, falling back on central control does not solve the economic allocation problem. Drawing on global experience[19] and adapting it to the uniquely resource scare yet highly controlled bulk water infrastructure context of MENA, there may be innovative ways of approaching the water resource rights and allocation problem. Given the complex underlying issues of legal pluralism and assumed water rights from historical use patterns, intermediate steps that bring legitimacy to water allocation decisions through collective action mechanisms are needed before moving to a system of individual water rights. The collective action proposal put forward here is to vest the "property rights" over local water in local governments along with a "cap-and-trade" policy regime among local jurisdictions.

The principle of "cap and trade," which has been used in energy markets to address the negative externality of carbon emissions for the ambient environment, can be adapted to the common pool problem of water. However, the specifics of a "cap-and-trade" policy framework for water, proposed in this report, have distinct institutional features, chief among which is that property rights for the purpose of trading or transferring water across different uses would remain with government agencies rather than private firms as is the case in carbon trading. That is, it is important to emphasize upfront that the idea being proposed does not involve privatization of water, but rather decentralization to local governments the decisions over the marginal reallocation of water across competing uses within nationally determined water allocations.

There is an emerging precedent for this in MENA. Within the extreme water scarce context of the United Arab Emirates, each of the federated emirates has jurisdiction over its own water resources and long-term financing of the water sector. This was originally related to their federated structure, the "cap" being the requirement to manage water within their own means, which today is overseen by the Federal Ministry of Energy and Infrastructure. This requirement for each emirate to resolve the problem of reconciling the competing claims on water by agriculture and cities led to diversity in the long-term water sector financing models and cooperation (the "trade" element). Although there is still a degree of unsustainable use of groundwater, withdrawals have been falling as more is invested in reusing treated wastewater for agriculture—a growing sector since 2010. Cooperation among the emirates, the "trade" element, is seen in the way Abu Dhabi imports water from the Northern Emirates and in a series of memorandums of understanding for strategic water connections enabling the exchange of water in case of emergencies, between Dubai and Abu Dhabi as well as between Dubai and the Northern Emirates.

Generalizing and further developing this example with the proposed "cap-and-trade" approach for other countries in MENA comes from thinking about water allocation decisions as tasks assigned to different government agents within the interdependent principal-agent framework laid out in part II and within the uniquely "networked" context of bulk water management in MENA set out in part I. The key idea is to assign the responsibility and authority over different aspects of water allocation based on variation in informational advantages across agents. The principle is the same as the one being used in carbon emission abatement policies of cap and trade: that is, to enable those agents who have more information and expertise about how to reduce carbon emissions to do it in least cost ways. However, the execution of the principle—of giving decision-making power to agents according to their information advantage—would be substantially different in the case of the water sector. In water, and especially in the institutional context of MENA, the proposed policy would rely on agents within government both to devise the caps using climate and water science, and to decide whether and where to engage in trade/exchange of water with other subnational jurisdictions.

Local governments, as representatives of the communities they serve, would employ decentralized information about the relative value of water to farmers and urban residents within their jurisdiction to identify potential gains from trade. National government agencies would set science-based "caps" to which each local government would need to adhere. Aggregate "macro" calculations of the status of the water resources in a country, and the science of their sustainability, can be used to set limits, or caps, on the amounts of water that can be consumed, abstracted, and polluted by different local jurisdictions. These caps would be enshrined in a national water strategy, through which national ministries would hold local government authorities accountable for adhering to national regulations over water use. Local government authorities, in turn, would be empowered to trade with each other, using their water entitlement under the national strategy as a starting point. Local governments would be held accountable by their constituents for their performance in managing these water entitlements, including identifying opportunities for gains from trade in water between local governments.

Just as the principle of "cap and trade" was devised using the logic of economic theory, and then applied in practice to carbon abatement policies, the idea proposed above is rooted in economic logic. Just as the application of cap and trade in energy markets has resulted in both successes and failures, depending on a variety of conditions in energy markets, so too is variation to be expected in the application of the logic to water. Outcomes of water management under the local government cap-and-trade framework proposed here would depend on the actual behavior and performance of local government agents. The key to whether good outcomes are obtained depends on the functioning of the local political market[20] through which leaders would emerge who would manage the local government's charge over water. If local political contestation yielded leaders who protested the caps imposed, or who captured the water entitlements to benefit local elites while leaving their constituents impoverished and insecure, the state would remain in the predicament in which it started. The contention behind the idea is that focused policy attention can go toward harnessing the *potential* of local political markets, where forces of contestation are already at play, to yield high-quality local leaders who can employ local information to win legitimacy and economic efficiency.

Local decision making by farmers and urban residents through their representatives in local governments has the potential to lend legitimacy to difficult trade-offs in the use of water between agriculture and WSS, compared to top-down directives from national ministries. Empowering local leaders in the policy area of managing their capped allocation of water, along with communication campaigns to encourage contestability on the basis of performance in managing water, could enable a shift in the equilibrium of low trust in society and government to a higher trust equilibrium. Such a shift is implied by available research on how contestation among local leaders can serve to coordinate expectations for higher performance. The process of local political contestation and the leaders who emerge from it serve to signal a shift in how others are behaving, which, in turn, changes individual behavior toward greater compliance with regulations (legitimacy) and trusting norms (Ostrom 2000; Acemoglu and Jackson 2015; Bidner and Francois 2013).

Communication around water scarcity and national water strategies. Communication requires investment in credible data and evidence (for example, on the hydrological cycle, infrastructure financing and future trends, and service delivery performance) as well as engagement of local political institutions—community and municipal leaders. Within the political and bureaucratic institutions through which citizens, public officials, service providers, bureaucrats, and political leaders form their beliefs or expectations, information about how others are behaving drives the transition between lower and higher equilibrium outcomes. Town halls and community meetings with local political leaders are needed, to communicate with citizens about the costs of supply-side investments to increase water resources, such as through desalination. Communication is also needed on the trade-offs in balancing water allocations between cities, agriculture, and other consumptive uses. Strategic communication can help gain acceptance for subsidy/tariff policy reforms to reduce the footprint of agriculture, and enable local government leaders to show how other state policies can address the livelihoods and income needs of farmers.

During the multiyear drought responses in São Paulo, Brazil, and Cape Town, South Africa, strategic communication by local government organizations complemented other reforms to reduce water use. In the case of Cape Town, as storage levels in the major dams fell, the city authority put in place a series of demand management measures through communication campaigns that changed norms by shocking people into fundamentally changing their water use. Transparency and public trust were built by sharing detailed and timely information about the water crisis through the "Water Dashboard," which gave weekly updates about total water usage in Cape Town, the city's augmentation plans, dam levels, and the approaching "Day Zero" date. Together these helped in reducing water use from 183 to 84 liters per person per day. Communication changed behavior by changing peoples' expectations of what others would do.

In the case of São Paulo, South America's largest city and home to 20 million people, elevated temperatures and lack of rain in 2014 caused the worst water crisis in more than 80 years. A communication campaign worked with communities and local leaders to explain the gravity of the situation and promote water savings. Across 39 municipal authorities, workshops on water saving were run with government entities and nongovernmental organizations. The communication campaign encouraged uptake of water-saving measures by customers and bridged the interests of farmers and nonfarming citizens through purchases of water from farmers.

Turning to an irrigation-specific example, in Mozambique, information campaigns on water use efficiency shifted norms in water use patterns, reducing conflict among farmers. Experiments in which farmers were provided information to help them avoid overwatering crops at early stages of the crop cycle significantly reduced the proportion of farmers across a scheme who self-reported having insufficient water. It also reduced the number of water-related conflicts in an irrigation scheme, compared to the number prior to the information campaign.[21]

The successes of these communication campaigns were due to the way they changed behavior by changing peoples' expectations of what others would do—they shifted underlying norms of behavior and addressed the informal institutions of legitimacy and trust.

NOTES

1. As defined by Falkenmark, Lundqvist, and Widstrand (1989).

2. Chapter 3 reports on 45 utilities covering around 60 percent of the region's population.

3. Water markets have seen limited application across the world (Australia, Chile, China, and the Western United States) and require high state institutional capacity for oversight and enforcement.

4. Structural transformation of the economies in MENA is already underway, with rising urbanization and falling per capita volumes of freshwater constraining agrarian livelihoods. Although fully addressing this transformation, such as how to re-equip those who are losing their livelihoods in the process, is beyond the scope of this report, it touches on it by addressing the overarching problem of governance by the state.

5. "Legitimacy" in this sense is defined in World Bank (2011).

6. Morocco: Talbi et al. (forthcoming); Jordan: Al Naber and Molle (2017).

7. See chapter 9 and https://www.worldvaluessurvey.org/wvs.jsp.

8. Mugisha, Berg, and Muhairwe (2007).

9. World Bank (2016) provides a review of the evidence on how transparency influences local political competition.

10. World Bank (2016).

11. See chapter 4 for agricultural water productivity and D'Odorico et al. (2020).

12. See, for example, Siegel (2015).

13. https://www.jordantimes.com/news/local/draft-water-law-stirs-public-anger.

14. Talbi et al. (forthcoming).

15. https://www.giz.de/en/worldwide/43179.html.

16. Kabagambe (2020).

17. Lombana Cordoba, Saltiel, and Perez Penalosa (2022).

18. Banerjee, Duflo, and Glennerster (2008).

19. The global experiences of water reallocations presented in chapter 7 show that although water use limits are generally set at a basin or aquifer scale (a hydrological unit), the role of enforcement and accountability for operating within that limit often falls to local (political) jurisdictions rather than technical water institutions.

20. See chapter 9 on local political contestation and chapter 11 on the role of local political markets in water management.

21. Christian et al. (2018).

REFERENCES

Acemoglu, D., and M. O. Jackson. 2015. "History, Expectations, and Leadership in the Evolution of Social Norms." *Review of Economic Studies* 82 (1): 1–34.

Al Naber, M., and F. Molle. 2017. "Controlling Groundwater over Abstraction: State Policies vs. Local Practices in the Jordan Highlands." *Water Policy* 19 (4): 692–708. https://doi.org/10.2166/wp.2017.127.

Banerjee, A. V., E. Duflo, and R. Glennerster. 2008. "Putting a Band-Aid on a Corpse: Incentives for Nurses in the Indian Public Health Care System." *Journal of the European Economic Association* 6 (2-3): 487–500.

Bel, G., and X. Fageda. 2009. "Factors Explaining Local Privatization: A Meta-Regression Analysis." *Public Choice* 139: 105–19. https://doi.org/10.1007/s11127-008-9381-z.

Bidner, C., and P. Francois. 2013. "The Emergence of Political Accountability." *Quarterly Journal of Economics* 128 (3): 1397–448.

Christian, P., F. Kondylis, V. Mueller, A. Zwager, and T. Siegfried. 2018. "Water When It Counts: Reducing Scarcity through Irrigation Monitoring in Central Mozambique." Policy Research Working Paper 8345, World Bank, Washington, DC.

Clarke, G., K. Kosec, and S. Wallsten. 2004. "Has Private Participation in Water and Sewerage Improved Coverage? Empirical Evidence from Latin America." Policy Research Working Paper 3445, World Bank, Washington, DC. https://openknowledge.worldbank.org/handle/10986/13898.

D'Odorico, P., D. D. Chiarelli, L. Rosa, A. Bini, D. Zilberman, and M. C. Rulli. 2020. "The Global Value of Water in Agriculture." *Proceedings of the National Academy of Sciences* 117 (36): 21985–993. doi:10.1073/pnas.2005835117.

Falkenmark, M., J. Lundqvist, and C. Widstrand. 1989. "Macro-Scale Water Scarcity Requires Micro-Scale Approaches." *Natural Resources Forum* 13: 258–67.

Galiani, S., P. Gertler, and E. Schargrodsky. 2005. "Water for Life: The Impact of the Privatization of Water Services on Child Mortality." *Journal of Political Economy* 113 (1): 83–120. https://doi.org/10.1086/426041.

Gerchunoff, P., E. Greco, and D. Bondorevsky. 2003. "Comienzos diversos, distintas trayectorias y final abierto: más de una década de privatizaciones en Argentina, 1990-2002." ILPES. http://hdl.handle.net/11362/7287.

Guasch, J. L., D. Benitez, I. Portabales, and L. Flor. 2014. "The Renegotiation of PPP Contracts: An Overview of Its Recent Evolution in Latin America." International Transport Forum Discussion Paper 2014/18, Organisation for Economic Co-operation and Development, Paris.

Joskow, P. L. 2007. "Regulation of Natural Monopoly." In *Handbook of Law and Economics*, vol. 2, edited by A. M. Polinsky and S. Shavell, 1227–348. Amsterdam: Elsevier. https://doi.org/10.1016/S1574-0730(07)02016-6.

Kabagambe, A. N. 2020. "Interim Report 2020: Africa Group 1 Constituency." World Bank, Washington, DC.

Lombana Cordoba, C., G. Saltiel, and F. Perez Penalosa. 2022. "Utility of the Future: Taking Water and Sanitation Utilities Beyond the Next Level 2.0 – A Methodology to Ignite Transformation in Water and Sanitation Utilities." World Bank, Washington, DC. http://documents.worldbank.org/curated/en/099325005112246075/P1655 860d146090dc097dc0165740604044.

Lyon, T. P., A. W. Montgomery, and D. Zhao. 2017. "A Change Would Do You Good: Privatization, Municipalization, and Drinking Water Quality." In *Academy of Management Annual Meeting Proceedings: Atlanta 2017*, edited by S. Taneja, 10499–501. Briarcliff Manor, NY: Academy of Management. https://doi.org/10.5465/AMBPP.2017.19.

Mugisha, S., S. V. Berg, and W. T. Muhairwe. 2007. "Using Internal Incentive Contracts to Improve Water Utility Performance: The Case of Uganda's NWSC." *Water Policy* 9: 10.2166/wp.2007.010.

Ostrom, E. 2000. "Collective Action and the Evolution of Social Norms." *Journal of Economic Perspectives* 14 (3): 137–58. doi:10.1257/jep.14.3.137.

Siegel, S. M. 2015. *Let There Be Water: Israel's Solution for a Water-Starved World*. New York: Thomas Dunne Books.

Talbi, A., C. Dominguez Torres, S. Bahije, D. de Waal, S. Dahan, R. Trier, and H. Benabderrazik. Forthcoming. "The New Normal of Allocating Water Scarcity: Adapting Water Resources Management and Services to the Changing Future." World Bank, Washington, DC.

World Bank. 2011. *World Development Report 2011: Conflict, Security, and Development*. Washington, DC: World Bank.

——. 2016. *High and Dry: Climate Change, Water, and the Economy*. Washington, DC: World Bank. https://openknowledge.worldbank.org/handle/10986/23665.

Abbreviations

ACLED	Armed Conflict Location & Event Data Project
AdE	Algerian Water Authority
BMLWE	Beirut and Mount Lebanon Water Establishment
BWE	Bekaa Water Establishment (Lebanon)
DEWA	Dubai Electricity and Water Authority
DIAM	Public Authority for Electricity and Water (Oman)
FLL	Field-Level Leadership
GDP	gross domestic product
JWU	Jerusalem Water Undertaking
l/c/d	liters per capita per day
m^3	cubic meters
MENA	Middle East and North Africa
MEW	Ministry of Electricity and Water and Renewable Energy (Kuwait)
NLWE	North Lebanon Water Establishment
NRW	nonrevenue water
NWC	National Water Company (Saudi Arabia)
O&M	operation and maintenance
ONA	National Agency of Sanitation (Algeria)
ONAS	National Sanitation Office (Tunisia)
ONEAD	National Office for Water and Sanitation (Djibouti)
ONEE	National Office of Electricity and Drinking Water (Morocco)
PPP	public-private partnership
PSP	private sector partnership
SOE	state-owned enterprise
SONEDE	National Company of Exploitation and Distribution of Water (Tunisia)
WAJ	Water Authority of Jordan
WCP	water conservation policy
WCT	water conservation technology
WSC	Water Services Corporation (Malta)
WSS	water supply and sanitation
WUA	water user association
WVS	World Values Survey

PART I

The Status Quo Institutions That Allocate Water

Economics studies how human societies allocate scarce resources across competing needs. This part of the report outlines and uses an economic approach to analyze how water is allocated in the Middle East and North Africa.

CHAPTER 1

An Economic View of Water Scarcity: The Inescapable Role of the State in Allocating Water

INTRODUCTION

Water scarcity in the Middle East and North Africa puts stress on societies and economies despite decades of large investments in the sector. This chapter lays out the tools of economics applied to water, which are then used in the following chapters to provide a fresh understanding of the problems and identify innovative solutions.

Governments in the Middle East and North Africa have received analytical evidence for decades warning them that the region cannot sustain its current trajectory of water allocation because the resource is becoming depleted. Furthermore, evidence shows that water allocations are inefficient, even within the resource constraint, and that needed investments in water infrastructure for economic growth and well-being cannot raise sustainable financing (World Bank 2007, 2018). However, little advice has been provided on the policy instruments that governments could use to change these allocation patterns and attract sustainable financing to invest in water. For example, in light of the environmental problems of resource depletion, should governments simply order the reduction of water consumption in agriculture? If they did, would agricultural water users comply with those orders, or would they raise the specter of political and social instability? Even when governments can control water allocation, such as through building and operating dams, how would a government decide the "optimal" allocation of water to serve the objectives of sustainable water management for economic growth, livelihoods, food security, health, and well-being for its people?

Economics is a field devoted to the questions of how to think about "optimal" allocation of scarce resources by individuals and society across competing needs, and what role governments could play in improving those allocations. A standard economic tool for thinking about optimality is whether any given allocation of resources could be changed to bring greater benefits in total, net of any costs incurred in changing those allocations. This is the notion of efficiency. Economics also offers tools for thinking about how to achieve other kinds of optimal allocations, with optimality viewed through the moral philosophical lenses of fairness, justice, and equity. These tools provide policy ideas for efficiently achieving the societal objectives of fairness, justice, and equity and developing them in light of the resource constraints.

This chapter lays out the foundational definitions needed for applying economic tools and terminology to water. The following chapters use these tools to understand how water is allocated, and how that allocation could be improved from the perspective of efficiency and equity (to paraphrase the objectives of moral philosophy, including fairness and justice).

WHAT IS THE PRICE OF WATER?

The allocation of resources in any economy, on a continuum between market-based and central planning institutions, is achieved through price signals. It is important to note that a resource can be priced through a fee charged for its use, as well as through restrictions on how much of the resource is used. A quantity constraint generates what in economics is called a "shadow" price, which is the price that users of water in effect pay through the constraint on the quantity of water they can use. Although the shadow price does not generate immediate revenue, it is reflected in the value of the underlying property, such as the agricultural land where water is being used, and thus shapes economic incentives to use water in a manner similar to regular prices.

Producers decide how much of a good to produce, and consumers decide how much to consume, using prices. Water can be priced using both direct price and quantity regulation instruments—a fee or tariff and a restriction on quantity. In economic terms, rapid depletion of water resources means that neither of these instruments has been sufficiently used to price and regulate water.

How water is priced and regulated depends on the institutional environment in which the consumer or producer is located. In cities, for example, the dominant "producers" of water for household use are the utilities that pipe water to households or provide public taps and drain away sewage water.[1] The consumers of household water and sanitation services pay a price for these water services through a combination of household-level water bills and the general fiscus of the state in which they reside (through payment of taxes, which may be diverted back to the utility).[2] In rural areas, the predominant use of water is for agriculture. The price of water in agriculture is primarily set through the quantity constraint—how water is shared among farmers to irrigate their crops, including through landownership and state-defined property rights over the water in the land (such as groundwater).

Demand for water in both urban and agricultural areas is also addressed by the producers who harvest water as a renewable resource, through environmental conservation, desalination, or investments in other technologies to reduce wastage of water, treat wastewater, and deliver the treated water to end users. The price signal for such producers is ultimately shaped by what households, farmers, and citizens are willing to pay through their bills or the fiscal resources of their state.

Challenges in Pricing Water: The Role of Property Rights

Economics typically studies the allocation of goods produced in competitive markets, in which producers enjoy private property rights over the means of production and sell their products to consumers for a price that allows them to stay in business and turn a profit. Water is a different product. Its physical and cultural properties are such that no country has relied entirely on market institutions for its allocation.

Across the world, including in the most advanced market economies, water resources are owned by states or public institutions. Significant sources of renewable water, such as rivers and lakes, are national property or local commons. Private property rights over water are limited and often linked to landownership. Water utilities that supply water for drinking, sanitation, and other household uses are typically state owned. If and when private firms are invited to build water infrastructure and operate utilities, the process of private sector participation involves negotiation with state agencies or regulators over the terms of production, supply, and pricing of water services.

Institutions of state, government, and local commons property governance thus play inescapably significant roles, even when parts of the production or supply of water services are privatized. It is not expected that privatization of water services would automatically deliver the efficient outcomes of other markets in the logic of economic theory, because the conditions for those efficiency results are absent in the markets for water.[3] States or government agencies must purposefully design those market conditions and the property rights that the logic of economic theory identifies as the conditions for efficient allocation of scarce resources.

The fact that market institutions based on private property rights are limited in the allocation of a commodity like water does not automatically mean that central planning offers a ready solution. Even a central planner needs policy ideas for how to manage the actions and behaviors of the large numbers of people who use water for their lives and livelihoods. Institutions—the formal and informal rules of the game—determine how millions of individual and collective actors (households, farmers, firms, and utilities) access, use, and manage water. Economic tools for examining how allocation decisions are made can help governments understand the current trajectories of water use by their citizens, and what policy instruments they can use to change those trajectories toward greater sustainability and improved well-being of their citizens. These tools use game theory of strategic interaction between actors or agents with different powers and authority to understand decision-making and associated outcomes.

Challenges in Pricing Water: The Role of Externalities

The problem of water scarcity in economies, including the most advanced market economies with strong institutions, is driven by lack of institutions to price the "externalities" associated with the consumption of water. Water is a common pool resource for which an individual's use of the resource involves a "negative externality" on the availability of the resource for others. Because the resource is scarce and commonly shared, one person's use of it has a social cost in the form of resource depletion. An individual user does not fully consider this cost when deciding how much of the resource to use.

In classical economics, a solution to this problem is for the central planner to assign property rights (Coase 1960). However, because of the physical characteristics of water resources, even if a policy maker wanted to establish clear property rights (abstracting for the moment from issues of equity or justice in such assignment of property rights), such rights over water are difficult to define and enforce (Copeland and Taylor 2009). Furthermore, the so-called Coase Theorem (of assigning property rights to solve the problem of externalities) is difficult to apply to the problem of managing water because of the many "transaction costs" among users of water.[4] North (1984, 7, his italics) provides the following definition: "Transaction costs are the costs of specifying and enforcing the *contracts that underlie exchange* and therefore comprise all the costs of political and economic organization that permit economies to capture the gains from trade." Transaction costs in turn are shaped by institutions, defined as both formal and informal rules of the game (North 1987). Governments need to establish property rights and contract enforcement as the formal rules of the game. Informal rules of the game are the norms of behavior prevalent among the vast numbers of players, such as among users of water as a resource.

In traditional rural societies that draw water for both household and agricultural use from a common property resource—such as a river, a community-owned well, or groundwater in privately owned land—water is priced by the rules and norms governing local behavior. Classic studies of local institutions that govern the "commons" describe self-governing irrigation institutions (Ostrom 1993, 2011). However, the prevailing local institutions may not have factored in the rapid depletion of water resources because of unsustainable use by growing populations and climate change, perhaps because this information is not available until it is "too late." Lab experimental studies (conducted with educated subjects in the United States, and thus a group that would have access to news and information) suggest that individuals are cognitively constrained in figuring out the "equilibrium" effects that arise by aggregating all individual behaviors (Dal Bo et al. 2018). That is, the externality in the consumption of water is "hidden," such that Ostrom-style institutions of local collective action to price water appropriately, to account for the externality in its consumption, may not have emerged in societies (Giordano 2009).

The scale of the externality problem of water and its links to climate change are nonmarginal and global, which also makes it difficult to apply the Coasian insight of establishing private property rights. The environment is a global public good over which private property rights cannot be defined. At the heart of the problem of public goods is that they are governed by political contracts that are not "justiciable"—they cannot be enforced by an ultimate court with supra-political authority.[5] If a contract among rival interest groups is not justiciable, it must be self-enforcing, and therein lies a Prisoner's Dilemma, in the language of game theory. Each group can extract private benefit by reneging—offering the common agent a little bit extra to serve its group interests at the expense of the other principals. Resolving this dilemma between groups, which ultimately arises from lack of legal enforcement by a third party, involves a system of norms and accompanying informal sanctions, to make credible their commitments to adhere to the agreement.

Challenges in Pricing Water: Natural Monopoly of Urban Utilities

The urban water supply and sanitation (WSS) sector is characterized by two features that profoundly shape its economic organization. The first characteristic, from a technological point of view, is that fixed and sunk costs constitute the overwhelming proportion of the total cost of supply compared to variable costs. This is caused by the sector's extreme capital intensity and the fact that WSS assets are specific and cannot be readily redeployed in other industries. Moreover, such assets are extremely long lived and can operate for centuries with little maintenance.[6]

Before a single drop of water can reach urban users,[7] dams, diversions, reservoirs, and wells must be built to capture and store the natural resource; aqueducts, sluices, and mains are needed to transport it over long distances from the production location to the consumption locations; and, finally, ditches and pipes are required to distribute water to each individual user. Moreover, used water is released back into the environment through a sewage system, which again features substantial capital costs. Variable cost components (also known as operational cost components) are mainly related to the energy employed for pumping the water from underground and transporting it, purifying it through physical and chemical treatments that raise its quality to meet human consumption standards, and powering the infrastructure necessary for reducing the contamination of wastewater. In addition, if users are charged by the volume they consume, another component of variable cost is the expense associated with metering and billing. The size of the workforce and the associated wage bill are relatively small.

In general, the prevalence of fixed costs over variable costs gives rise to scale economies that can potentially lead to the emergence of natural monopolies, which is often the case in the WSS sector. Indeed, meaningful and sustainable competition is possible only in locations that can rely on a multiplicity of water sources of sufficient capacity.[8] Even in such circumstances, multiple providers can be present only in the upstream vertical phases of production related to water capture, storage, and transportation, whereas distribution networks and sewage systems would remain natural monopolies. Even the most favorable situation would remain far from the conditions of perfect competition, and especially the cheapest sources might be able to earn substantial rents. This situation occurs because the consumer price is determined by the marginal cost of the most expensive water source. Thus, the inframarginal sources would earn so-called Ricardian rents merely because of the topography of their location. Such rents do not remunerate any investment or compensate for any risk sustained in the production process; they constitute a simple redistribution from users to the entities that control the best water sources (see Noll 2002, 49–50).

The economies of scale associated with a piped water distribution system are such that bypassing it through decentralized supply using tanker trucks or bottled water is almost always overly expensive. The latter can become viable competitors only for high-quality water uses (drinking and personal hygiene) and not for activities such as washing, cleaning, or gardening, which can be done effectively with lower quality water.

The second characteristic of the sector is that water consumption by an agent can generate substantial negative externalities on other users, especially at the local level (see also chapter 5 of this report). These externalities can take the form of reduced quality, reduced quantity, or increased cost of obtaining and treating water. Considering the first, a large share of water withdrawn from the environment is neither consumed nor destroyed; after use, it simply goes back to the environment dirtier and more contaminated.[9] Downstream users are therefore affected by upstream consumption because their water is the wastewater of the latter. Not just downstream users but also the upstream users can suffer from lack of proper disposal and treatment once they have used the water. That is, residents of a city without adequate sanitation and sewage management will suffer from their own use of water. Second, unsustainable consumption (the sum of current uses—including maintenance of the ecosystem of the source—is above the replenishment rate) progressively reduces available quantities and water becomes a nonrenewable resource. Finally, current use might increase the cost of providing the resource in the future, for example because the groundwater table sinks and thus the energy cost of pumping increases or the quality of the water resource deteriorates as it becomes more saline. Negative externalities can be exerted on the same type of consumer (for example, between two cities that capture their water from the same river) or between various types of users (for example, urban dwellers and farmers).

The prevailing technology and engineering of supplying water and sanitation to densely populated urban communities creates the conditions for a "natural monopoly." The average cost of production, that is, the supply of water and sanitation to households, tends to decline as more households are added to a piped network, making it efficient to have a single firm operate an urban water utility. In addition to these issues of economies of scale, the long life of the infrastructure of piped water networks means that the state cannot credibly commit not to expropriate private investments in the future. Taken together, these technical characteristics of the "production function" of piped water systems mean that states or governments are deeply involved even when a private firm operates the utility. Private firms will not enter the market of piped water and sanitation without state guarantees to protect their investments and ensure that they earn sufficient returns to cover their costs. States or government institutions in turn represent consumer interests relative to a monopoly producer of water and sanitation services. Because consumers cannot switch between different providers of piped water and sewage services, monopoly utilities would have incentives to price "too high" from the perspectives of fairness and justice.

Weak public institutions do not imply better performance by private agents when the forces of competition are missing, as in a natural monopoly. Private providers of utility services often have incentives to "subvert" the government that is expected to regulate them (Engel, Fischer, and Galetovic 2014). Government regulation of water and sanitation utilities, regardless of whether a utility operates as a state-owned enterprise or a private firm, is thus essential and occurs in every country in the world. Governments ultimately set rules for pricing water and sanitation services and standards for the quality of water supply and treatment and disposal of sewage. Understanding how government institutions function in these areas is thus inescapable for reform leaders and their external development partners who seek to improve the outcomes of water and sanitation services.

IDENTIFYING REFORM DIRECTIONS USING AN ECONOMIC LENS

How should reform leaders and their external development partners think about policy actions to address the long-standing problems of water scarcity and service delivery in the Middle East and North Africa? The special features of water—the challenges of establishing property rights, addressing externalities, and regulating natural monopolies—require understanding how producers and consumers of water behave strategically, under beliefs and expectations about how others are behaving. This is the arena studied using the tools of game theory of strategic interaction among a large number of actors with different objectives and authority.

In the following chapters, the report describes the status quo institutions that allocate water and uses game theory tools to examine why institutions function the way they do, and what policy actions can improve their functioning to achieve better allocations of water. Institutions are described as the objectives, beliefs, and expectations of different actors who wield power over how to allocate water. The report seeks to answer the following questions:

- *Hydraulic infrastructure investments.* Who are the key actors who have power over deciding when and where to build dams and reallocate source water between urban household needs, rural agriculture, and industry?
- *Irrigation.* Who are the key actors who have power over deciding on the availability and use of water for irrigation? Who are the actors who implement irrigation policies and regulations over the use of water owned as part of the land?
- *Watershed and environmental management.* Who are the key actors who have power over policies to manage watersheds and the environment for the sustainability of water as a resource?
- *Household water and sanitation services.* Who are the key actors who have power over the policies governing WSS utilities? Who are the actors who implement utility policies and deliver services?
- *Wastewater and pollution management.* Who are the key actors who have power over deciding on investments in sewage management, treatment of wastewater, and regulation of pollutants disposed into water?

Each of these policy areas involves the actions of a vast number of people, such as public officials who manage utilities, households and farmers who decide how much and whether to pay for water, and ministry officials who design policy and manage the implementation of hydraulic projects and environmental regulations. Their actions in turn shape the outcomes of interest (sustainability of water resources; social goals of access to water and sanitation for all; and productivity in agriculture for livelihoods, food security, and economic growth). The report uses the economic tools of game theory to examine the incentives and norms that shape the behavior of agents in each of these policy areas, and thence the outcomes of interest.

NOTES

1. There are also producers of bottled water and tankers that can supply water, but these producers would ultimately depend on the supply of water from utilities, or access to a body of water legally owned or regulated by the state (notwithstanding issues of legal plurality—see chapter 7).

2. When water bills collected by utilities cannot cover their costs of operating, the state budget or fiscal resources are used to cover the costs of the utility.

3. A powerful result from the logic of economic theory is that market institutions that enable decentralized and voluntary exchange among individuals are likely to allocate resources for greater net gains to society compared to allocation decisions made by a central planner. This logical argument has also found empirical support in variation across countries in economic growth and prosperity, with market-oriented reforms associated with more healthy economies (see the review in Rajan and Zingales 2003). However, water is a commodity with physical properties such that decentralized and voluntary exchange do not happen under the conditions needed for efficient results. For example, even in the case of delivery of water by private tankers to individual households, which may appear to be a decentralized and voluntary exchange, access to the source of water is not voluntary, with property rights over the commodity being ill-defined, violating a fundamental condition for market efficiency.

4. Coase (1960) was clear in his argument, frequently referred to by economists as the Coase Theorem, that its results hold only under the assumption of zero or low transaction costs.

5. This point about "justiciability" is drawn from Dixit (1996, 2003, 2018). The lack of enforceability of political contracts by an independent third party is also the argument in Acemoglu (2003) on why a Political Coase Theorem is infeasible.

6. An extreme example is the Aqua Virgo aqueduct in Rome, which is still used after 2,000 years to bring water to the monumental fountains of the city.

7. Traditional rural communities may use natural water sources directly.

8. This situation resembles what we find in the electricity sector in which wholesale competition is possible upstream in generation, and the truly natural monopoly is given by the electric grid. In the WSS context, various water sources compete in the supply of bulk water.

9. Storage facilities such as dams and reservoirs also affect the local environment, altering the variability and temperature of river flows and the ecosystems that depend on them. Spillage can cause problems if the resource is released into the environment without any control and does not run off or percolate into the soil quickly enough. When water is very slow moving, it becomes a breeding ground for microorganisms and insects that can cause serious diseases.

REFERENCES

Acemoglu, D. 2003. "Why Not a Political Coase Theorem? Social Conflict, Commitment, and Politics." *Journal of Comparative Economics* 31 (4): 620–52.

Coase, R. H.1960. "The Problem of Social Cost." *Journal of Law and Economics* 3: 1–44.

Copeland, B. R., and M. S. Taylor. 2009. "Trade, Tragedy, and the Commons." American Economic Review 99 (3): 725–49.

Dal Bó, P., and G. R. Fréchette. 2018. "On the Determinants of Cooperation in Infinitely Repeated Games: A Survey." *Journal of Economic Literature* 56 (1): 60–114.

Dixit, A. K. 1996. *The Making of Economic Policy: A Transaction-Cost Politics Perspective*. Cambridge, MA: MIT Press.

Dixit, A. K. 2003. "Some Lessons from Transaction-Cost Politics for Less-Developed Countries." *Economics & Politics* 15 (2): 107–33.

Dixit, A. K. 2018. "Anti-corruption Institutions: Some History and Theory." In *Institutions, Governance and the Control of Corruption*, edited by K. Basu and T. Cordella, 15–49. London: Palgrave Macmillan.

Engel, E., R. D. Fischer, and A. Galetovic. 2014. *The Economics of Public-Private Partnerships: A Basic Guide*. Cambridge: Cambridge University Press.

Giordano, M. 2009. "Global Groundwater? Issues and Solutions." *Annual Review of Environment and Resources* 34: 153–78.

Noll, R. G. 2002. "The Economics of Urban Water Systems." In *Thirsting for Efficiency: The Economics and Politics of Urban Water System Reform*, edited by M. M. Shirley, 43–63. Washington, DC: Elsevier Science for the World Bank.

North, D. C. 1984. "Transaction Costs, Institutions, and Economic History." *Zeitschrift Für Die Gesamte Staatswissenschaft/Journal of Institutional and Theoretical Economics* 140 (1): 7–17.

North, D. C. 1987. "Institutions, Transaction Costs and Economic Growth." *Economic Inquiry* 25 (3): 419–428.

Ostrom, E. 2011. "Reflections on 'Some Unsettled Problems of Irrigation.'" American Economic Review 101 (1): 49–63.

Ostrom, E., and R. Gardner. 1993. "Coping with Asymmetries in the Commons: Self-Governing Irrigation Systems Can Work." Journal of Economic Perspectives 7 (4): 93–112.

Rajan, R. G., and L. Zingales. 2003. *Saving Capitalism from the Capitalists: Unleashing the Power of Financial Markets to Create Wealth and Spread Opportunity*. New York: Crown Business.

World Bank. 2007. *Making the Most of Scarcity: Accountability for Better Water Management Results in the Middle East and North Africa*. MENA Development Report. Washington, DC: World Bank.

World Bank. 2018. *Beyond Scarcity: Water Security in the Middle East and North Africa*. MENA Development Report. Washington, DC: World Bank.

CHAPTER 2

Middle East and North Africa: Diversity of Economic and Hydrological Context

The countries in the Middle East and North Africa (MENA) are some of the most water scarce in the world (figure 2.1). As well as being among the hottest and driest countries, they have experienced declining or more variable levels of rainfall and diminishing inflows of water along shared rivers and in shared aquifers, which have led to shrinking water resource endowments. Population growth and climate change will only make this situation worse in the future.[1]

The level of water stress is reported under Sustainable Development Goals indicator 6.4.2 as the ratio of freshwater withdrawals to available freshwater resources. The majority of countries in MENA are in the *critical* category of water stress (map 2.1), meaning that where annual water withdrawals exceed available renewable water resources. The three main ways countries can exceed these apparent limits of ecological sustainability are by tapping so-called fossil groundwater (sources of groundwater that are not renewable), diverting surface water flows from downstream areas or the environment (for example, from wetlands), or investing in various forms of desalination and wastewater reuse. In extreme cases, such as some of the Gulf Cooperation Council countries, freshwater withdrawals are between 4 and 40 times the available freshwater, primarily because of the use of fossil groundwater, desalination, and wastewater reuse.

The region has seen its population grow from just over 100 million people in 1960 to more than 450 million in 2018, and the medium forecast for the population in 2050 is estimated at more than 720 million. Within the next decade, all the countries in MENA will fall below the water scarcity threshold of 1,000 cubic meters per person per year. Figure 2.2 shows water scarcity measured using the Falkenmark indicator of per capita water availability (Falkenmark, Lundqvist, and Widstrand 1989), revealing remarkable variation in water scarcity, albeit in a region that, compared to rest of the world, is the most water scarce.

Figure 2.1 Renewable water resources per capita per year, by economy, 2017

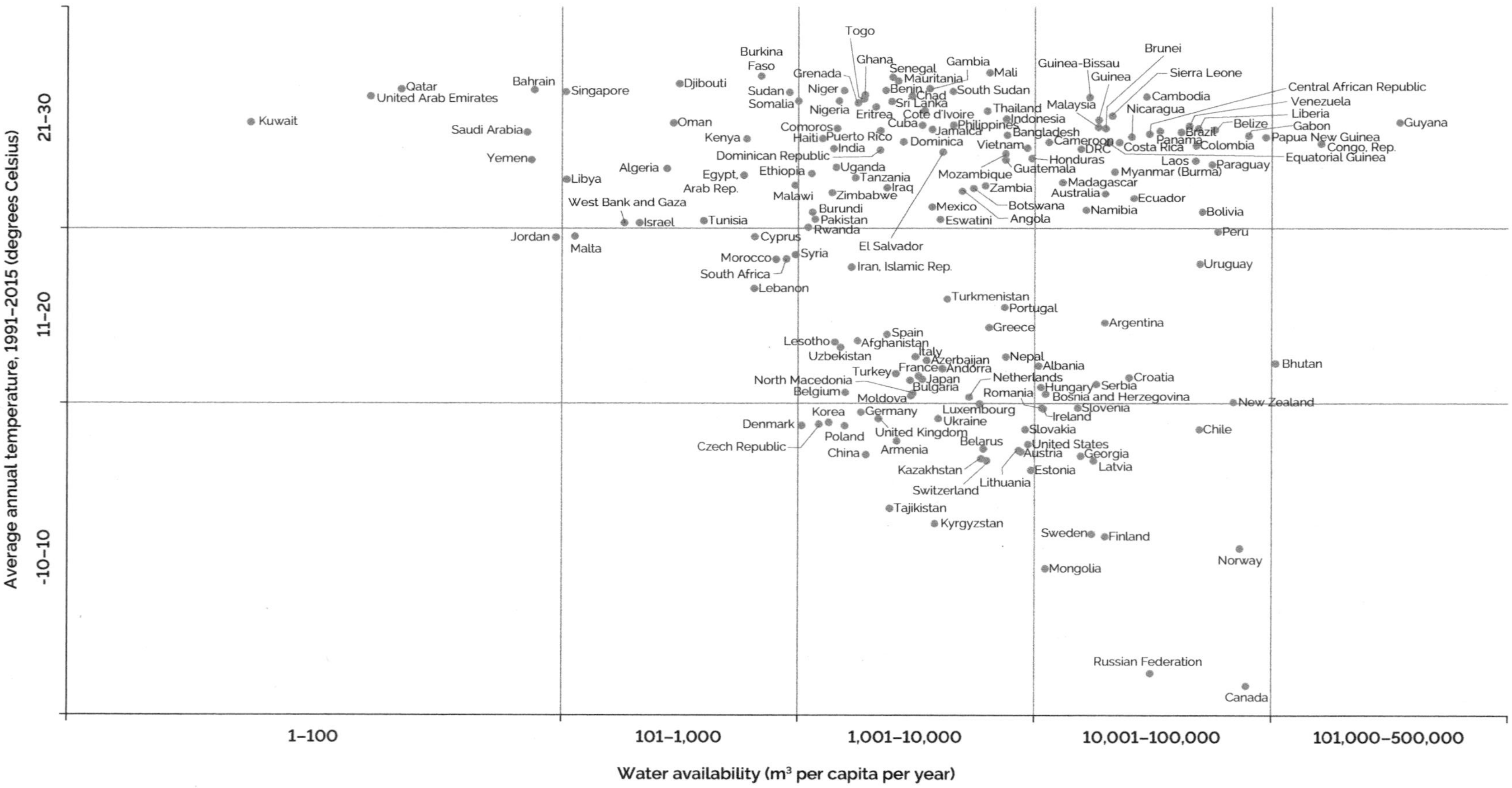

Average annual temperature, 1991–2015 (degrees Celsius)

Water availability (m³ per capita per year)

Sources: For temperature, Food and Agriculture Organization of the United Nations, AQUASTAT (https://climateknowledgeportal.worldbank.org). World Bank Climate Change Portal (https://climateknowledgeportal
.worldbank.org/country)

Note: m³ = cubic meters.

Map 2.1 Water stress around the world

Sustainable Development Goal 6.4.2

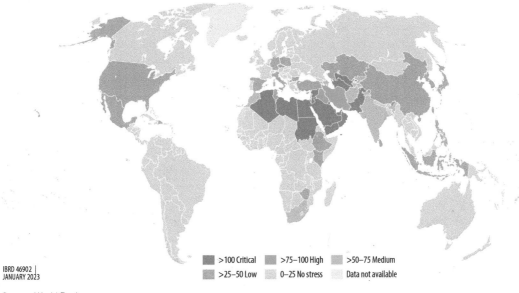

■ >100 Critical	■ >75–100 High	■ >50–75 Medium
■ >25–50 Low	■ 0–25 No stress	■ Data not available

IBRD 46902 |
JANUARY 2023

Source: World Bank.

Figure 2.2 Renewable water resources per person per year, Middle East and North Africa, 2018

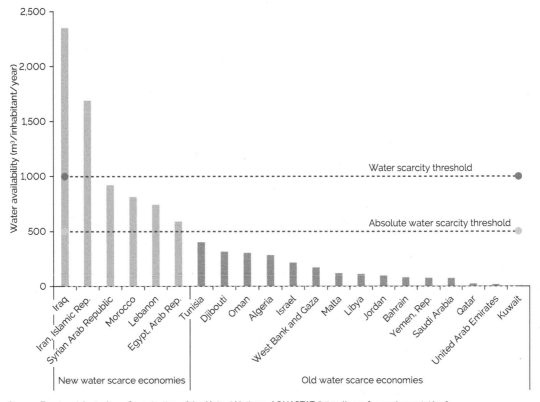

Source: Food and Agriculture Organization of the United Nations, AQUASTAT (https://www.fao.org/aquastat/en/).
Note: m³ = cubic meters; MENA = Middle East and North Africa.

Before describing the detailed institutional aspects of supply and demand in chapters 3 and 4, the typology in table 2.1 provides a broad framing for making sense of the diversity of countries in MENA. From this economic heterogeneity, some broad insights emerge on the way in which economic circumstances shape water use and how water scarcity shapes economies. The economic circumstances range from conflict-afflicted, low-income Republic of Yemen to high-income hydrocarbon exporters such as Qatar. Vulnerabilities may be obscured in oil producing countries that can spend their way out of problems, or vulnerabilities may be exacerbated in countries affected by fragility, conflict, and violence, where failure to address water scarcity contributes to fragility and conflict, and water systems are disproportionately likely to be casualties of direct or indirect violent conflict—compared to other regions of the world.[2]

"Old water scarce" countries—those below the absolute water scarcity threshold—are the more urbanized countries in the region. Although the high-income countries in the region—the majority of which are oil exporters with large urban expatriate migrant populations— might be expected to be more urbanized, even middle-income economies such as Djibouti, Jordan, Libya, and the West Bank and Gaza are highly urbanized, with more than three-quarters of people living in towns and cities. Only the Republic of Yemen, the single low-income fragile country in this group, still has two-thirds of its population living in rural areas. The higher level of urbanization among old water scarce countries is correlated with lower national rates of per capita water withdrawals (figure 2.3) because these

Table 2.1 Typology of economies: A starting point for unpacking the underlying challenges and opportunities

Typology		Economy	Total population (million)	Rural Share (%)
Old water scarce	Fragile lower-income and middle-income countries and economies	Djibouti	1	22
		Libya	7	20
		West Bank and Gaza	5	24
		Yemen, Rep.	31	64
	Middle-income countries	Algeria	46	28
		Jordan	10	9
		Tunisia	12	31
	High-income countries	Bahrain	2	11
		Israel	9	7
		Kuwait	4	0
		Malta	0.5	5
		Oman	5	16
		Qatar	19	1
		Saudi Arabia	35	16
		United Arab Emirates	10	14
New water scarce	Fragile lower-income and middle-income countries and economies	Iraq	38	30
		Lebanon	7	12
		Syrian Arab Republic	16	47
	Middle-income countries	Egypt, Arab Rep.	101	57
		Iran, Islamic Rep.	86	30
		Morocco	38	38

Source: Harmonized List of Fragile and Conflict Affected Situations FY19, World Bank (https://thedocs.worldbank.org/en/doc/892921532529834051-0090022018/original/FCSListFY19Final.pdf).

Figure 2.3 Urban population share of water withdrawals versus per capita water withdrawals, Middle East and North Africa

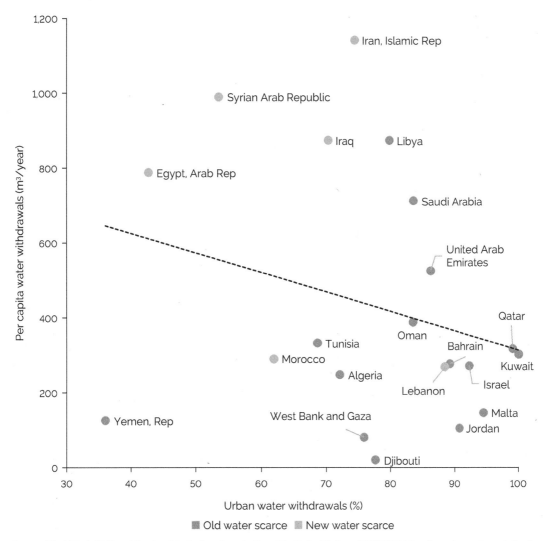

Sources: World Bank 2018 and Food and Agriculture Organization of the United Nations, AQUASTAT (https://www.fao.org/aquastat/en/).
Note: m³ = cubic meters.

economies rely less on water intensive rural livelihoods. As a result, however, most old water scarce countries rely heavily on cereal imports for over 80 percent of their needs. In this group, only Tunisia (60 percent) and Algeria (70 percent) are less reliant on cereal imports.

The *high-income* countries in this group have spent heavily on nonconventional water, aiming to "de-couple" water supply from climate-dependent freshwater availability. As part of this transition to nonconventional water use, they have developed national water grids for bulk water transfers. Five countries (Bahrain, Kuwait, Malta, Qatar, and the United Arab Emirates) are more than 75 percent reliant on nonconventional water sources in their overall water supply mix (figure 2.4). Agriculture is increasingly supplied from treated wastewater, and it is transitioning to higher levels of crop water productivity, for example, in fruit and vegetable production. Key areas of policy dialogue are (1) whether to fund the sector from tariffs or taxes as the shift toward full cost recovery tariffs has stalled

Figure 2.4 Share of nonconventional water in total water withdrawals, Middle East and North Africa

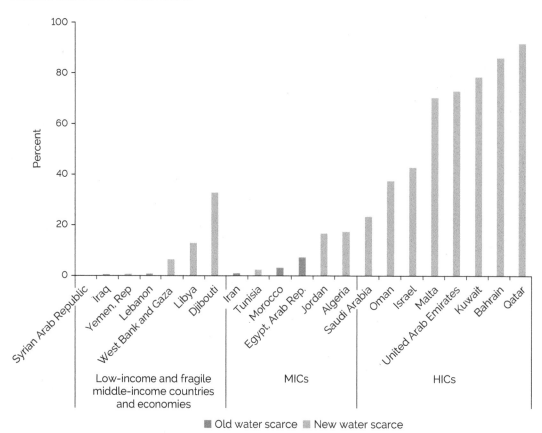

Sources: For nonconventional water, Global Water Intelligence (https://www.globalwaterintel.com); for conventional water, Food and Agriculture Organization of the United Nations, AQUASTAT (https://www.fao.org/aquastat/en/).
Note: HICs = high-income countries; MICs = middle-income countries.

in most countries because of objections from consumers, and (2) how to curb the high energy costs of nonconventional water systems and reduce their carbon footprint.

The *middle-income* countries in this group have started to invest in nonconventional water, including bulk water transfer systems to provide desalinated water to demand centers and move wastewater from demand centers back to agriculture. Utility supply is intermittent and has led to coping strategies to supplement utility supply, such as storage tanks, tanker truck water, and bottled water—particularly during the dry summer months. Agriculture is still a source of livelihoods, but over the past decades water has been reallocated to urban areas as rural populations have diminished. Key areas of policy dialogue are (1) whether, in the face of objections from medium and large irrigators, to reallocate more water from agriculture rather than building new sources of nonconventional water; and (2) how to increase tariffs to meet at least operation and maintenance costs in light of the rising recurrent deficits driven by the addition of nonconventional water sources.

In old water scarce *fragile* countries, national water governance has been constrained by conflict. These countries rely heavily on aid and have limited scope for or progress on sector reform. They have only started the transition to nonconventional water, but bulk water transfer systems are already a core part of coping with water scarcity in key demand centers. Utility supply is subject to significant disruptions and has led to widespread and year-round use of coping strategies such as storage tanks, tanker truck water, and bottled water. Financing for operation and maintenance is under severe stress. Agriculture is a declining source of livelihoods, except in the Republic of Yemen, where agriculture is a mainstay of livelihoods. Key areas of policy dialogue for fragile countries are (1) how to stem the decline in services, and (2) how to regain sector oversight of policy and reform in the context of protracted crisis.

All the *new water scarce* countries are middle-income countries. The five most populous countries—Iraq, the Syrian Arab Republic, the Arab Republic of Egypt, the Islamic Republic of Iran, and Morocco—have sizable agrarian populations (figure 2.5) and are home to over 70 percent of the region's rural population of 167 million. These five countries channel more than three-quarters of their water withdrawals to agricultural irrigation—nearly five times the amount of water channeled to agriculture by old water scarce countries. They also account for the vast majority of surface water withdrawals (163 billion cubic meters per year) compared to old water scarce countries (5 billion cubic meters per year) and produce half or more of their cereal needs. At one extreme, cereal production in the Arab Republic of Egypt is almost entirely dependent on irrigation; at the other, rainfed agriculture supports 85 percent of Morocco's cereal production. All the countries in this group, including Lebanon, are self-sufficient in fruits and vegetables and, except Iraq, also export them. Only a small proportion of total water withdrawals in these countries comes from desalination or wastewater reuse, mostly in dry, coastal areas.

In the nonfragile middle-income countries in the new water scarce group, weak water governance has been ineffective in limiting the amount of water abstracted by agriculture, leading to pockets of boom/bust exploitation and irreversible deterioration in water quality. Emergency reallocations to urban areas are made in dry years, leading to protests by irrigators. Inter-basin water transfers have been developed to respond to both localized irrigation and urban water needs. Key areas of policy dialogue are (1) how to limit the amount of water used by agriculture, (2) how to finance the inevitable increase in nonconventional water and associated energy costs, and (3) how to make timely adjustments to tariffs in anticipation of higher sector costs.

In the fragile middle-income countries, utility supply is intermittent, with large spatial and socioeconomic inequities. More water scarce subnational regions have widespread use of coping

Figure 2.5 Rural population share versus renewable water resources per capita

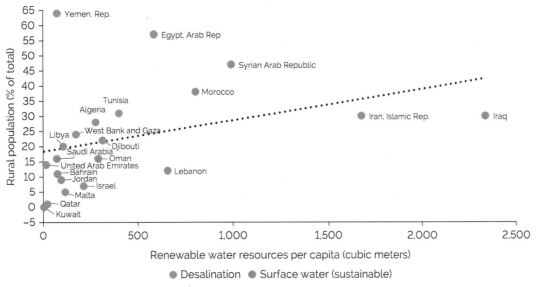

Source: Food and Agriculture Organization of the United Nations, AQUASTAT (https://www.fao.org/aquastat/en/).

strategies, including household storage tanks and resorting to water tankers and bottled water. Water governance is weak and a potential risk multiplier leading to imbalances across subpopulations (for example, between hosts and refugees in Lebanon) and governorates (for example, north versus south in Iraq), with significant externalities emerging in water quality and quantity. Weak water governance and poor water infrastructure performance are leading to (premature) spending on nonconventional water, particularly in water scarce parts of these countries despite their lower levels of water stress relative to old water scarce countries. Key areas of policy dialogue are (1) how to level out the growing disparities in the water available for agriculture and services across subnational governorates in the face of an uptick in protests from water rich donor regions or water stressed recipient regions, and (2) how to finance rehabilitation, upgrading, and targeted expansion of existing water infrastructure, which is in poor condition because of both conflict and decades of underinvestment in maintenance.

Common features across old and new water scarce countries are that they are withdrawing water at unsustainable levels and importing a large amount of "virtual" water. MENA's imports of virtual water—the water embodied in the production of agricultural commodities—doubled between 1998 and 2010. The 255 billion cubic meters of virtual water imported in the form of agricultural produce are equivalent to *more than half* of MENA's annual renewable water resource endowment and equal to total annual agricultural withdrawals (map 2.2). Until recently, imports of virtual water have been spurred by falling real prices of agricultural commodities, including wheat (Antonelli and Tamea 2015).

Relying on the rising levels of virtual water imports has enabled policy makers in the region to avoid tackling sensitive and interlinked reforms affecting both the food and water security sectors. Although the 2007–08 food price crisis did not translate into a dip in virtual water imports, fiscal space for subsidizing imports is far more constrained across the middle-income countries in the region in the post-COVID-19 period (UN ESCWA 2021). This tightening points to the need to resolve trade-offs related to the food, water, and energy nexus, which are subject to upward cost pressure across the board.

A common feature across all the old and new water scarce countries is the unsustainability of their water withdrawals, which are mainly of groundwater (figure 2.6). In the extreme cases of Libya and

Map 2.2 Net virtual water trade with the Middle East and North Africa as a percent of total water trade

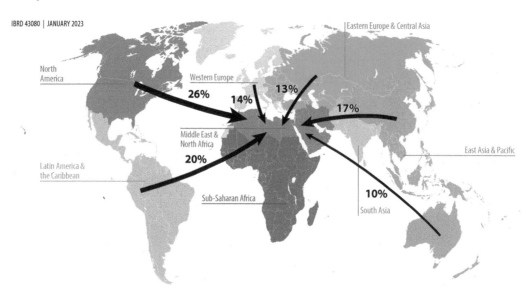

Source: World Bank 2017.

Figure 2.6 Sustainability of water withdrawals in the Middle East and North Africa, by source

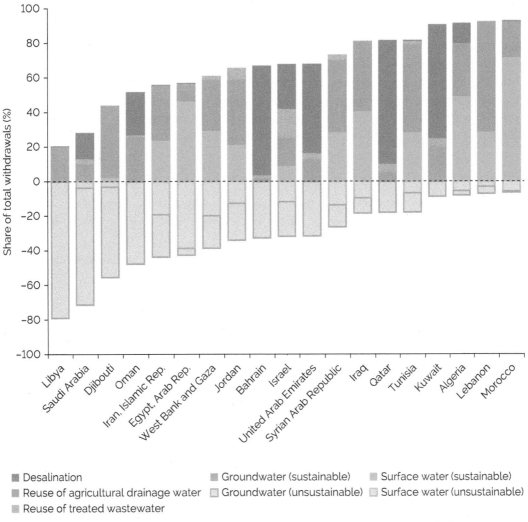

Legend:
- Desalination
- Reuse of agricultural drainage water
- Reuse of treated wastewater
- Groundwater (sustainable)
- Groundwater (unsustainable)
- Surface water (sustainable)
- Surface water (unsustainable)

Source: World Bank 2017.

Saudi Arabia, these withdrawals are far greater than available renewable resources and are sourced from "fossil" aquifers—sources of water that are not significantly replenished by current rainfall. The extent to which these fossil sources of water may present an opportunity to buffer water resource needs temporarily is further explored in chapter 5. However, resorting to groundwater, particularly deep fossil sources of groundwater, involves relatively high energy costs for pumping water to demand centers.

Although the key drivers of water scarcity are related to demographics and economic growth, the cost of climate-related inaction is higher in MENA than in other regions of the world. Climate change will also drive temperatures in MENA higher than the projected global averages. The World Bank (2016) estimates that a business-as-usual scenario, in which water is managed and allocated under the current regimes, could cost MENA between 6 and 14 percent of gross domestic product by 2050. The estimated global average reduction of gross domestic product is less than 1 percent by 2050, which highlights the relative vulnerability of water scarce regions such as MENA and the urgent need to improve water management.

By 2030, average annual per capita water resource availability across MENA will fall below the absolute water scarcity threshold of 500 cubic meters per person per year. With ever-growing pressure on water resources, what opportunities do new water scarce economies have to learn from old water scarce countries—including from their mistakes? Given the absence of water markets, what types of institutional solutions could help countries address the pressing policy concerns of intersectoral water allocations and long-term financing of services? This report aims to answer these questions. The rest of this part of the report first describes how supply-side water institutions have emerged in response to water scarcity (chapter 3), the characteristics of water demand (chapter 4), and the externalities emerging from the current water management systems (chapter 5).

NOTES

1. World Bank, Climate Change Knowledge Portal, https://climateknowledgeportal.worldbank.org. Temperature drives evaporation, diminishing the sitting water in a dam, and transpiration, the amount of water plants need to grow.

2. The Pacific Institute Water Conflict Chronology reports more instances of water being a casualty of conflict in MENA than in the entire rest of the world (http://www.worldwater.org/conflict/list/).

REFERENCES

Antonelli, M., and S. Tamea. 2015. "Food-Water Security and Virtual Water Trade in the Middle East and North Africa." *International Journal of Water Resources Development* 31 (3): 326–42. http://dx.doi.org/10.1080/07900627.2015.1030496.

Falkenmark, M., J. Lundqvist, and C. Widstrand. 1989. "Macro-scale Water Scarcity Requires Micro-scale Approaches: Aspects of Vulnerability in Semi-arid Development." *Natural Resources Forum* 13 (4): 258–67.

Food and Agriculture Organization of the United Nations, AQUASTAT (https://www.fao.org/aquastat/en/).

UN ESCWA (United Nations Economic and Social Commission for Western Asia). 2021. "Liquidity Shortage and Debt: Obstacles to Recovery in the Arab Region." Policy Brief 2, UN ESCWA, Beirut, Lebanon. https://digitallibrary.un.org/record/3978987.

World Bank. 2016. *High and Dry: Climate Change, Water, and the Economy.* Washington, DC: World Bank. https://openknowledge.worldbank.org/handle/10986/23665.

World Bank. 2018. *Beyond Scarcity: Water Security in the Middle East and North Africa.* MENA Development Series. World Bank, Washington, DC.

World Bank. 2018. World Development Indicators. Washington, DC: World Bank. https://databank.worldbank.org/source/world-development-indicators.

CHAPTER 3

Supply-Side Institutions That Build Large Infrastructure but Fail to Reduce Water Stress

ORIGINS AND EVOLUTION OF WATER INSTITUTIONS IN THE MIDDLE EAST AND NORTH AFRICA

The people of the Middle East and North Africa (MENA) have been tackling the endemic problem of water scarcity and variability for millennia through remarkable innovations. Six thousand years ago, the Sumerians channeled and regulated the flow of water and silt from the Tigris and Euphrates using reed dams, palm trunks, and mud to irrigate and fertilize the fields surrounding the ancient city of Ur. In cities and towns, technology for the management of water supply and sanitation is evident as far back as 2,500 years ago in the Persepolis Complex founded by Darius the Great. In the ceremonial capital of the Achaemenid Empire, in modern day Shiraz in the Islamic Republic of Iran, water was supplied through qanats, which harvested water from hills through systems of connected wells, tunnels, and sewage networks to convey runoff and wastewater out of the city.

Along with these technologies, institutions emerged for managing water. These institutions have evolved from their two main uses: water for agriculture and water for domestic supply.

Throughout history, institutions for investing in and managing large-scale irrigation water have been linked to centralized forms of power: pharaohs, sultans, emperors, kings, colonial administrations, and post-independence central governments (Wittfogel 1957). Investments on the Nile to regulate its flood waters go back at least 4,000 years. The level of annual flooding of the Nile had a big impact on Egyptian agricultural productivity and the tax revenues that could be raised from agriculture. King Menes (2500 BC) carried out a major water diversion built by widening a natural channel, now called

Bahr Yousuf canal, from present day Asyut to Lake Qarun, a depression that is below sea level. This diversion helped to prevent high flood years from destroying crops. To assess taxes more "fairly," later Ptolemaic rulers of Egypt (305–30 BC) built temples along the Nile and installed nilometers in them.

Unlike in other areas of the world with more benign climates (wetter and cooler) where farm-level working capital drove agricultural productivity,[1] irrigation water was a binding constraint to growth of agricultural production across much of MENA.

In the 19th and early 20th centuries, powerful technical bureaucracies were formed, such as the Egyptian Department of Public Works and the Directorate General of Irrigation in Iraq. These technical agencies became schools of engineering practice, greatly expanding the capacity to design and develop hydraulic infrastructure. The Egyptian Department of Public Works constructed major irrigation canals (Ibrahimiya, Ismailia, and Mahmoudiyah), the Delta Barrages to expand and improve irrigation in the mid-19th century, and the Aswan Low Dam in the late 19th century to allow growing multiple crops per year in the Nile Delta. The Directorate General of Irrigation in Iraq, established in 1917, initially focused on flood control, including diverting flood waters into the Tharthar and Habbaniyah depressions.

During the 20th century, swept along in a worldwide uptick in dam building, states added increasing hydroelectricity for industrialization to their list of interventions, creating a positive feedback loop—more water infrastructure, more agricultural output, more industrial output, and more tax revenue. This feedback loop was accelerated by sovereign states' ability to borrow against future tax revenues, spurring a "hydrologic mission" led by powerful centralized state institutions for water investment and management (Molle, Mollinga, and Wester 2009). States gained popular support from mega projects and the associated expansion of services. The Aswan High Dam in the Arab Republic of Egypt, Karun and Sefidrud Dams in the Islamic Republic of Iran, Mosul Dam in Iraq, and other dams across the region were iconic symbols of state technical capacity enabling the expansion of both irrigated agriculture and electricity production. Between independence and the 1980s, Morocco more than doubled the number of dams, expanded irrigation area from 70,000 to more than 800,000 hectares, and added more than 1,000 megawatts of hydroelectric capacity (Bourblanc and Mayaux 2016).

By contrast, institutions for investing in and managing the domestic water and sewer systems of towns and cities emerged through a bottom-up process linked to local political institutions. Throughout the Ottoman period (17th to early 20th century), as urban centers grew across the region so did the need for local public services, ranging from keeping public order to building and managing markets, streets, and water systems. Cities such as Tripoli, in present day Lebanon, had relative autonomy from the central power in Istanbul, with dignitaries drawn from guilds, traders, and landowners forming the *jama'a al-bilâd*, the city assembly (Lafi 2007). These assemblies appointed a chief of the town, *cheikh al-bilâd*, who managed local services, urban taxes, and the relationship with the Ottoman governor. Although fiscal power was highly centralized in the Ottoman state (Tosun and Yilmaz 2008), these types of local assemblies, which emerged in various forms across MENA, drew on local taxes and contributions for investment in services, including water supply and sanitation systems. During the Ottoman Tanzimat modernization reforms in the second half of the 19th century, these urban assemblies were formalized as municipal councils (*baladiyya*), which persisted through the colonial mandate period and still form the first mile of government in many places across MENA today. As cities grew and managing water supply and sanitation became more complicated, concessions and public companies for managing water were introduced. For example, during the colonial mandate period in Morocco, beginning in 1912, water supply and sanitation in the cities of Casablanca, Meknes, Rabat, Salé, and Tangiers were managed under a concession with a private sector consortium led by the French company Lyonnaise des Eaux.

These two quite distinct origins of formal water management institutions evolved rapidly over the 20th century, buffeted by the colonial mandate period, independence, continued massive growth of urban areas, and increasing water scarcity. Overall, there was a trend toward national-level institutions with a strong emphasis on investing in infrastructure for both irrigation and water supply and sanitation (WSS) services.

Toward the end of the 20th century, a number of factors began to challenge this centralized water management model, including that the scope for storing renewable water resource endowments plateaued, returns to investment diminished, lack of maintenance of past infrastructure became apparent, debt repayments reduced fiscal space, and environmental concerns about dams began to be voiced. Some countries in the region embarked on a period of reform, introducing participatory approaches and basic demand-side interventions whereby, for example, greater responsibility for management of irrigation was shifted to water user associations (WUAs) and user charges for operation and maintenance (O&M) costs were levied on irrigators (Ghazouani, Molle, and Rap 2012). Interventions were often paired with subsidies to promote uptake of more efficient irrigation technologies, such as sprinklers or drip systems.

Unlike in other water scarce parts of the world, particularly federal countries where provincial governments contested and forced greater decentralization of water management and investment, central governments in MENA were able to retain their influence on water management. The limits to expanding opportunities for rural livelihoods led to a period of rapid urbanization, calling for the expansion of urban WSS services. Spurred by the Millennium Development Goals, countries financed the rapid expansion of urban piped water services to reach near universal coverage.[2] The expansion of urban services required additional storage, bulk water conveyance infrastructure, and, more recently, expansion of nonconventional water (desalination and wastewater reuse plants). It provided not only a new line of supply-side infrastructure business for centralized ministries and agencies driving the hydraulic mission but also the pretext to centralize control of water and sanitation services, which from the Ottoman period to the latter half of the 20th century had been managed by municipal institutions. By the end of the 20th century, national WSS utilities had emerged in most countries across MENA—a trend that has continued, with national utilities or holding companies in 14 of 21 countries in the region.

Because of the focus on large-scale infrastructure and the increasing complexity of water systems, in many places, the role of municipalities in managing water has faded into the background and along with it the water sector's more direct political links with local people. However, it is also evident across MENA that municipal institutions persist as the first mile of government (see the appendix). Later chapters of the report come back to this point.

The remainder of this chapter first describes the scale of investment in infrastructure expansion across MENA over the past half century. It then describes signs of stress that are emerging from the region's heavily supply-driven approach to water management.

INDUSTRIAL-SCALE EXPANSION OF WATER-RELATED INFRASTRUCTURE

Dams and Irrigation Systems

The completion of the Aswan High Dam in Egypt in the early 1970s, and the development of dams that followed, increased MENA's total dam storage capacity nearly fourfold (figure 3.1). Large public investments in dam storage supported the expansion of supply for multiple uses, including agriculture, industry, and domestic water supply, as well as the production of hydroelectricity.

Along with the uptick in dam storage, a series of bulk water transport projects were developed to move water from sources to demand centers. For example, the first phase of what is now known as the King Abdullah Canal in Jordan was completed in 1961 to transport water from the Yarmouk River in the north for irrigation schemes along the Jordan Valley. The canal later became a source for the Greater Amman area. In Israel in 1964, the 130-kilometer National Water Carrier was completed to transfer water from the Sea of Galilee in the north of the country to the highly populated center and arid south.

Figure 3.1 Total freshwater capacity and withdrawals in the Middle East and North Africa, 1960–2020

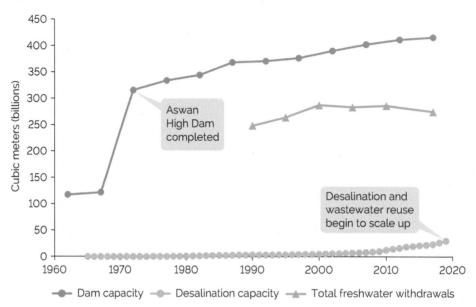

Sources: Food and Agriculture Organization of the United Nations, AQUASTAT (https://www.fao.org/aquastat/en/); Global Water Intelligence, GWI desalination database (https://www.globalwaterintel.com/articles/topic/desalination).

Most of the water infrastructure in Israel is integrated with the National Water Carrier through a network of bulk water pipes that enable efficient use and regulation of the country's water supply. These systems can also combine the use of large rivers, natural depressions, and canal infrastructure to regulate huge variations in annual flows, such as in the Euphrates/Tigris system (Abdullah et al. 2020). Over the intervening decades, these and many other bulk water transport systems have been constructed across the countries in MENA, enabling a high degree of control and even trade in water with neighboring countries and territories.

In addition to dam storage and bulk surface water transport projects, the region has seen significant public and private investment in groundwater exploitation. In oil exporting countries, public investment in groundwater has been for all uses, including agriculture. In Libya, the Great Man-Made River, built in the 1980s for an estimated US$25 billion, supplies 95 percent of the water used in the populated north of the country from the Nubian and other sandstone aquifers through a network of nearly 3,000 kilometers of pipes. In middle-income countries, investment in groundwater has been through combined public and private investment. For example, with its proximity to Casablanca and access to European markets, groundwater in the Sahel of Doukkala pumped from a coastal aquifer drove development in what became one of the most productive agricultural zones in Morocco. Even in 2000, the Food and Agriculture Organization of the United Nations stated that MENA has "virtually no more freshwater to develop" (FAO 2000, 50). By 2017, the continuous development of groundwater across MENA supplied more than 106 billion cubic meters a year, or a third of freshwater withdrawals.

Nonconventional Water: Desalination and Wastewater Reuse

As opportunities to expand dam capacity and exploit groundwater have decreased[3] and demand has continued to rise (World Bank 2018a), there has been a sharp increase in the supply of nonconventional water—desalinated water and wastewater reuse (figure 3.2). The Gulf Cooperation Council countries

Figure 3.2 Desalination and reuse capacity in the Middle East and North Africa, 1960–2020

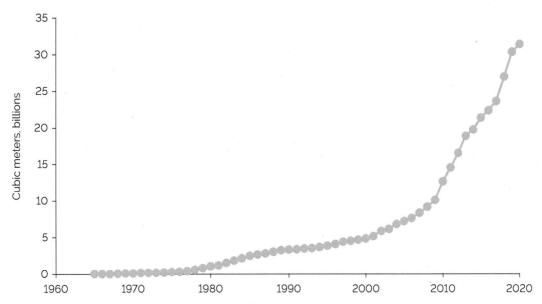

Source: Global Water Intelligence, GWI desalination database (https://www.globalwaterintel.com/articles/topic/desalination).

were early adopters, investing heavily in desalination in the 1980s, pausing in the 1990s, and then ramping up investment again from 2000 onward, including the largest plant in the world—the Ras Al Khair in Saudi Arabia. Israel initiated large investments in desalination from the early 2000s. In Algeria, following a series of violent protests over water shortages, between 2002 and 2004 the government signed a series of public-private partnership contracts for large desalination plants that were constructed over the following decade.[4] As of 2020, nearly half of the installed capacity for water desalination in the world is in MENA (figure 3.3).

Starting later than investment in desalination, investment in wastewater reuse in MENA has seen a sharp increase since 2010. Wastewater reuse is a less precise term than desalination, covering basic reuse, reuse with tertiary treatment for removal of pathogens, and triple-barrier reuse (that is, using ultrafiltration or microfiltration followed by reverse osmosis and ultraviolet disinfection or ozonation). The process deployed is matched with the intended reuse. The higher the quality of treated wastewater, the more expensive is the process. The two main applications of treated wastewater in MENA are agricultural irrigation (47 percent) and landscape irrigation (37 percent). The amount used for potable water is negligible. Egypt has been the largest investor in wastewater treatment and reuse for agricultural irrigation, with installed capacity of more than 4 billion cubic meters per year. This water is channeled to land near the wastewater treatment plants for growing nonedible plants such as jojoba, jatropha, flax, olives, and timber. The United Arab Emirates has the largest applications of wastewater reuse for landscape irrigation.

The cumulative capacity of nonconventional water sources across MENA is more than 30 billion cubic meters per year. This capacity amounts to investments of about US$86 billion,[5] with over 90 percent in eight countries,[6] and more than half of that 90 percent in Saudi Arabia and the United Arab Emirates. Desalination plants make up about 60 percent of the volume, and wastewater reuse plants about 40 percent. Wastewater reuse is expected to expand faster than desalination because it has become a widely accepted practice and many countries have established regulations and

Figure 3.3 Global share of desalinated water capacity, 2021

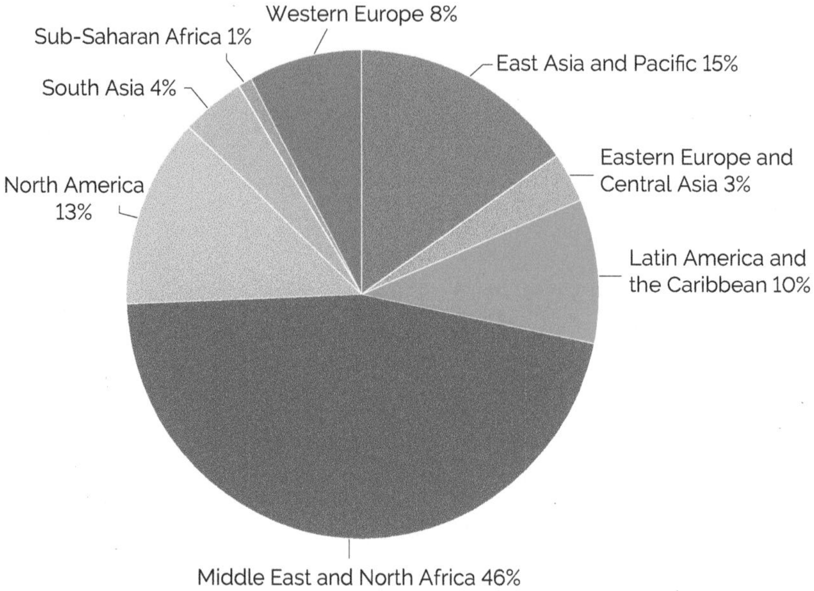

Western Europe 8%
Sub-Saharan Africa 1%
South Asia 4%
North America 13%
East Asia and Pacific 15%
Eastern Europe and Central Asia 3%
Latin America and the Caribbean 10%
Middle East and North Africa 46%

Source: Global Water Intelligence, GWI desalination database (https://www.globalwaterintel.com/articles/topic/desalination).

standards on the uses of wastewater. In the face of continued economic and population growth as well as climate impacts, countries plan to invest in another 10 billion cubic meters of capacity by 2025.

The expansion of investment in nonconventional water has been driven and overseen by central ministries across MENA. The private sector has dominated construction and manages a large share of the O&M of both desalination and wastewater treatment plants providing water for reuse. However, the "off-takers" purchasing nonconventional water are almost exclusively state-owned enterprises (SOEs). This split in the nonconventional water structure is referred to as vertical unbundling and mirrors institutional developments in the electricity sector. Most of the very large desalination projects in the Gulf have applied the independent water plant model using long-term build-operate-transfer contracts. The exception is Saudi Arabia, which preferred awarding projects on an engineering, procurement, and construction basis to retain state ownership and operation of plants through its Saline Water Conversion Corporation.

The centralization of WSS institutions, integration with bulk storage and transmission infrastructure, and more recent investment in desalination and wastewater treatment have created highly "networked" bulk water systems in which moving water around countries has become routine and, in many countries, detached from traditional river basin management models. Saudi Arabia has 8,400 kilometers of bulk water pipelines. Bulk water pipelines in the United Arab Emirates transport more than 4 billion cubic meters of water a year, over half of which comes from desalination plants and the rest from groundwater. Even middle-income countries such as Iraq, Jordan and Morocco have multiple inter-basin transfer mechanisms and pipelines moving water from sources to demand centers. This networked nature of bulk water systems has given central governments an enhanced set of levers with which to allocate water among its competing uses and, with those levers, centralized responsibility for resolving water allocation dilemmas. The dilemmas involve the competing uses to which water should flow (agriculture, cities, or the environment) and the policy conditions attached to those flows (quantity and price restrictions).

Expansion of Piped Water and Sewage Networks

In addition to the industrial-scale expansion of bulk water supply, MENA has also seen significant expansion of water utility piped water and sewage networks. Data for network connectivity do not go back as far as those for bulk water infrastructure. Between 2000 and 2017, however, about 118 million people were connected to water networks provided by public utilities, and an estimated 85 million were connected to sewer networks (figure 3.4).

Only five economies—Algeria, Jordan, Libya, the Syrian Arab Republic, and the West Bank and Gaza—saw a decline in the proportion of people with piped water access from 2000 to 2017 (figure 3.5, panel a). Two countries—Libya and Syria—have experienced widespread violent conflict and destruction of infrastructure, leading to a decline in the absolute number of people with access to piped water (World Bank, ICRC, and UNICEF 2021). The large drop in access in the West Bank and Gaza is due to sea water intrusion in the Gaza aquifer, which has made it too salty to use as a source of domestic drinking water (World Bank 2018b). During this period, Jordan hosted an estimated 1.6 million refugees from

Figure 3.4 Water and sewer network connections in the Middle East and North Africa, 2000–17

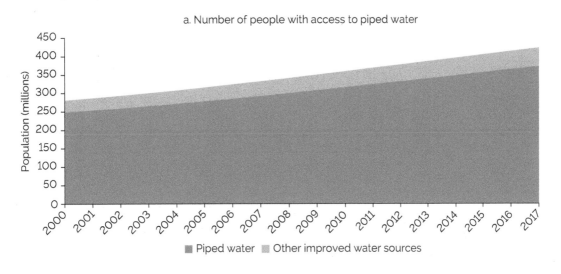

a. Number of people with access to piped water

■ Piped water　■ Other improved water sources

b. Number of people with access to sewers

■ Sewer　■ Septic tank　■ Other improved

Source: World Health Organization/United Nations Children's Fund Joint Monitoring Program (https://washdata.org/monitoring/methods/facility-types).

Figure 3.5 Change in access to piped water and sewage connections, Middle East and North Africa, 2000–17

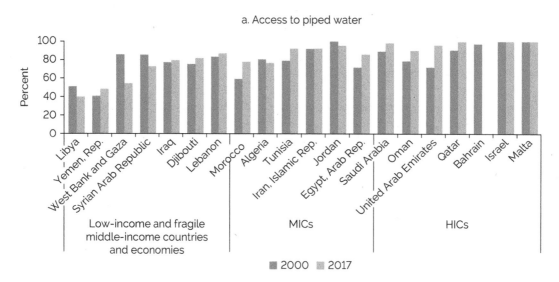

a. Access to piped water

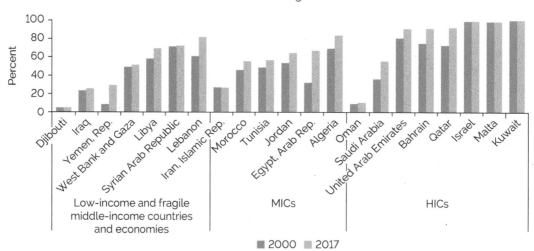

b. Access to sewage connections

Source: World Health Organization/United Nations Children's Fund Joint Monitoring Program (https://washdata.org/monitoring /methods/facility-types).
Note: In panel a, data are missing for Kuwait for both years and for Bahrain for 2017. HICs = high-income countries; MICs = middle-income countries.

neighboring conflict zones and still saw an increase of 3.6 million in the number of people connected to piped water services. Algeria also saw an increase—with 6.6 million people gaining access. The growth in the proportion of the population with sewage connections (figure 3.5, panel b) reflects the growth in infrastructure but not whether the sewage is being treated. The distinction between WSS infrastructure expansion and the quality of services is discussed further in chapter 4 on demand-side behavior.

The expansion of access to water—both bulk water and network infrastructure—has been supported by development partners with more US$20 billion in gross disbursements to countries across MENA between 2002 and 2019. Nearly all aid flows to the water sector in MENA have been project rather than program based (UN-Water and WHO 2019).[7] Eighty percent of this official development assistance has been for expansion and rehabilitation of infrastructure: large

WSS systems (54 percent), basic WSS (10 percent), and agricultural water (16 percent).[8] Over the period, US$3.5 billion (18 percent) was spent on water sector policy and governance, including legislation, regulation, planning, and management, as well as on transboundary management of water, institutional capacity development, and activities supporting the integrated water resource management approach. However, little of the assistance was targeted specifically at water resources conservation (1 percent) or river basin development (1 percent).

SIGNS OF DISTRESS IN MANAGING SUPPLY-SIDE INFRASTRUCTURE

Supply-side interventions through infrastructure expansion have provided only a short-term solution to scarcity, eventually and paradoxically enabling increased water demand (Damania et al. 2017; Di Baldassarre et al. 2018). As water availability increases, consumption tends to increase—which is known in economics as the Jevons paradox. Higher consumption not only may lead to unsustainable exploitation of water resources but also increases the scale of potential economic damage caused by droughts when extended dry shocks occur and the infrastructure fails users who are highly dependent on dam storage.

The following subsections summarize the signs of stress emerging from the heavily supply-driven approach, which are evident from the operational status of dams and irrigation systems as well as the financial and operational performance of WSS service providers. Beyond these, chapter 5 discusses a set of negative externalities.

Dams

Two symptoms of the lack of recurrent investment in dams across the region are the loss of storage capacity due to sedimentation and growing concerns about dam safety.

Sediment management was a central problem in some of the region's earliest water management structures, highlighting the ever-present need for sustainably managing sediment alongside water supplies. In Jordan, Petra's well-known water harvesting and conveyance structures functioned thanks to sediment settling tanks that allowed for the periodic removal of sediment. In Egypt, sediment release contributed to soil fertility management.

In modern-day MENA, sediment continues to present a major challenge in managing water storage infrastructure. Despite patchy reporting on sedimentation rates, existing data suggest that some of the region's large dams have lost about half their water storage capacity to sedimentation (table 3.1).[9] In the Maghreb, about 35 percent of the reservoirs with capacity greater than 1 million cubic meters have life spans of less than 50 years because of siltation (Sadaoui et al. 2018). In Morocco, the countrywide water storage capacity lost to sedimentation is estimated at about 70 million cubic meters per year (Houzir, Mokass, and Schalatek 2016). Reservoirs in the Mashreq region face similar challenges, with the King Talal Dam in Jordan having lost about a fifth of its initial storage capacity to sedimentation (El-Radaideh, Al-Taani, and Al Khateeb 2017). In some cases, sediments trapped behind dams pose environmental hazards because they contain heavy metals and other toxic substances.

Alongside sedimentation, dam safety poses increasing concerns, with the recent emergency rehabilitation of Mosul Dam making international headlines. Since the beginning of its operation in the 1980s, the dam has suffered seepage problems and destabilization, which require continued interventions to reduce the risk of failure and subsequent catastrophic flooding that could affect millions of people downstream (Milillo et al. 2016).

Irrigation

Expansion of large-scale irrigation systems in the region accelerated in the 1960s, reaching nearly 25 million hectares by 2018, and is still taking place in selected areas, such as parts of Egypt

Table 3.1 Selected dams ranked by sedimentation rates in the Middle East and North Africa region

Country	Name of dam	River	Operational since	Estimated reservoir capacity (million cubic meters)	Sedimentation (latest known) (%)
Iran, Islamic Rep.	Karoun 1	Karoun	1976	3,139	53.9
Iran, Islamic Rep.	Karoun 3	Karoun	2004	2,970	42.1
Iran, Islamic Rep.	Sefidroud	Sefidroud	1961	1,800	38.9
Morocco	Mohammed V	Moulouya	1967	725	35.4
Iran, Islamic Rep.	Karkheh	Karkheh	2001	5,575	31.1
Iran, Islamic Rep.	Zayanderoud	Zayanderoud	1970	1,450	13.8
Morocco	Mansour Eddahbi	Draa	1972	592	10.6
Iran, Islamic Rep.	Dez	Dez	1962	2,856	9.0
Morocco	Bin El Ouidane	El Abid	1953	1,484	6.7
Morocco	Sidi Mohamed Ben Abdellah	Bouregreg	1974	1,025	4.5
Morocco	Oued El Makhazine	Loukkos	1979	807	4.2
Morocco	Al Massira	Oum Er R'Bia	1979	2,760	3.0
Algeria	Gargar	Rhiou	1988	450	2.9
Morocco	Idriss 1°	Inaouene	1973	1,217	2.5
Jordan	Wadha (Unity)	Yarmouk River	2007	55	0.6
Syrian Arab Republic	Unity (Wadha)	Yarmouk River	2007	55	0.6
Jordan	Mujib	Wadi Al Mujib	2003	31.2	0.3
Jordan	Karamah	Wadi Al Mallaha	1998	52.52	0.1

Source: Food and Agriculture Organization of the United Nations' Geo-referenced Database on Dams, AQUASTAT (https://www.fao.org/aquastat/en/databases/dams).

(Borgomeo and Santos 2019). Although they resulted in an increase in the area equipped for irrigation, these investments have been constrained by water scarcity and quality issues. As shown in figures 3.6 and 3.7, only three-quarters of the area equipped for irrigation is actually irrigated. For example, in Tunisia, cropping intensity in irrigated areas is 60 percent of the potential because of water-related constraints (shortages; salinity); in Algeria, actual irrigated area might be less than 50 percent of the

Figure 3.6 Expansion of irrigated area across the Middle East and North Africa and area irrigated, 1997–2017

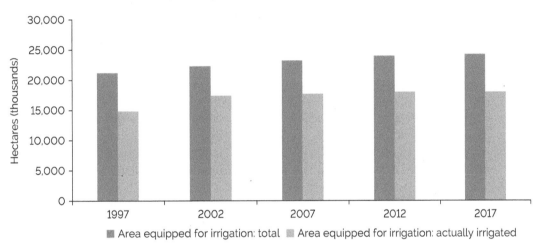

Source: Food and Agriculture Organization of the United Nations, AQUASTAT (https://www.fao.org/aquastat/en/).

Figure 3.7 Expansion of irrigated area, by economy, 2017

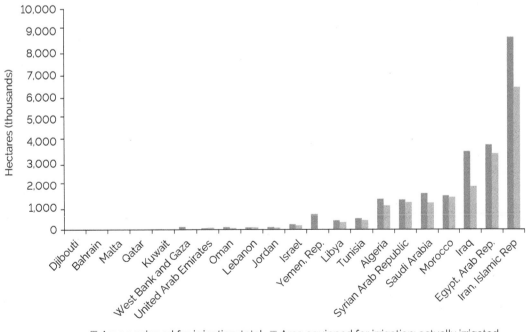

Source: Food and Agriculture Organization of the United Nations, AQUASTAT (https://www.fao.org/aquastat/en/).

area equipped for irrigation (Molle, Sanchis-Ibor, and Avellà-Reus 2019). In Iraq, which faces declining quantities of water availability in the Tigris and Euphrates, reports suggest that salinity has negatively affected 70 percent of agricultural land, with as much as 30 percent of the land abandoned (FAO 2011). Across the region, just over 5.3 million hectares are reported to be salinized by irrigation.[10]

Since the late 20th century, irrigation infrastructure expansion, which was originally managed by centralized government irrigation agencies, has been accompanied by a push for decentralized participatory management linked to irrigation modernization programs. Despite the long tradition of communal management of irrigation structures in the region, these recent attempts at increasing water user participation have faced challenges (Khadra and Sagardoy 2019).

First, although intended to play a key role in the implementation of irrigation modernization programs, the decentralized WUAs received much less institutional support compared with the modernization of irrigation networks and on-farm systems.

Second, the ways the roles and responsibilities for irrigation have been decentralized to WUAs have varied greatly across countries and even across areas within countries, including (1) the level of irrigations system (primary, secondary, or tertiary canals) delegated to WUAs to manage O&M, (2) the aspects of operation and/or maintenance assigned to WUAs, and (3) whether WUAs or central irrigation agencies collect irrigation service fees. In many cases, these factors have limited the autonomy of the WUAs and, in some cases, led to a disconnect between roles and responsibilities. For example, unlike in countries such as Italy and Spain, which have delegated whole irrigation systems to WUAs, countries in MENA have not transferred the management of major irrigation works (main canals, large pumping stations, and irrigation dams) to WUAs. In Morocco and Tunisia, irrigation agencies manage major hydraulic works on main irrigation systems. In the case of Egypt, works at even lower levels (branch and secondary canals) remain under public management. In Jordan, central irrigation agencies still collect irrigation service fees, and WUAs simply manage the allocation of available water among irrigators (van den Berg et al. 2016). Notably, decentralization in MENA has not included delegation of water rights to WUAs.

Third, decentralization efforts were predicated on the argument that increased user participation would contribute to enhanced cost recovery and maintenance of irrigation infrastructure. Limited evidence exists to support this argument. Because of the partial and uneven nature of decentralization, little consolidated information is available on O&M coverage across countries and, even where it exists, matching the data with the varied delegation of roles and responsibilities is difficult. A drive to increase irrigation fees in Tunisia in the late 1990s is credited with covering O&M costs, and there are some bright spots in other countries (for example, the Tadla scheme in Morocco). However, other areas in Morocco and other countries in the region have not achieved O&M cost coverage—with rates of cost coverage between 5 and 60 percent (Molle, Sanchis-Ibor, and Avellà-Reus 2019). The result is a recurring burden on state finances, which are used periodically to revamp and rehabilitate aging and dilapidated infrastructure.

Last, governments justified the modernization programs by the water they would save through improving irrigation networks as well as increasing on-farm use of irrigation technologies such as drip irrigation. Governments offered generous subsidies to irrigators (between 40 and 100 percent) for purchasing irrigation equipment. Despite evidence that productivity has increased as a result of modernization programs, they have not led to water savings (chapter 7 discusses why these savings did not materialize in most cases).

Water Supply and Sanitation

The stress in managing WSS service delivery manifests in terms of service provider finances (recurrent deficits and accumulated debt) as well as in key operational indicators. Today, despite their common origins as municipal entities, the institutional arrangements for WSS service provision have become extremely diverse across MENA, ranging from highly centralized to highly decentralized and everything in between. At one extreme, such as in Iraq and Kuwait, a central government ministry manages WSS service delivery. At the other extreme, service provision arrangements are still highly decentralized. The West Bank and Gaza has more than 300 WSS service providers, which are managed by departments of municipalities and even village councils. Many economies in the region still have pockets where municipalities run the services either because they have resisted attempts to aggregate them into larger subnational utilities (Israel and Lebanon) or because they are remote (Algeria). In the United Arab Emirates, the individual emirates have taken a leading role in a decentralized city-state model of WSS service provision. Between the two extremes are national SOE models (Algeria, Bahrain, Djibouti, Malta, Oman, and Tunisia) and subnational governorate- or regional-level SOEs (Egypt, the Islamic Republic of Iran, Lebanon, and Jordan) that have been formed by clustering the services originally managed by municipalities.

As well as vertical unbundling, which is the separation of bulk water production from distribution, some countries have horizontal unbundling of WSS services. In Algeria and Tunisia, water services and sewage services are delivered by separate SOEs—although Algeria has reintegrated water and sewage services into joint subsidiaries of the national SOEs. Bahrain, Qatar, Kuwait, and the United Arab Emirates, where desalination is the major water source, have integrated water and electricity delivery into a single SOE because of the high energy demands of desalination.

Institutional diversity also occurs within countries. For example, Morocco's particularly diverse service provision setup has four categories of WSS service providers: the national public company, the National Office of Electricity and Drinking Water, managing bulk water and supplying 28 percent of customers; private concessionaires supplying customers in Casablanca, Rabat, Tangiers, and Tetouan (38 percent of customers); municipal utilities (31 percent); and municipalities providing services directly (3 percent). Some smaller municipalities provide sewer services directly, despite a policy to transfer these services to the national public company. Morocco's law on decentralization[11] also retains the core idea of the municipality as the service authority with ultimate responsibility for public services that can be delegated to a public or private entity—although few formal contracts exist today.

Compared to the expansion of bulk water infrastructure, the expansion of piped water and wastewater networks has been more piecemeal, using private contractors to hook up unserved neighborhoods and new housing developments, or through organic growth in connecting new houses, apartments, and industries to the network. The main exception to this piecemeal approach has been the program of new city developments in Egypt, where the central Ministry of Housing, Utilities and Urban Communities allocated funding to set up more than 20 new networks and utilities through the New Urban Communities Authority.

Within this complex institutional environment, a picture of WSS financing can be viewed top-down from the perspective of public financial flows or bottom-up from the utilities. The challenge in MENA is the limited publicly available data on public budgets and utility finances. Public budgetary data capture only recurrent subsidies from the public purse, not service provider debt or tariff revenues.[12] Although only five utilities across MENA publish their annual audited financial statements online,[13] this report collected data on 45 utilities; these data provide a bottom-up picture of WSS financing covering services to over 60 percent of the people across MENA, albeit with key limitations. This low level of transparency, financial accountability, and compliance with international generally accepted accounting standards is itself a barrier to sector governance.

Nevertheless, a picture emerges of the stresses on WSS service providers. The operating cost recovery ratio, the proportion of basic operating expenditures covered by customer tariffs, is a core starting point for understanding service provider finances and was available for 45 service providers (figure 3.8).

Figure 3.8 Operating cost recovery ratio for selected utilities and years across the Middle East and North Africa

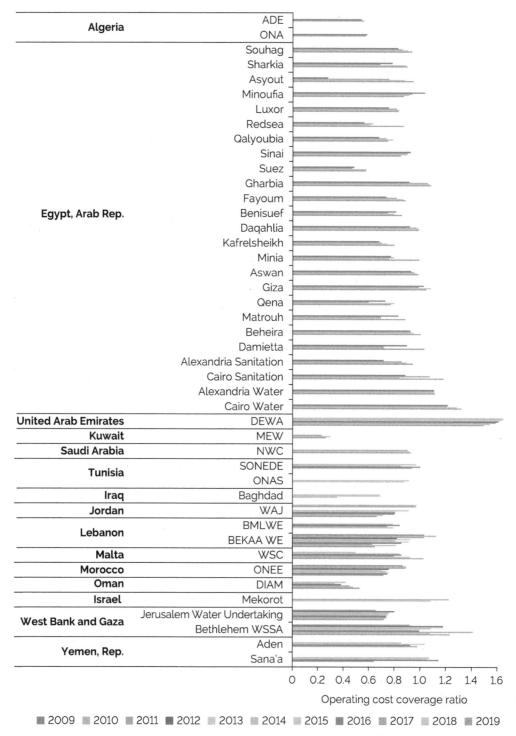

Source: World Bank, MENA Water Report database.
Note: See annex A for a list of utilities included in this figure.

Of these, 41 could not consistently cover their basic operating expenditures from customer tariffs, with general taxation covering on average a quarter of operating costs and as much as three-quarters in Kuwait.

Even with subsidies included, only three of the utilities could consistently cover their basic operational costs. Some subsidies were insufficient to cover operational costs or were not provided consistently. In these cases, service providers are forced to take on debt from local banks or advances from ministries of finance, or they do not pay their suppliers, such as electricity distribution companies. With energy representing a major cost driver for water pumping and treatment, water utilities are particularly exposed to rising energy costs. For example, in Jordan following the Arab Spring, electricity tariffs for pumping and treating water increased more than threefold by 2018, accounting for half of total water utility operating expenses (World Bank 2019).

Only four of the service providers could consistently cover their basic operating expenditures from customer tariffs. In a relatively low-cost, low-tariff (US$0.11/cubic meter) conventional water context, Alexandria and Cairo, in Egypt, could consistently cover the operating costs of water supply—although not wastewater services. By contrast, in a relatively high-cost, high-tariff (US$2.58/cubic meter) nonconventional water context, the Dubai Electricity and Water Authority (DEWA) was consistently able to cover its operating expenditures. Qatar Electricity and Water Company (QWEC) is a fully integrated WSS and electricity utility that cross-subsidizes the WSS costs from electricity tariff revenues.

The different contexts of Cairo and Dubai illustrate the changes in sector governance that underpin moving from conventional water abstracted from a passing river to nonconventional water with seawater desalination as the main source. These changes in sector governance go beyond a 20-fold increase in the tariff and are not even specifically linked to the transition in technology from conventional to nonconventional water. Rather, the paradigm shift in sector governance lies in the respective roles of the state and its utilities. Before making the shift, governments fund most of the capital expenditure and utilities manage the recurrent financing of O&M. After the shift, utilities like DEWA play a central role in managing O&M *and* the long-term financing of service delivery. In this latter role, utilities, empowered with a higher degree of financial and administrative independence, use revenues[14] to finance O&M and pay leases on any public-private partnerships and debt financing. Doing so can enable them to issue debt on the international financial markets, which comes with the requirement of a much higher level of financial transparency because it opens them to scrutiny by the credit rating agencies.

The handful of utilities in MENA that have made this shift have successfully raised finance from capital markets. Based on their audited financial statements, they have raised an estimated US$10 billion from capital markets mainly in the form of bonds.[15] Some utilities in MENA, however, have only partially made the shift toward taking responsibility for the long-term financing of WSS services and are as a result in a bind. These utilities have had thrust upon them the responsibility for long-term financing but without the revenues (from tariffs and/or taxes) to match that responsibility. The mismatch between responsibility and revenues has led to the accumulation of debt from a combination of recurrent deficits and liabilities for lease payments to supply-side public-private partnerships. The at-risk water sector–related debt[16] is estimated at US$8 billion and expected to rise as countries pursue energy intensive supply-side interventions—mainly desalination and wastewater reuse projects—through various forms of public-private partnership with sovereign guarantees. In Jordan, for example, water-related debt is equivalent to 15 percent of gross domestic product and expected to increase in the coming years if it is not resolved.

These signs of stress also manifest as deferred maintenance of existing publicly managed parts of the production and distribution system. For example, the levels of nonrevenue water (NRW) remain stubbornly high across countries in MENA, with half of the service providers reporting that over 30 percent of the water they produce is not billed to customers (figure 3.9). The optimal level of NRW

Figure 3.9 Nonrevenue water of selected utilities in the Middle East and North Africa

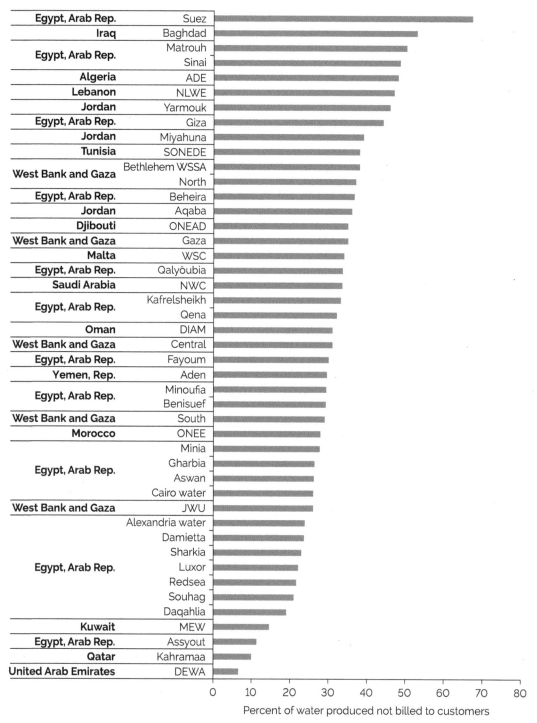

Percent of water produced not billed to customers

Sources: Annual financial statements from country utilities; World Bank calculations.

should be determined using financial/economic analysis (that is, when the marginal cost of saving a cubic meter of water equals the marginal cost of supplying it), suggesting that the higher the reliance on desalinated water, the lower the optimal NRW target.

This chapter has described how the formal institutions for managing water in MENA have two separate origins: central authorities that have driven the expansion of infrastructure and municipal governments that provide water supply and sanitation services to local populations. As centralized institutions have driven supply-side infrastructure expansion and taken over service delivery, the role of municipalities and their connections with local water management have diminished.

Over the past couple of decades, investment in dams and groundwater exploitation has plateaued and given way to expanding nonconventional water—both desalination of seawater and reuse of wastewater. The level of water-related infrastructure development—dams, control structures, bulk water carriers, desalination, and wastewater reuse schemes—has led to the increasingly "networked" nature of bulk water management. This hyper-centralization puts a great deal of responsibility on the central government entities tasked with allocating water resources and financing the sector.

Signs of stress exist in the O&M of this supply-side infrastructure across dams, irrigation systems, and WSS. In the case of dams and irrigation systems, the signs of stress primarily manifest in lack of maintenance of infrastructure.

In the case of WSS service providers, expansion into nonconventional water, for which they bear most of the cost, stresses them financially and in turn leads to deferred maintenance and high levels of NRW. Although expanding the use of nonconventional water is an important way for countries in MENA to escape the confines of their shrinking renewable water resource endowments, the transition comes with higher service delivery costs. Other than the handful of utilities in MENA empowered by the state to take charge of long-term financing of service delivery, the transition to nonconventional water is driving up WSS service providers' recurrent annual deficits and debt. The result is a mismatch between responsibilities and revenue, and it looks to be a growing problem across MENA as more countries continue to pursue supply-side interventions without addressing demand-side questions.

NOTES

1. For example, the growth of mixed farming in 18th and 19th century England.

2. A key theme explored later is that access to infrastructure is not the same as access to services.

3. Most MENA countries have a large share of surface water stored in reservoirs but low volumes of water stored in dams per capita. That is, they have stored all the water available to store (World Bank 2018a).

4. From the Pacific Institute Water Conflict Chronology (http://www.worldwater.org/conflict/list/); Global Water Intelligence, GWI desalination database (https://www.globalwaterintel.com/articles/topic/desalination).

5. Current prices for 2020.

6. Saudi Arabia, the United Arab Emirates, Kuwait, Qatar, Libya, Algeria, Oman, and Israel.

7. Organisation for Economic Co-operation and Development, "Financing for Sustainable Development," https://www.oecd.org/dac/financing-sustainable-development/.

8. "Financing for Sustainable Development."

9. Food and Agriculture Organization of the United Nations' Geo-referenced Database on Dams, AQUASTAT, https://www.fao.org/aquastat/en/databases/dams.

10. AQUASTAT.

11. 1976 Charte Communale.

12. The two main sources of publicly available data on public expenditure are the Classification of the Functions of Government (COFOG) and the World Bank BOOST database. Data for Malta and Israel are available in COFOG and data for Jordan are available through BOOST.

13. They are DEWA (Dubai), DIAM (Oman), Mekorot (Israel), QWEC (Qatar), and Water Services Corporation (Malta).

14. Revenues can come from both water tariffs and subsidies paid from general taxation to utilities.

15. Utilities raising debt through local or international bonds included DEWA (United Arab Emirates), QWEC (Qatar), Water Authority of Jordan (Jordan), Water Services Corporation (Malta), and Mekorot (Israel).

16. This estimate is based on debt that meets both of the following criteria: (1) the operating cost coverage ratio is less than 1, and (2) the sovereign credit rating is below investment grade.

REFERENCES

Abdullah, M., N. Al-Ansari, N. Adamo, V. K. Sissakian, and J. Laue. 2020. "Floods and Flood Protection in Mesopotamia." *Journal of Earth Sciences and Geotechnical Engineering* 10 (4): 155–73.

Borgomeo, E., and N. Santos. 2019. *Towards a New Generation of Policies and Investments in Agricultural Water in the Arab Region: Fertile Ground for Innovation*. Rome: Food and Agriculture Organization of the United Nations, and Colombo, Sri Lanka: International Water Management Institute.

Bourblanc, M., and P.-L. Mayaux. 2016. "Comparing Hydrocracies in Morocco and South Africa: Water Reform and Bureaucratic Restructuring in a Neo-liberal Context." In *Water Regimes Questioned from the "Global South": Agents, Practices and Knowledge*, edited by S. Dasgupta, R. de Bercegol, O. Henry, B. O'Neill, F. Poupeau, A. Richard-Ferroudji, and M.-H. Zérah, 47. New Delhi: Centre for Policy Research.

Damania, R., S. Desbureaux, M. Hyland, A. Islam, S. Moore, A.-S. Rodella, J. Russ, and E. Zaveri. 2017. *Uncharted Waters: The New Economics of Water Scarcity and Variability*. Washington, DC: World Bank. https:// openknowledge.worldbank.org/handle/10986/28096.

Di Baldassarre, G., N. Wanders, A. AghaKouchak, L. Kuil, S. Rangecroft, T. I. E. Veldkamp, M. Garcia, P. R. van Oel, K. Breinl, and A. F. Van Loon. 2018. "Water Shortages Worsened by Reservoir Effects." *Nature Sustainability* 1 (11): 617–22. https://doi.org/10.1038/s41893-018-0159-0.

El-Radaideh, N., A. A. Al-Taani, and W. M. Al Khateeb. 2017. "Status of Sedimentation in King Talal Dam, Case Study from Jordan." *Environmental Earth Sciences* 76 (3): 132.

FAO (Food and Agriculture Organization of the United Nations). 2000. "New Dimensions in Water Security: Water, Society and Ecosystem Services in the 21st Century." Land and Water Development Division, FAO, Rome. http://www.fao.org/3/x4687e/x4687e.pdf.

FAO (Food and Agriculture Organization of the United Nations). 2011. *Iraq: Agriculture Sector Note*. FAO Investment Centre Country Highlights Report 4. Rome: FAO. https://www.fao.org/3/i2877e/i2877e.pdf.

Ghazouani, W., F. Molle, and E. Rap. 2012. "Water Users Associations in the Near-East Northern Africa Region: IFAD Interventions and Overall Dynamics." Project Report Submitted to the International Fund for Agricultural Development by the International Water Management Institute, Colombo, Sri Lanka.

Houzir, M., M. Mokass, and L. Schalatek. 2016. "Climate Governance and the Role of Climate Finance in Morocco." Heinrich Böll Stiftung, Washington, DC.

Khadra, R., and J. A. Sagardoy. 2019. *Irrigation Governance Challenges in the Mediterranean Region: Learning from Experiences and Promoting Sustainable Performance*. Cham, Switzerland: Springer. https://doi .org/10.1007/978-3-030-13554-6.

Lafi, N. 2007. "The Ottoman Municipal Reforms between Old Regime and Modernity: Towards a New Interpretative Paradigm." In *First International Symposium on Eminönü,* 348–55. Istanbul: Eminönü Belediyesi. https:// halshs.archives-ouvertes.fr/halshs-00146210.

Milillo, P., R. Bürgmann, P. Lundgren, J. Salzer, D. Perissin, E. Fielding, F. Biondi, and G. Milillo. 2016. "Space Geodetic Monitoring of Engineered Structures: The Ongoing Destabilization of the Mosul Dam, Iraq." *Scientific Reports* 6: 37408. https://doi.org/10.1038/srep37408.

Molle, F., P. P. Mollinga, and P. Wester. 2009. "Hydraulic Bureaucracies and the Hydraulic Mission: Flows of Water, Flows of Power." *Water Alternatives* 2 (3): 328–49.

Molle, F., C. Sanchis-Ibor, and L. Avellà-Reus, eds. 2019. *Irrigation in the Mediterranean: Technologies, Institutions, and Policies*. Global Issues in Water Policy 22. Cham, Switzerland: Springer.

Sadaoui, M., W. Ludwig, F. Bourrin, Y. Le Bissonnais, and E. Romero. 2018. "Anthropogenic Reservoirs of Various Sizes Trap Most of the Sediment in the Mediterranean Maghreb Basin." *Water* 10 (7): 927. https://doi.org/10.3390/w10070927.

Tosun, M. S., and S. Yilmaz. 2008. "Decentralization, Economic Development, and Growth in Turkish Provinces." Policy Research Working Paper 4725, World Bank, Washington, DC. https://openknowledge.worldbank.org /handle/10986/6979.

UN-Water (United Nations–Water) and WHO (World Health Organization). 2019. *National Systems to Support Drinking-Water, Sanitation and Hygiene: Global Status Report 2019*. UN-Water Global Analysis and Assessment of Sanitation and Drinking Water (GLAAS) 2019 Report. Geneva: WHO.

van den Berg, C., and S. Kh. H. Agha Al Nimar. 2016. *The Cost of Irrigation Water in the Jordan Valley*. World Bank, Washington, DC. https://openknowledge.worldbank.org/handle/10986/23997.

Wittfogel, K. A. 1957. *Oriental Despotism: A Comparative Study of Total Power*. New Haven, CT: Yale University Press.

World Bank. 2018a. *Beyond Scarcity: Water Security in the Middle East and North Africa*. MENA Development Series. Washington, DC: World Bank.

World Bank. 2018b. "Toward Water Security for Palestinians: West Bank and Gaza Water Supply, Sanitation, and Hygiene Poverty Diagnostic." World Bank, Washington, DC. https://openknowledge.worldbank.org/handle /10986/30316.

World Bank. 2019. "Implementation Completion and Results Report on IBRD Loans with the Concessional Financial Facility Support in the Aggregate Amount of US$500 Million to the Hashemite Kingdom of Jordan for the First and Second Programmatic Energy and Water Sector Reforms Development Policy Loans." Report ICR00004657, World Bank, Washington, DC. https://documents1.worldbank.org/curated /en/222301546546705732/pdf/icr00004657-12282018-636818041906584165.pdf.

World Bank, ICRC (International Committee of the Red Cross), and UNICEF (United Nations Children's Fund). 2021. "Joining Forces to Combat Protracted Crises: Humanitarian and Development Support for Water Supply and Sanitation Providers in the Middle East and North Africa." World Bank, Washington, DC. https://openknowledge.worldbank.org/handle/10986/35122.

CHAPTER 4

Demand-Side Behavior That Challenges States' Ability to Raise Finance and Regulate Water

DRIVERS OF WATER DEMAND

The two major drivers of water demand in countries across the Middle East and North Africa (MENA) region are irrigation and domestic water supply, with industrial withdrawals in third place. Despite being the most water scarce region, MENA has a higher proportion of water consumed by agriculture (83 percent) than the world average (70 percent). Demand from industry is low (5 percent) compared to the world average of 20 percent (figure 4.1). Where it is higher, it is often linked to oil production.

This chapter describes how the two main competing demands have developed over time, contrasting the demand for irrigation water in a vast arid region in which water is a binding constraint to production with the relatively predictable yet growing water needs of cities. How these two consumptive uses interact to create synergies between cities and agricultural areas depends on the presence of a long-term financing mechanism that will support countries to go beyond the ecological limits of conventional water endowments.

Water: A Binding Constraint to Agriculture in a Vast Arid Region

At the aggregate level, MENA is the most water scarce region in the world. However, hydrological variability over space and time means that there is a huge range of average annual renewable water

Figure 4.1 Water withdrawals, by sector and economy

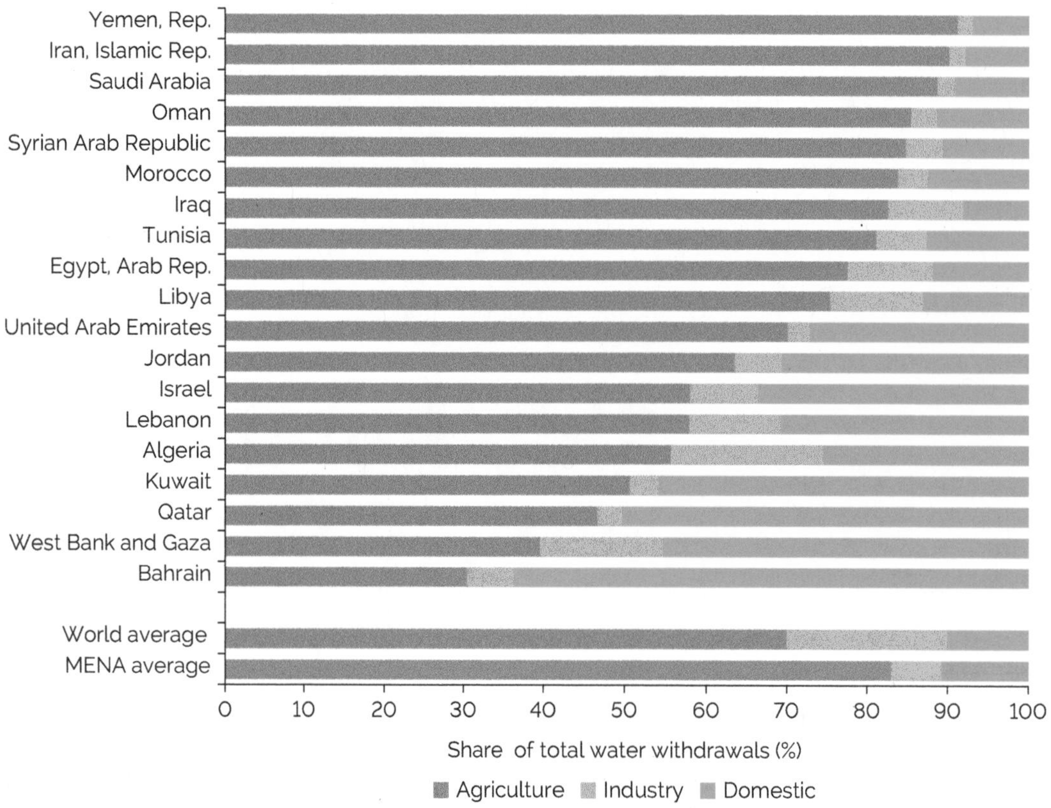

Source: World Bank 2017.
Note: MENA = Middle East and North Africa.

resources available by country. In absolute terms, for example, the Islamic Republic of Iran has nearly 7,000 times the annually renewable water resources of Kuwait. These very different water endowments have shaped rural livelihoods for millennia, ranging from nomadic pastoralism in the arid Arabian Peninsula to flood-recession grain production along the major rivers in the region. Between these extremes are small but diverse agroecological zones and micro-climates that have supported rainfed agriculture at higher latitudes and altitudes as well as traditional irrigation systems in the foothills and valleys of the mountainous areas.

These water endowments alone were not enough to create the demand for agricultural water seen today. It is evident both from a historical perspective—the accounts of historians—and in more recent times—from the data—that the supply of irrigation infrastructure itself has facilitated demand for agricultural water.

In the 19th century, the limited public investment in and maintenance of irrigation systems (with the exception of the Arab Republic of Egypt) are thought to have severely constrained growth of agricultural production and economic growth across the region. Distinct from Western Europe, where individual farm-level working capital drove growth in mixed farming, agricultural productivity across MENA, beyond the areas suitable for rainfed agriculture (just 3.5 percent of the region's arid landmass), required public investment in irrigation infrastructure to enable growth in agricultural productivity.

In the post–World War II period, the massive public investment in dams and irrigation canals, described in the previous chapter, was followed by private investment in groundwater exploitation, especially as advances in technology brought down the costs of exploration and drilling. This second wave of irrigation investment, initiated by farmers (small and large) beginning in the 1970s and 1980s, was often to supplement the supply of surface irrigation water because of (1) annual variation in publicly supplied surface water availability, (2) lack of maintenance of public irrigation infrastructure, and (3) overexpansion of public irrigation infrastructure schemes.

Access to groundwater "liberated" irrigators from the hierarchical state-controlled surface water irrigation systems and diminished reliance on traditional collective management systems (Kuper et al. 2016). Spurred by the opportunity to expand agricultural production, countries promoted groundwater exploitation, providing subsidies for drilling wells and cheap sources of energy for pumping water. The opportunity also led to countries losing control of agricultural water abstractions and the externalities they cause—a central theme returned to throughout this report.

In this vast arid region, water rather than land is a key constraint to production, (Di Baldassarre et al. 2018). Only 5.5 percent of the region's landmass is cultivated, split between 3.5 percent that is rainfed agriculture and just 2 percent that is irrigated (map 4.1).

Policy makers provided and farmers supplemented publicly provided water with investment in groundwater. Peaking in the early 2000s at above 260 billion cubic meters a year, three times the agricultural water withdrawals of the 1960s, agricultural withdrawals fell back slightly to an estimated 252 billion cubic meters a year by 2018.

Led by countries with large agrarian populations and supported by green revolution technologies, gross agricultural output (by weight) grew by nearly four times over this period (figure 4.2) and agriculture's value added grew by more than five times.[1] Confirming the basic logic of policy makers, in 2018 the region's irrigated area contributed nearly twice as much (US$98.5 billion) to agricultural valued added as did rainfed areas (US$50.5 billion).[2] Limited data are available on the incomes of famers practicing

Map 4.1 Land cover classification of the Middle East and North Africa, 2015

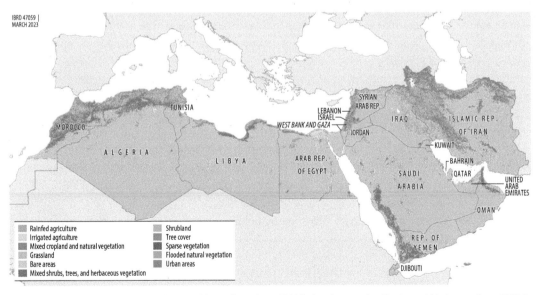

Source: Copernicus Climate Change Service, Climate Data Store (2019). *Land cover classification gridded maps from 1992 to present derived from satellite observation.* https://doi.org/10.24381/cds.006f2c9a10.24381/cds.006f2c9a. Accessed on 01-Feb-2023.

Figure 4.2 Gross agricultural output, by economy, 1961–2018

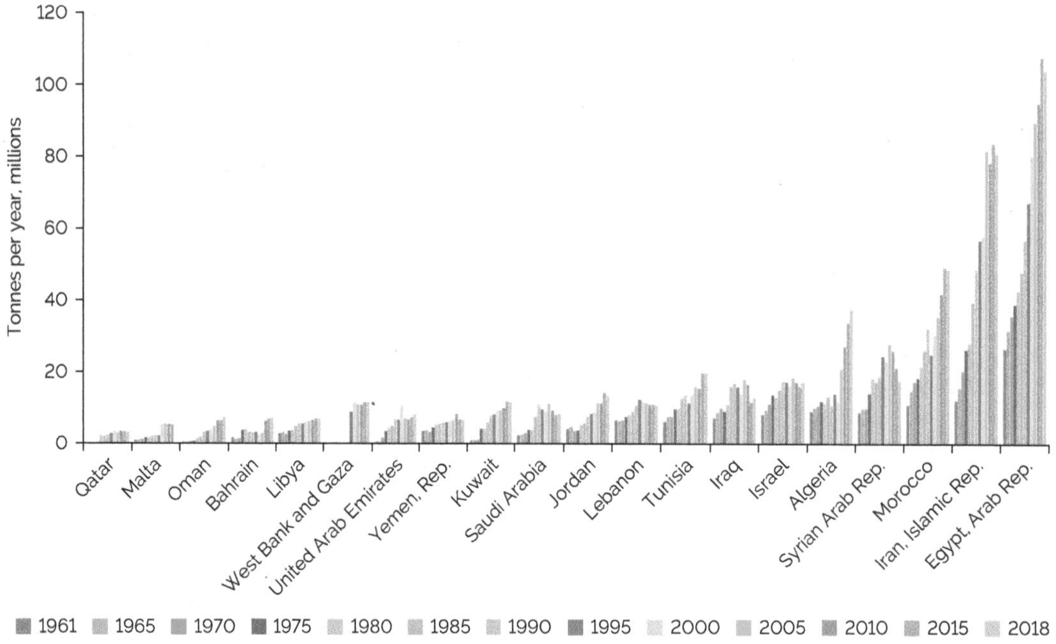

Source: Food and Agriculture Organization of the United Nations, FAOSTAT (https://www.fao.org/faostat/en/#home).

irrigated versus rainfed agriculture, but a study in Tunisia estimates that the incomes of irrigators were on average three times those of rainfed farmers (Hamdane 2019).

As water supplies to agriculture have plateaued across the region, the constrained demand has influenced farmers' behavior, encouraging more efficient water use. Aided by government support for modernizing irrigated agriculture, overall economic water productivity (agricultural value added over agricultural water withdrawals) in the region has increased by 60 percent in real terms over the past 20 years. By 2018, regional agricultural water productivity averaged US$0.39 per cubic meter. However, this high-level water productivity indicator varies widely across countries. Putting aside countries for which data on both water consumption and gross domestic product (GDP) are dated, the contribution of each cubic meter of water to the gross value added of irrigated agriculture ranges from less than US$0.10 per cubic meter in Libya to more than US$2.00 per cubic meter in Israel: a more than 20-fold difference (figures 4.3 and 4.4).

This variation shows an inverse correlation between water scarcity and water productivity. This inverse correlation has been driven by behavioral responses to scarcity, including improvements in (1) irrigation technology—the shift from open channel flood irrigation to pressurized drip irrigation; (2) the crop mix grown—the production of higher-value horticultural crops (fruits and vegetables) has increased at a faster rate than the production of grains; and (3) improvements in crop husbandry—such as the introduction of netting and polytunnels to reduce losses from evapotranspiration.

The shift in the crop mix has happened in tandem with large growth in virtual water imports. Virtual water imports—the water imported within food and other agricultural commodities—doubled to 255 billion cubic meters between 1998 and 2010, an amount equivalent to the region's annual agricultural water withdrawals (Antonelli and Tamea 2015). At an aggregate level, complementary shifts in policy, which have increased imports of cereals, have enabled more land and water to be dedicated to growing higher-value crops such as fruits and vegetables (figures 4.5 and 4.6). Thus, although economic

Figure 4.3 Irrigation water productivity, by economy

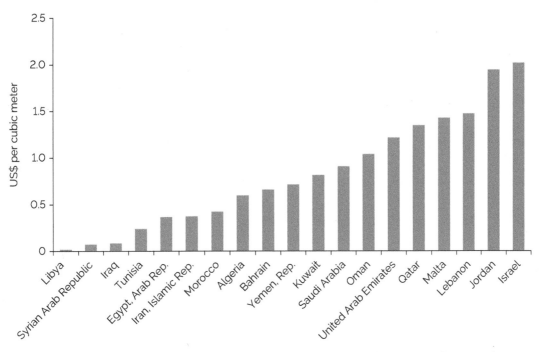

Sources: Food and Agriculture Organization of the United Nations, AQUASTAT (https://www.fao.org/aquastat); World Development Indicators.

Figure 4.4 Irrigation water productivity and per capita agricultural water withdrawals, by economy

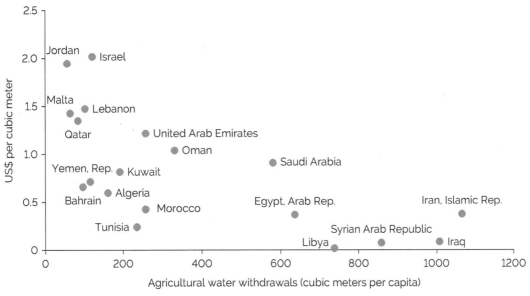

Sources: Food and Agriculture Organization of the United Nations, AQUASTAT (https://www.fao.org/aquastat); World Development Indicators.

water productivity has increased, it has also left countries across the region more exposed to changes in global cereal prices.

While agricultural output has grown and water productivity has improved, structural transformation of the region's economies means that the contribution of agriculture to GDP has waned in relative terms.

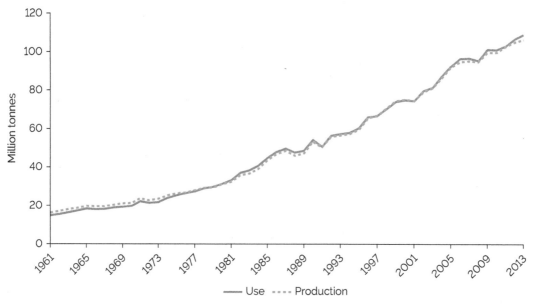

Figure 4.5 Domestic production and use of fruits and vegetables across the Middle East and North Africa, 1961–2013

Source: OECD and FAO 2018.

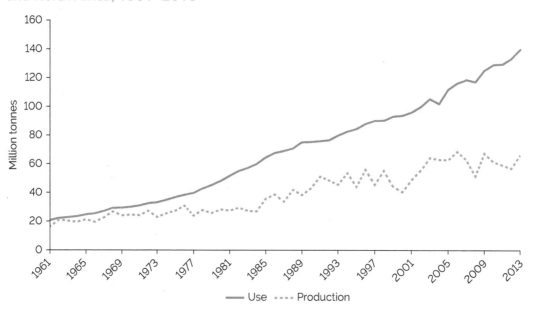

Figure 4.6 Domestic production and use of cereals across the Middle East and North Africa, 1961–2013

Source: OECD and FAO 2018.

This decrease has occurred even in economies with a significant agrarian population (figure 4.7). Meanwhile, growth in the service and industrial sectors has increased, driven by urbanization. In countries with large agrarian populations, agriculture's contribution to GDP is less than half what it was in the 1970s when many of the dams and irrigation systems were being designed and constructed (figure 4.7).[3] Yet agriculture in these countries is still a key source of employment, an important part of rural cultural heritage, and potentially a means of promoting spatial development.

Figure 4.7 Agriculture sector's share of GDP and total employment in countries with rural populations over 10 million

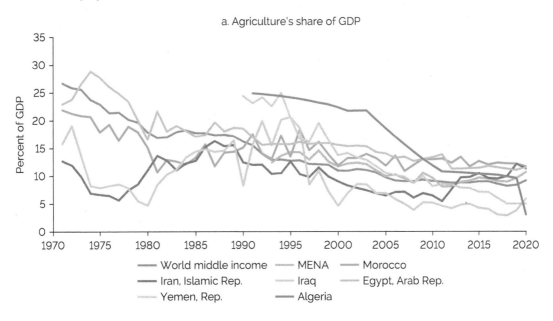

a. Agriculture's share of GDP

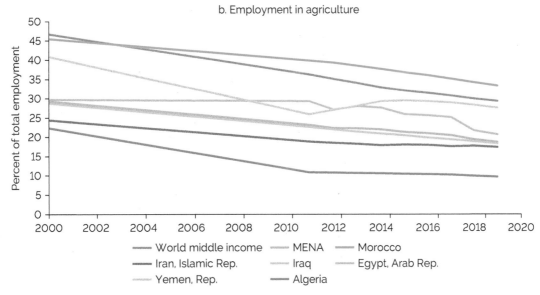

b. Employment in agriculture

Source: World Bank.
Note: MENA excludes high income. In panel b, employment in agriculture is the modeled International Labour Organization estimate.
GDP = gross domestic product; MENA = Middle East and North Africa.

By 2018, total water withdrawals consumed by agriculture contributed only a modest 3 percent to regional GDP. Although it is more productive than rainfed agriculture, irrigated agriculture did not contribute more than 11 percent of GDP in any country in the region (figure 4.8), even in countries where agriculture accounts for over 75 percent of total water withdrawals. Along with several countries in Central and South Asia, water withdrawals per unit of GDP in the agrarian middle-income countries of MENA are among the highest in the world (Kochhar et al. 2015).

In a water-scarce context such as MENA, this situation raises obvious questions: (1) Is the current allocation of water across the economy optimal? (2) Could water be used for activities with more value

Figure 4.8 Proportion of total water withdrawals allocated to agriculture and relative contributions to GDP of irrigated and rainfed agriculture, 2018

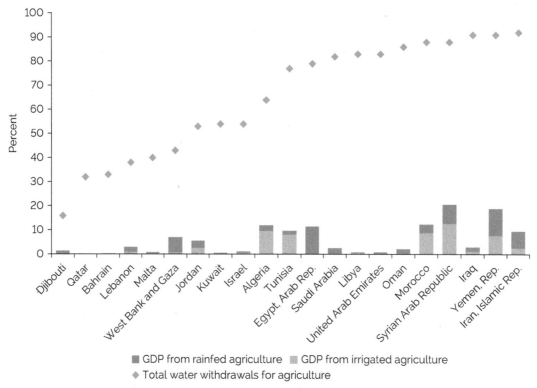

■ GDP from rainfed agriculture   ■ GDP from irrigated agriculture
◆ Total water withdrawals for agriculture

Source: Food and Agriculture Organization of the United Nations, AQUASTAT (https://www.fao.org/aquastat).
Note: GDP = gross domestic product.

added? (3) Is the growth of the service and industrial sectors being held back by lack of water? and (4) Should more water be allocated to domestic water supply to avoid having to invest in desalination plants, which would push up costs? Whereas in the past the benefits of growing agricultural irrigation were captured through taxation, other potential uses of water may now yield higher levels of GDP per unit of water and concomitant higher levels of tax revenues.

In the absence of markets, the economic valuation of water across different uses (agriculture, domestic, and industry) is not straightforward, involving the estimation of shadow prices for water. Global studies report that the average cost of irrigation water to farmers is between US$0.01 and US$0.02 per cubic meter—the range also seen across most of MENA. Attempts to estimate the value generated by irrigation water suggest that it is an order of magnitude more than these average irrigation charges. Where there are market transactions, in times of scarcity, municipal and industrial users of water have paid two orders of magnitude more than these average irrigation charges (D'Odorico et al. 2020).

However, the complexities of such technical economic analysis obscure the more fundamental question that is central to this report: If there is not a functional market for water, *who* should make the decisions on the allocation of water? This is a question of political choice. Countries in the region need to find ways to balance the social and cultural values ascribed to rural livelihoods with the economic roles of cities and the reluctance of both farmers and city dwellers to pay more for services. Before exploring this question further in part II of the report, the next section examines how demand-side behavior of domestic water supply to cities challenges states' ability to raise long-term infrastructure finance.

Cities' Predictable Yet Growing Demand for Water

Although irrigated agriculture has been the dominant source of water demand, cities' water demand has grown steadily. According to the World Bank's World Development Indicators, MENA's urban population grew from 40 million in 1962 to 300 million in 2020. With this urban growth has come an increased but predictable demand for modern piped water services. Although data are available only for the past 25 years, the demand for domestic water supply increased from 19 billion cubic meters in the early 1990s to just over 32 billion cubic meters in 2018—which accounts for just over 10 percent of MENA's total water withdrawals.

In contrast to the extremely wide range of agricultural water withdrawals per capita across countries, withdrawals for domestic water supply per capita fall within a much narrower band. Half of the countries fall in the range of 84–284 liters per capita per day (l/c/d). Average withdrawals across countries in MENA are just under 200 l/c/d, close to the Organisation for Economic Co-operation and Development average of 220 l/c/d (figure 4.9). Countries at the low end of the consumption range, such as the Republic of

Figure 4.9 Domestic water withdrawal, by country grouping and quartile of the distribution

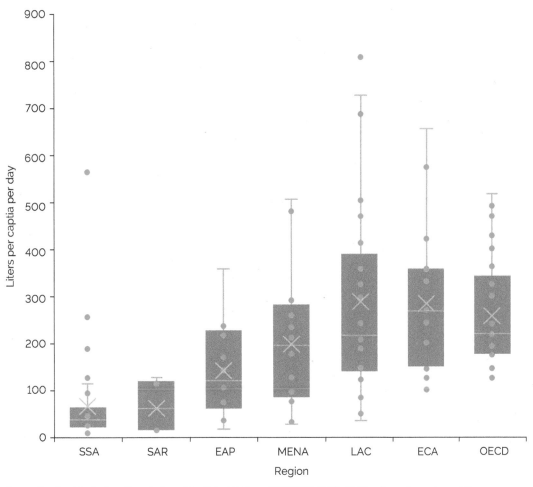

Source: Food and Agriculture Organization of the United Nations, AQUASTAT, 2013–17 (https://www.fao.org/aquastat).
Note: The regions follow World Bank definitions, with OECD countries presented as a separate group. EAP = East Asia and Pacific; ECA = Europe and Central Asia; LAC = Latin America and the Caribbean; MENA = Middle East and North Africa; OECD = Organisation for Economic Co-operation and Development; SAR = South Asia; SSA = Sub-saharan Africa.

Yemen (26 l/c/d), have service providers that are struggling to function (Abu-Lohom et al. 2018). The vast majority of households there (80 percent) use alternative sources of supply, such as bottled or tanker water. Countries at the high end, such as Bahrain (505 l/c/d), have virtually unconstrained demand with low tariffs (US$0.21 per cubic meter) and high recurrent subsidies.

Across the economies of MENA, there is a correlation between higher tariffs and lower per capita water withdrawals (figure 4.10). Setting aside contexts such as the Republic of Yemen, which has absolute supply constraints, economies that have established domestic tariffs of at least US$0.60 per cubic meter for the first 100 l/c/d have below-average domestic and industrial withdrawals.[4]

This correlation raises the question of whether higher tariffs make water difficult for poorer households to afford. Using the prevailing tariffs and household income data for each country, the cost of 100 l/c/d was assessed for households in different quintiles. The results show that the poorest 20 percent of households pay between four and nine times higher proportions of their incomes than the wealthiest 20 percent. Common thresholds used to assess the affordability of water supply and sanitation (WSS) services are in the range of 3 percent to 5 percent of household expenditure. Based on this rudimentary affordability test, and given that this calculation was possible only for the water component of tariffs, the poorest quintile of households in Tunisia, the United Arab Emirates, and West Bank and Gaza were only marginally below the 3 percent threshold (figure 4.11).[5] A criticism of this method of assessing affordability is that it fails to account for differences in the quality of services provided to households and the widespread service quality problems across many economies in MENA.

Despite the significant expansion of bulk water infrastructure—dams, transmission pipelines, and desalination plants—and water distribution networks connecting homes, about a quarter of households across the region (100 million people) do not, or cannot, use this infrastructure as their main source

Figure 4.10 Higher tariffs, lower water withdrawals per capita

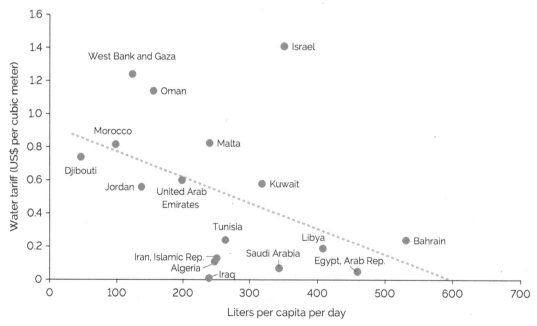

Source: World Bank staff calculations.
Note: Tariffs are for the equivalent of 100 liters per capita per day.

Figure 4.11 Cost of 100 liters per capita per day relative to income consumption quintile, by economy

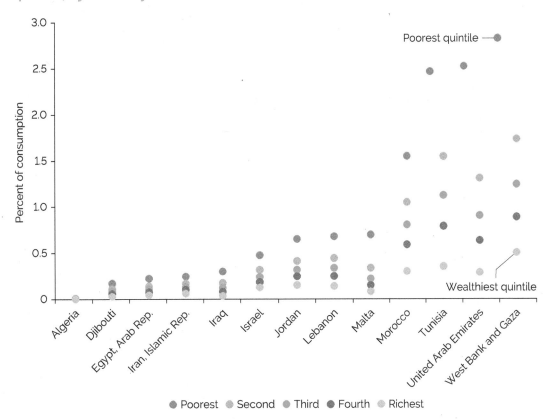

Sources: United Nations Children's Fund, Multiple Indicator Cluster Surveys (https://mics.unicef.org/surveys); U.S. Agency for International Development, various years; World Bank, World Development Indicators; UN DESA 2017; Euromonitor; Government of Israel Ministry of Foreign Affairs; Integrated Public Use Microdata Series 2011 (https://international.ipums.org) (household size); International Benchmarking Network (tariffs).

of drinking water. The two main reasons for not using utility piped water are service interruptions and poor water quality—due to microbial contamination or that it is too saline to use. In recent surveys in Algeria, Iraq, Jordan, and Tunisia, a quarter of households reported that they had experienced days with insufficient water in the past month.[6]

Households experiencing service interruptions and/or water quality issues supplemented their piped network water with alternative sources, including bottled water, tanker truck water, and other sources of nonnetwork water (figure 4.12). A public expenditure review in Lebanon reported that the public utilities capture only a quarter of household expenditure, with the other three-quarters going to water trucks or bottled water (World Bank 2010). In Jordan, households that purchased bottled water, including those in the poorest quintiles, spent as much on bottled water—collectively US$155 million a year—as they did on their water utility bills. In West Bank and Gaza, because the water provided through the utility network is so saline, most households buy 250–500 liters of water each week, not just for drinking but also for cooking and bathing, at a cost of US$7.00–US$9.00 per cubic meter.

Even where people do use utility water, they commonly treat the water before using it. The type of "point-of-use" water treatment reflects the specific type of water quality problem faced. For example, in Egypt, households treat water by allowing it to stand and settle to remove sediment before filtering whereas, in Iraq and Jordan, half of all households filter utility water. Although few systematic water

Figure 4.12 Primary source of drinking water, circa 2000 and circa 2015

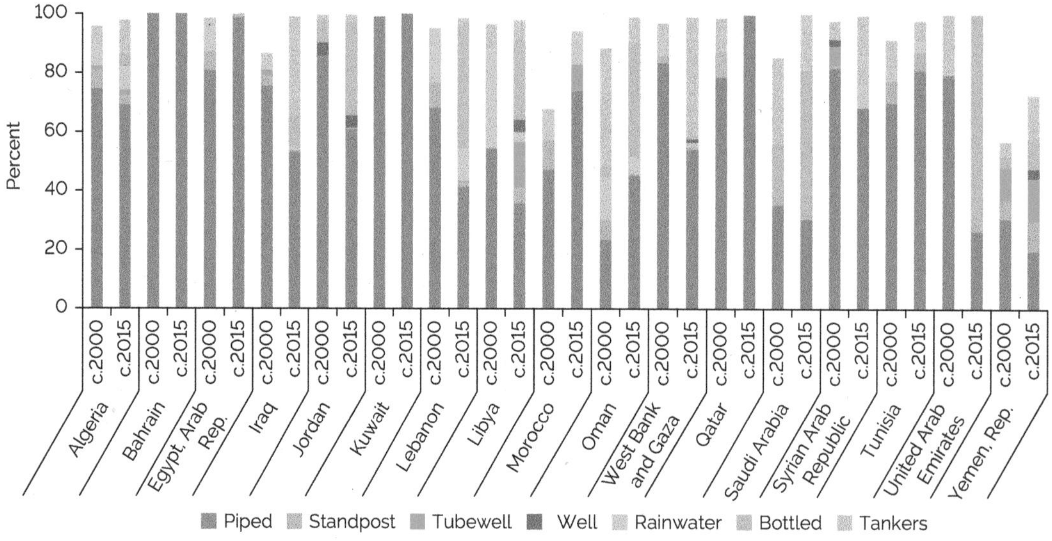

Source: Joint Monitoring Programme for Water Supply, Sanitation and Hygiene, World Health Organization and United Nations Children's Fund.
Note: Unimproved sources are excluded.

quality surveys have been conducted to compare sources, nationally representative household surveys in Iraq and Lebanon confirmed the presence of microbial contaminants in a quarter and half of the pipe water samples, respectively.[7] However, they also showed comparable amounts of microbial contamination in bottled water and much higher levels of microbial contamination in tanker truck water.

These supplementary sources of water, often multiple times more expensive than utility-provided water, and the costs associated with point-of-use treatment increase the real costs of coping with poor water supply services and have a material impact on affordability well beyond the incidence of utility tariffs (World Bank 2010, 2018, forthcoming).

Particularly over the past decade since the Arab Spring, reform leaders have struggled with the question of whether to improve services first and then raise tariffs, or to raise tariffs to improve services. The data on both the quality of services and willingness of consumers to pay are limited across the region—compared to other regions. Not only is the number of household surveys limited but those surveys also do not report on the volumes of water actually used from utilities. Conversely, utility billing systems that can capture data on the volume of water used by households do not categorize households by income stratum or whether the households use other sources of water. These types of data would be essential in helping reform leaders figure out what public utilities could do to improve services and "win back" market share.

HOW THE TWO MAIN CONSUMPTIVE USES OF WATER—IRRIGATED AGRICULTURE AND CITIES—INTERACT AND SHAPE LONG-TERM FINANCING OPTIONS

The consumptive uses of water for agriculture and cities compete for the same water resources. As water scarcity increases and the structure of economies changes, the trade-offs involved in allocating water to agriculture or cities come into ever sharper focus.

With the development of most of the available freshwater resources in the region, escaping country-level water resource endowments has pushed old water scarce countries in MENA to supplement conventional with nonconventional water resources. New water scarce countries are now following suit. In old water scarce countries like Israel and Jordan, freshwater is increasingly channeled first through WSS systems and then provided to agriculture after it has been treated for reuse. Although not eliminating the need for investing in desalination, this practice has helped push back the speed and scale at which desalination capacity has had to be developed.

In the experience of old water scarce countries in MENA, the viability of the WSS subsector business model is a prerequisite for domestic and industrial water demand and foundational to financing the synergies with agriculture. In the most financially sustainable cases, the decision to invest in desalination has initially been financed from general taxation but then shifted back to the water sector—through tariffs for urban WSS. In the countries that have done so (Dubai, Israel, Malta, and the United Arab Emirates), synergies between water for cities and water for agriculture have been created (Siegel 2015). In these cases, the WSS business model covers the costs of both desalination and wastewater treatment, providing additional low-cost water to agriculture—a step toward developing a circular economy.

As well as ensuring a viable WSS subsector, this "substitution" of freshwater flows to agricultural irrigation with recycled wastewater has meant placing caps on agricultural water abstractions. For countries that have not managed to contain agricultural water abstractions, urban expansion has driven the need for further supply-side investments in desalination, pushing up costs in the WSS subsector, and/or generated negative externalities—the subject of the next chapter.

NOTES

1. World Bank, World Development Indicators (2015 constant prices).

2. Food and Agriculture Organization of the United Nations, AQUASTAT, 2013–17 (https://www.fao.org/aquastat); World Bank staff calculations.

3. The exception is the Islamic Republic of Iran, which has been subject to sanctions, including of its oil exports.

4. Industrial tariffs are higher than domestic tariffs, but data on average tariffs including industry were not available.

5. Coverage of wastewater services is not as universal as that of water services in MENA.

6. UNICEF, Multiple Indicator Cluster Surveys (https://mics.unicef.org/surveys); U.S. Agency for International Development, Demographic and Health Surveys, various years.

7. The presence of *E. coli* with counts above 1 colony forming unit per 100 milliliters. The surveys were the Lebanon Water Quality Survey 2016 and the Iraq Multiple Indicator Cluster Survey 2018 (https://mics.unicef.org/surveys).

REFERENCES

Abu-Lohom, N. M., Y. Konishi, Y. Mumssen, B. Zabara, and S. M. Moore. 2018. "Water Supply in a War Zone: A Preliminary Analysis of Two Urban Water Tanker Supply Systems in the Republic of Yemen." Discussion Paper, Water Global Practice, World Bank, Washington, DC. https://documents1.worldbank.org/curated/pt/434091532620702995/pdf/128907-WP-P165727-Water-Supply-in-a-War-Zone-PUBLIC.pdf.

Antonelli, M., and S. Tamea. 2015. "Food-Water Security and Virtual Water Trade in the Middle East and North Africa." *International Journal of Water Resources Development* 31 (3): 326–42. http://dx.doi.org/10.1080/07900627.2015.1030496.

D'Odorico, P., D. D. Chiarelli, L. Rosa, A. Bini, D. Zilberman, and M. C. Rulli. 2020. "The Global Value of Water in Agriculture." *Proceedings of the National Academy of Sciences* 117 (36): 21985–993. doi:10.1073/pnas.2005835117.

Di Baldassarre, G., N. Wanders, A. AghaKouchak, L. Kuil, S. Rangecroft, T. I. E. Veldkamp, M. Garcia, P. R. van Oel, K. Breinl, and A. F. Van Loon. 2018. "Water Shortages Worsened by Reservoir Effects." *Nature Sustainability* 1 (11): 617–22. https://doi.org/10.1038/s41893-018-0159-0.

Hamdane, A. 2019. "Tunisia." In *Irrigation in the Mediterranean: Global Issues in Water Policy*, vol 22, edited by F. Molle, C. Sanchis-Ibor, and L. Avellà-Reus. Cham, Switzerland: Springer. https://doi.org/10.1007/978-3-030-03698-0_2.

Kochhar, K., C. Pattillo, Y. Sun, N. Suphaphiphat, A. Swiston, R. Tchaidze, B. Clements, S. Fabrizio, V. Flamini, L. Redifer, H. Finger, and an IMF Staff Team. 2015. "Is the Glass Half Empty or Half Full? Issues in Managing Water Challenges and Policy Instruments." Staff Discussion Note SDN/15/11, International Monetary Fund, Washington, DC.

Kuper, M., N. Faysse, A. Hammani, T. Hartani, S. Marlet, M. F. Hamamouche, and F. Ameur. 2016. "Liberation or Anarchy? The Janus Nature of Groundwater Use on North Africa's New Irrigation Frontiers." In *Integrated Groundwater Management,* edited by A. J. Jakeman, O. Barreteau, R. J. Hunt, J. D. Rinaudo, and A. Ross, 583–615. Cham, Switzerland: Springer. https://doi.org/10.1007/978-3-319-23576-9_23.

OECD and FAO (Organisation for Economic Co-operation and Development and Food and Agriculture Organization of the United Nations). 2018. *OECD-FAO Agricultural Outlook 2018-2027*. Paris: OECD. https://doi.org/10.1787/agr_outlook-2018-en.

Siegel, S. M. 2015. *Let There Be Water: Israel's Solution for a Water-Starved World*. New York: Thomas Dunne Books.

UN DESA (United Nations Department of Economic and Social Affairs, Population Division). 2017. "Household Size and Composition Around the World 2017 – Data Booklet." United Nations, New York. https://www.un.org/en/development/desa/population/publications/pdf/ageing/household_size_and_composition_around_the_world_2017_data_booklet.pdf.

World Bank. 2010. "Republic of Lebanon Water Sector: Public Expenditure Review." World Bank, Washington, DC. https://openknowledge.worldbank.org/handle/10986/2877.

World Bank. 2017. *Beyond Scarcity: Water Security in the Middle East and North Africa*. MENA Development Series. Washington, DC: World Bank.

World Bank. 2018. "Toward Water Security for Palestinians: West Bank and Gaza Water Supply, Sanitation, and Hygiene Poverty Diagnostic." World Bank, Washington, DC. https://openknowledge.worldbank.org/handle/10986/30316.

World Bank. Forthcoming. "Jordan: Fiscal Public Expenditure Review." World Bank, Washington, DC.

CHAPTER 5

Externalities: Status and Trends of Water Depletion and Pollution

IDENTIFICATION OF EXTERNALITIES IS A FIRST STEP TOWARD VALUING WATER

This chapter identifies two major types of negative externalities related to water in the Middle East and North Africa (MENA): water depletion and water pollution. As shown in table 5.1, the first type of externality arises when water is used as a *source*, specifically, when it is unsustainably withdrawn from freshwater bodies to irrigate crops or provide drinking water supplies to cities. In simple terms, if water withdrawals exceed replenishment over a multiannual time horizon, a water source is being depleted. Aquifers are more vulnerable to depletion because of their underground and invisible nature, which makes management solutions challenging (Bierkens and Wada 2019).

The second type of externality arises when water is used as a *sink*. Unwanted output and waste from production and consumption, such as sewage discharges or discharges from oil extraction facilities, are disposed of in freshwater bodies such as rivers, lakes, and aquifers. When the capacity of the water environment to absorb these unwanted products and waste is exceeded, then negative externalities arise. Both types of externalities have "hidden" costs, that is, costs that are not reflected in water and pollution tariffs or in the costs users face to extract or discharge water.

Although this chapter focuses on negative externalities, water-related externalities can also be beneficial, or both harmful and beneficial, depending on the location of the users. The case of return flows from irrigation is an example of a positive externality arising from the spatial variability of water supply and demand. In the Arab Republic of Egypt, for example, irrigators in the Nile Delta benefit from the irrigation water returned to the drainage systems from agricultural lands in Upper Egypt (El Agha, Molden, and Ghanem 2011). These return flows also contribute to maintaining an adequate salt balance and flush pollution.

Table 5.1 Water as a "source" and a "sink" and related negative externalities

Type of water use	Type of negative externality	Examples of hidden costs
Sink	Water pollution	• Burden of waterborne diseases • Declining crop yields because of salinity
Source	Water depletion	• Disappearing aquatic ecosystems and fisheries • Increasing cost of groundwater withdrawal

Source: World Bank.

Examples of water resource depletion and pollution across MENA are many and profound. They are evident at all levels, from the macro regional transboundary level, through growing inequalities within countries, to local cases in which new water sources drive an unmanaged boom followed by a bust. Figure 5.1 demonstrates these nested sets of negative externalities, which are described in more detail in the following sections. In many places, depletion and pollution occur simultaneously, as observed in the Shatt al-Arab River at the confluence of the Tigris and Euphrates Rivers. Recognizing these externalities is a key step toward more comprehensive valuation of water. Thus, this chapter also attempts to quantify their magnitudes in terms of costs for society, the environment, and the economy.

WATER DEPLETION

The evidence of depletion is manifold, coming from global hydrological models, remote sensing from satellites, and local reports of wells running dry and streams and wetlands disappearing. Global hydrological and water resource models suggest that about 50 percent of the region's water withdrawals are unsustainable and contributing to depletion (World Bank 2018). These water withdrawals exceed natural groundwater replenishment rates and/or infringe on environmental flows, that is, they do not leave enough water in rivers and streams to maintain healthy aquatic ecosystems. Although these models do not provide locally specific information, they unequivocally identify the MENA region as a global hot spot of depletion at present and also under future climate and population scenarios (Wada and Bierkens 2014). Map 5.1 shows the results from one such global hydrological and water resource model. By combining information on groundwater availability and water use, the model suggests that from 1990 to 2010 groundwater levels declined almost everywhere in MENA, with some areas showing average declines of as much as 1 meter per year.

Satellite remote sensing is another method for monitoring water. In particular, observations from the Gravity Recovery and Climate Experiment satellite mission allow for detection of areas where groundwater storage shows negative trends over multiannual timescales. These observations indicate decreasing water storage across the MENA region (Joodaki, Wahr, and Swenson 2014; Rodell et al. 2018; Voss et al. 2013). Observations from the north-central Middle East (the Islamic Republic of Iran, Iraq, and the Syrian Arab Republic) highlight a loss of groundwater storage of about 13 (+/ −1.6) cubic kilometers per year in volume (the volume withdrawn unsustainably) over six years from 2003 to 2009 (Voss et al. 2013). In the Northwest Sahara, Richey et al. (2015) observe a decline of 2.7 cubic kilometers per year over 2003–12. Finally, parts of the Arabian Peninsula's Paleogene and Cretaceous aquifers are experiencing depletion of −2.8 (+/−0.8) cubic kilometers per year (Sultan et al. 2019). To put these numbers in context, these losses in groundwater storage are equivalent to 7 percent of the region's annual water withdrawals and a little more than the current installed desalination capacity in the region.

Satellite imagery also shows large reductions in the extent of surface waterbodies, such as lakes and wetlands. The data in figure 5.2, based on earth observations, show the change in water-related ecosystem extent in MENA countries as of 2016 compared to the baseline period of 2001–05.[1] Although these ecosystems cover a small share of MENA's land surface, they provide important natural habitats and ecosystem services, including purification and flood control. Egypt and Iraq emerge as hot spots

Figure 5.1 Examples of nested sets of negative externalities in the Middle East and North Africa

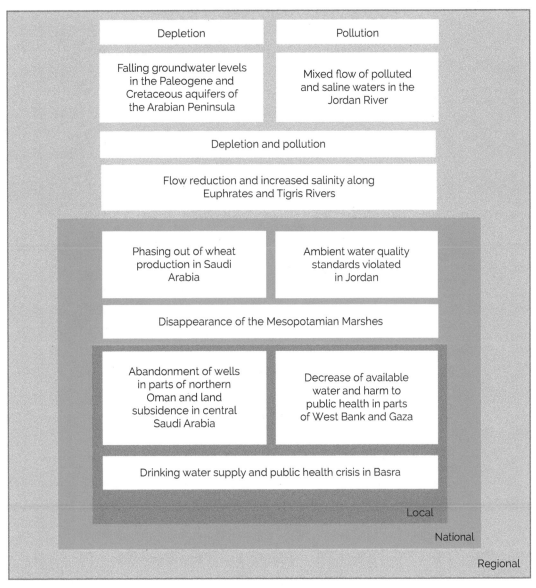

Sources: Regional: Hillel et al. 2015 (mixed flow of polluted and saline waters in the Jordan River); Wada and Heinrich 2013 (falling groundwater levels in the Paleogene and Cretaceous aquifers). National: Ouda 2014 (disappearance of wheat production in Saudi Arabia); Schyns et al. 2015 (ambient water quality standards violated in Jordan). Local: Abulibdeh et al. 2021 (abandonment of wells in parts of Oman); Othman and Abotalib 2019 (land subsidence in Saudi Arabia); UNEP 2020 (West Bank and Gaza).

Map 5.1 Average groundwater stress in the Middle East and North Africa, 1990–2010

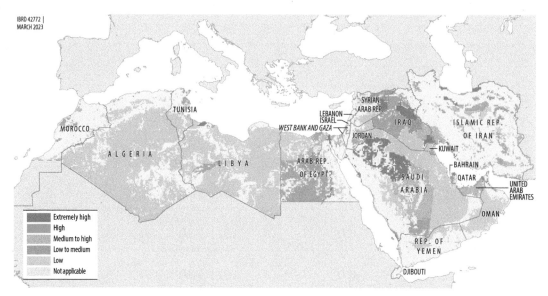

Source: Analysis and calculations from geospatial data sets developed by Stichting Deltares in cooperation with the University of Utrecht in the Netherlands. Permission granted by Stichting Deltares and the University of Utrecht; permission required for reuse.
Note: Groundwater stress is estimated as *ABS/(RCH-fxRCH)*, where *ABS* is groundwater abstraction estimated with the PCR-GLOBWB model, *RCH* is groundwater recharge simulated by PCR-GLOBWB, and *f* is the fraction of *RCH* reserved to meet environmental flows. Groundwater stress is estimated using long-term averages to control for the effects of interannual variability. State levels correspond to the administrative units for each country in the Global Database of Administrative Areas.

Figure 5.2 Change in the extent of water-related ecosystems, 2001–05 to 2016

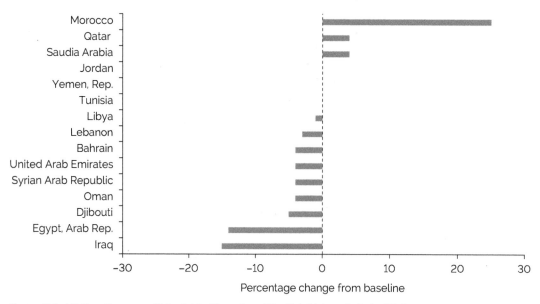

Source: United Nations, Progress on Water-Related Ecosystems (https://sdg6data.org/indicator/6.6.1).

where the extent of water-related ecosystems has declined by more than 10 percent over the past 20 years.

Local evidence of depletion across the region confirms the findings from global water resource models and remote sensing. In Syria, local monitoring suggests that groundwater levels have been declining since the 1980s, and some wells have had to be abandoned altogether. For example, in large aquifers under Aleppo, the groundwater level has fallen by 1.5 meters per year over the past 25 years (Aw-Hassan et al. 2014)—see figure 5.3. As pumping increased and replenishment patterns remained stationary (stable precipitation levels), Aleppo's groundwater account has become depleted. Similar trends are reported from other parts of Syria, including the eastern provinces where expansion of groundwater-fed irrigation in the 1990s led to an increase of wells from 135,000 in 1999 to more than 213,000 in 2007, with subsequent drying of springs such as the Fijeh and Ras al-Ain springs (Daoudy 2020).

Groundwater monitoring across Jordan highlights similar levels of depletion. Of Jordan's 12 groundwater basins, 10 are being exploited at a rate faster than they can be replenished (abstraction far exceeds the aquifers' safe yields), according to official government data (MWI 2017), as shown in table 5.2. Overall, groundwater is being withdrawn at twice the rate of replenishment. In terms of depletion rates, data from more than 100 wells suggest that aquifer levels declined by about 1 meter per year, with peaks of 9 meters per year, from 1960 until 2011 (USGS 2014). If these rates of decline continue, average saturated aquifer thicknesses (a simple measure of how much water is stored in an aquifer) are forecast to decline by 30 to 40 percent by 2030.

Figure 5.3 Water table level and annual precipitation at Tel Hadya Research Station, Aleppo, Syrian Arab Republic, 1984–2010

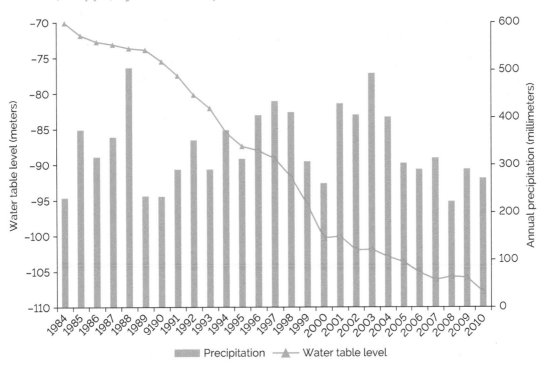

Source: Aw-Hassan et al. 2014.

Groundwater basin	Safe yield	Abstraction	Deficit
Amman-Zarqa	87.5	164.98	–77.48
Araba North	3.50	6.56	–3.06
Araba South	5.50	10.90	–5.40
Azraq	24.0	69.66	–45.66
Dead Sea	57.0	83.85	–26.85
Disi	125.0	141.58	–16.58
Hammad	8.0	1.59	6.41
Jafer	27.0	35.53	–8.53
Jordan Side Valley	15.0	45.64	–30.64
Jordan Valley	21.0	27.04	–6.04
Sirhan	5.0	0	5.00
Yarmouk	40.0	54.53	–14.53

Source: MWI 2017, 9.

Across the main aquifers in Morocco, withdrawals are typically much greater than aquifers' renewable potential, including in the key aquifers of Souss and Haouz (Hssaisoune et al. 2020). Overexploitation is leading to a dramatic decline in the water table of up to 64 meters in 25 years in the Saiss aquifer, and 24 meters in 34 years in the Souss aquifer (Benabdelfadel 2012). Overall, estimates suggest that the rate of depletion is 862 million cubic meters per year, equivalent to about 9 percent of all water withdrawals in the country.[2] Groundwater overuse in Morocco has led to a series of negative externalities, including abandonment of agriculture in the Souss area by farmers who could not keep up with the increasing depth to water in their wells and related pumping costs (Closas and Villholth 2016), lower access to drinking water supplies for some rural communities, and aquifer salinization (Benabdelfadel 2012). The Chaouia region is a case in point. Following the expansion of wells to support citrus production in the 1970s and 1980s, intensive groundwater pumping led to seawater intrusion in the aquifer closer to the coast and dropping groundwater levels inland. To adapt, farmers had to shift to more salinity-tolerant but less profitable crops, such as cauliflower and maize. This rapid decline in good-quality groundwater compromised the entire agricultural value chain in the area. The number of cooperatives exporting fruit and vegetables dropped from 120 in 1980 to 3 today, pushing farmers to urban areas in search of employment (Faysse et al. 2011).

Ample local reports of drying lakes, wetlands, and rivers are further local symptoms of widespread overuse of surface water resources. The MENA region hosts some of the most emblematic examples of wetland and lake decline in relation to water depletion, such as the Mesopotamian Marshes in southern Iraq and the Dead Sea. Drained to less than 10 percent of their original area because of politically motivated drainage works in southern Iraq in the late 1980s and early 1990s (UNEP 2001), the Mesopotamian Marshes now face reduced water supplies and loss of the flood pulses because of increasing upstream damming and diversions and related marine ingression, with direct impacts on ecosystem services and the livelihoods that depend on them (Al-Mudaffar Fawzi et al. 2016). The Dead Sea is another striking example. Increasing water use for mineral extraction and upstream damming and diversions—thought to have reduced the Jordan River's inflow to 10 percent of its original discharge into the Dead Sea—led to a drop in its elevation of 28 to 30 meters since the 1960s, with pervasive impacts on lake-related industries, including tourism and mining (EcoPeace Middle East 2018; Wurtsbaugh et al. 2017).

Water depletion has the potential to result in complete exhaustion of water resources, raising questions about a potential "exhaustion date," especially of nonrenewable groundwater resources. The concerning trends described earlier result in an obvious question related to the proximity to this exhaustion limit: How much groundwater is left? Answering this question is challenging, not least because of the uncertainties surrounding groundwater storage and future levels of withdrawals. A first-order approximation for two major aquifers in the region shows the impact that large uncertainties in groundwater "stocks" and depletion rates can have on estimates of "exhaustion dates" (table 5.3).

It is important to note that groundwater withdrawals could end well before the aquifer is completely "empty." Groundwater use has physical limits because not all the groundwater might be extractable or usable. The usable volume depends on the quality (mostly salinity) of the groundwater, whereas its extractability depends on the depth at which groundwater pumping needs to take place and other aquifer characteristics (Bierkens and Wada 2019). The costs of withdrawals increase with depletion.[3]

POLLUTION OF FRESHWATER AND MARINE RESOURCES

Three main sources of pollution threaten water quality: domestic wastewater, industrial effluents, and agricultural runoff. These sources of pollution give rise to externalities in the social (public health and burden of waterborne diseases), environmental (loss of biodiversity), and economic (declines in fish catches, lower yields, and cleanup costs) dimensions. Untreated domestic wastewater remains a public health issue and a major source of human and environmental externalities. On average across the region, more than 50 percent of domestic wastewater is discharged untreated into the environment (World Bank 2018). Although country-level estimates of wastewater flows and treatment capacity are uncertain because of reporting gaps, a first-level assessment was conducted by the Center for Environment and Development for the Arab Region and Europe in 2019 following the definition of

Table 5.3 When will it run out? Large uncertainties about overall groundwater stocks and depletion rates make it difficult to identify the "exhaustion dates" of aquifers

Aquifer	Countries	Estimated exploitable reserves (million cubic meters)	Depletion rate (cubic kilometers per year)	Estimated years to exhaustion
Arabian Aquifer System	Bahrain, Iraq, Jordan, Oman, Qatar, Saudi Arabia, United Arab Emirates, Yemen, Rep.	500,000–2,185,000	15.5	32–140
Northwestern Sahara	Algeria, Libya, Tunisia	1,280,000	2.7	475

Sources: Foster and Loucks 2006 (exploitable reserves); Richey et al. 2015 (depletion rates).

Sustainable Development Goal 6.3.1 (see AbuZeid et al. 2019; UN-Habitat and WHO 2021), and is presented in figure 5.4. These estimates show significant gaps in domestic wastewater treatment in the region, which engender public health and environmental contamination risks. Wastewater pollution can even become a transboundary problem, not just along the permanent rivers such as the Euphrates but also along seasonal rivers such as the Wadi Samen, which flows from Hebron in West Bank and Gaza to Shoket in Israel.

Water pollution from industry and agriculture is also a major source of negative externalities. Despite the lack of countrywide estimates of industrial water pollution, evidence from across the region shows that it is a widespread problem. First, industrial pollution in the form of produced water[4] from oil fields, and oil spills and seepage from oil pipelines, is causing pollution in Iraq (Amin Al Manmi et al. 2019) and Libya (Abdunaser 2020), among others. In southern Iraq, analysis of satellite imagery from 2018 highlights the presence of an oil spill in Basra, indicating that it was a potential source of a drinking water contamination event that caused more than 100,000 people to be hospitalized (HRW 2019). In Kuwait, groundwater remains contaminated from the destruction of oils wells during the Gulf War (Mukhopadhyay et al. 2017). Waterbodies close to densely industrialized areas are particularly vulnerable, such as the Zarqa River in Jordan (Jordan Ministry of Environment 2017) and the Litani River in Lebanon (Darwish et al. 2021).

Agricultural pollution mainly takes the form of excessive nutrients and salinity, which are already degrading the water quality of MENA's largest rivers. Nitrogen pollution is considered one of the greatest externalities of economic growth (Kanter and Searchinger 2018; Zhang et al. 2015). In water, it can manifest as nitrate, nitrite, and ammonium nitrate, among other compounds, all of which are harmful for human health and ecosystems when present in sufficient concentrations (Damania et al. 2019). In MENA, nitrogen losses from manured agricultural lands to freshwater courses are about 25 percent of the applied fertilizer, much greater than the global average of 11 percent. Releases of phosphate, another major agricultural pollutant, into the environment are about 12 percent of the phosphorus applied as fertilizer, in line with the global average of 12 percent (FAO and IWMI 2018).

Salinity is a widespread problem across MENA, limiting agricultural production and in some cases also damaging drinking water sources. In the Nile, water quality analysis indicates excessive concentrations of salts from agricultural runoff activities, in addition to heavy metals from untreated industrial discharge

Figure 5.4 Safely treated wastewater flows from households

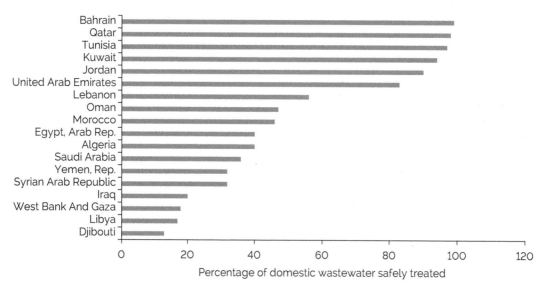

Source: AbuZeid et al. 2019.

(Abdel-Satar, Ali, and Goher 2017). High salinity levels have also been recorded in the Tigris and Euphrates Rivers system, in the Jordan River, and in many aquifers in MENA. In Morocco, seawater intrusion and irrigation aggravate the salinization of aquifers, with at least 30 percent of the country's groundwater resources being degraded because of pollution and salinization (Hssaisoune et al. 2020).

Emerging pollutants are the latest worrying addition to the set of externalities related to water in MENA. These pollutants include a range of chemical products of anthropogenic origin, such as pharmaceuticals, household cleaning products, agricultural products, and microplastics, which make it into the region's waterways without being removed by wastewater treatment processes. As observed in other parts of the world (Damania, Desbureaux, and Zaveri 2020), pharmaceuticals, personal care products, and microplastics are the most commonly occurring contaminants in the region's freshwater bodies (Ouda et al. 2021). The presence of these contaminants gives rise to negative externalities that will also likely affect countries' wastewater reuse potential, because many wastewater treatment plants are not designed to remove these harmful chemicals of anthropogenic origin (Piña et al. 2020). Research has shown that wastewater treatment plants can play a role in releasing microplastics into the environment (Sun et al. 2019). Therefore, proper accounting of these environmental externalities is a key aspect to guide the selection of wastewater treatment technologies and to remove them.

Although MENA accounts for about 50 percent of global desalinated water, it accounts for 70 percent of brine production. In absolute terms, the region produces almost 100 million cubic meters per day of brine, approximately double the amount of drinking water produced (Jones et al. 2019). This imbalance suggests that desalination plants in the region operate at very low efficiency, converting only 25 percent of the intake water into drinking water and the remaining 75 percent into brine, which needs to be disposed of. This low efficiency is a result of the low-efficiency desalination technologies used in the region (mostly thermal), but, more important, it is a direct result of the expansion of desalination in the closed, shallow seas of the Gulf and the Red Sea. The more desalination expands, the more brine is produced. The most economical way of disposing of the brine is to discharge it untreated back into the sea, as is done almost ubiquitously across MENA, where it increases overall salinity levels. The high salinity levels at the plant intakes mean that desalination is more energy intensive, and thus costly and less efficient. These high levels present yet another stark reminder that trade-offs often exist between the benefits of water supply augmentation and environmental quality, and that the externalities generated by supply-side solutions can be circular, reducing economic benefits and technical feasibility in the long term.

Beyond lower desalination efficiency and the economic externality of desalination costs, brine discharge also has serious impacts on marine biodiversity and ecosystems. The discharge of brine and other chemicals used in the desalination process leads to alterations in the chemical properties of seawater around desalination plant outlets, posing a threat to marine ecosystems (Petersen, Frank, et al. 2018). In MENA, these effects have been measured in the Red Sea, where higher salinity levels had an observed impact on coral physiology and bleaching (Petersen, Paytan, et al. 2018); in the Arabian/Persian Gulf, where numerical models show significant spatial and temporal variability of increases in salinity (Campos et al. 2020); and in the Mediterranean (Kenigsberg, Abramovich, and Hyams-Kaphzan 2020). Marine organisms can also be entrained or impinged at the desalination plant seawater intakes (World Bank 2019).

COMPOUND EFFECTS OF WATER-RELATED EXTERNALITIES

As well as the temporal dimension—what is overused today cannot be used tomorrow—all the externalities described above have spatial dimensions. Linking a series of these externalities together can lead to cascade or compound effects.

In Iraq, the Tigris and Euphrates Rivers system, for example, suffers multiple local breaches of both overabstraction and pollution of water, which get compounded. Salinity increases as the rivers move downstream, peaking in the Shatt al-Arab, because of the compound effect of agricultural drainage channels with high salinity and reduced volumes of freshwater flows. Salinity levels downstream of Baghdad exceed the threshold for drinking water quality (Rahi and Halihan 2018), compromising water supply security for domestic and agricultural uses further downstream. Moreover, the low summer flows of water allow tidal surges from the Arabian/Persian Gulf to increase salinity further in the Shatt al-Arab to half that of seawater even 60 kilometers inland at Basra (Ewaid et al. 2020). As a result, in Basra, although the vast majority of households have a piped connection, only 1 percent of households use it as their primary source of drinking water because the municipal water is of such poor quality. The rest purchase water from private water vendors who desalinate the water and sell it at a high price (see figure 5.5).

Another example of the spatial nature of externalities arising from water management efforts relates to irrigation efficiency improvements. Improvements in efficiency do not typically result in reductions in consumption among irrigators, but they do reduce return flows to downstream users (Grafton et al. 2018). In Morocco, the adoption of drip irrigation in the Souss and Tensift basins has reduced recoverable return flows to overexploited aquifers, thus exacerbating groundwater depletion and resulting in higher water consumption because of crop intensification and increased irrigated area owing to improved control of water through advanced irrigation technology (Molle and Tanouti 2017). Thus, an intervention to enhance water-use efficiency cascades to a larger number of water users in the basin, exacerbating water depletion. The spatial nature of externalities is also visible at the transnational scale, where water development in one country can alter the river flow regime (for better or for worse) in a downstream country. These examples show that, unless the spatial nature of externalities is considered, water policy can backfire or cause significant negative impacts on certain users.

Figure 5.5 Iraq: Households' main source of drinking water, by governorate

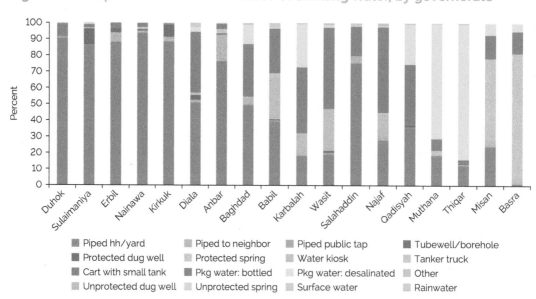

Source: United Nations Children's Fund, Multiple Indicator Cluster Surveys, 2018 (https://mics.unicef.org/surveys)
Note: hh = household; pkg = packaged.

HIDDEN COSTS OF WATER-RELATED EXTERNALITIES

The negative externalities of water depletion and pollution extend to human health, the environment, and the economies of MENA. These costs materialize not only in the form of economic losses but also in mortality and animal and plant species extinction. Although it is not possible to provide a comprehensive assessment of these costs, existing estimates and data sets provide a preliminary analysis using a triple bottom line approach (economy, environment, and society).

Water-Related Negative Externalities Cost Tens of Billions Every Year

The economic cost of negative externalities related to water pollution due to inadequate water supply and sanitation coverage alone is large, with one estimate placing it at US$21 billion every year. The estimated economic costs include health care costs, lost productive time due to sickness, premature mortality, and the value of time savings that would result if improved water and sanitation facilities were closer to home. The cost of the human health externality is greatest in conflict-affected Libya, the Republic of Yemen, Iraq, and West Bank and Gaza (figure 5.6). These costs provide a likely lower bound because they do not include the environmental externalities related to the degradation of aquatic ecosystems and related fisheries arising from lack of sanitation infrastructure.

Groundwater depletion also causes significant economic losses. As aquifers are depleted, exploitation costs increase because of the increased energy required to pump groundwater from greater depths and the additional costs required to treat the low-quality, brackish water produced by overexploited aquifers. In some parts of MENA, the cost of groundwater pumping might reach the cost of desalinating water (more than US$1 per cubic meter) by 2050 (Turner et al. 2019).

Major Environmental and Biodiversity Risks Caused by Depletion and Pollution

Water overuse and pollution are major causes of freshwater species decline in the region. Across the Arabian Peninsula, 17 percent of known freshwater species (both fauna and flora) are threatened with

Figure 5.6 Economic losses from inadequate water supply and sanitation

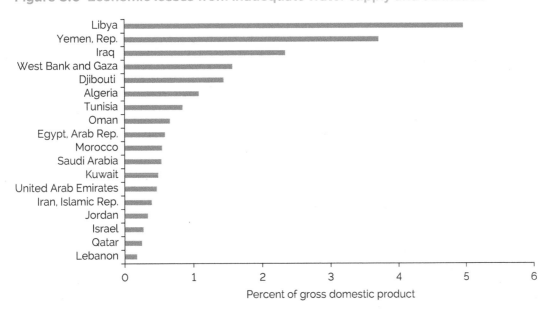

Source: Sadoff et al. 2015.

extinction, and a further 3 percent are near threatened (Cox et al. 2015). Similar levels of biodiversity risk are reported for Northern Africa and the Mashreq (Darwall et al. 2014). Little has been done in MENA to protect aquatic ecosystems from these risks: across the region, the area of natural wetlands is also declining, with most sites having no or low protection status (Leberger et al. 2020).

Water overuse also increases vulnerability to drought, in turn heightening the risk of deforestation and cropland expansion. Groundwater often acts as a safety net in times of drought, providing farmers the additional water they need to irrigate their crops in dry periods. However, when this resource becomes depleted, farmers are more vulnerable to drought and more likely to resort to adaptation options that further damage the environment. Economic analysis of the impacts of droughts in MENA suggests that, in the face of drought, farmers are likely to cut down forests to recoup the agricultural losses, in a vicious cycle of water insecurity that further increases negative externalities (Damania et al. 2017; Taheripour et al. 2020).

Far-Reaching Impacts on Human Health and Society

The effects on human health are major negative externalities of water use in MENA. Water pollution arising from inadequate water supply and sanitation services leads to death and morbidity (figure 5.7). Mortality rates attributable to unsafe water, unsafe sanitation, and lack of hygiene are low in most high-income MENA countries, but they are much higher in conflict-affected countries. Contaminated drinking water is a leading cause of death among children under five, with especially high rates in Syria and the Republic of Yemen. In some MENA countries, diarrheal diseases due to inadequate water, sanitation, and hygiene services cause the deaths of 5 to 15 percent of children younger than five (figure 5.8).

Figure 5.7 Mortality rate attributed to exposure to unsafe water, sanitation, and hygiene services, 2016

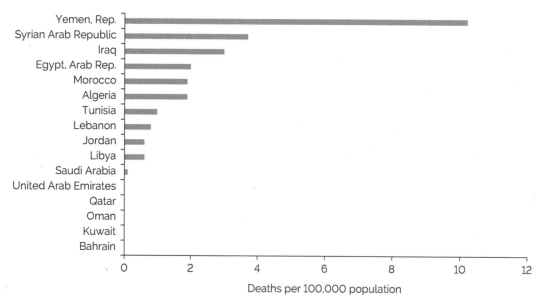

Deaths per 100,000 population

Source: Prüss, Neira, and Bos 2016.
Note: Data were not available for Djibouti or West Bank and Gaza.

Currently, the Republic of Yemen is undergoing the largest documented cholera epidemic in modern times (Camacho et al. 2018).

Negative externalities also impose a cost on social and political dynamics. During a crisis, these externalities materialize suddenly and can contribute to instability and violence in circumstances characterized by preexisting grievances. When thousands of people were hospitalized in Basra in 2018 because of contaminated water, riots erupted over poor access to services and other governance issues. These riots were just the most recent and visible example of the social cost of water externalities. In other parts of Iraq, people have been forced to leave their homes because their water supplies disappeared or became too saline (IOM and Deltares 2020). In Algeria, people regularly protested in front of government buildings during the 2002–04 drought (Ward and Ruckstuhl 2017). In Jordan, plans to convey water to urban centers through the Disi conveyance system have left groundwater users in the southern Mudawarra area to face the consequences of groundwater depletion, leading to farm closures (Liptrot and Hussein 2020). In the Republic of Yemen, depletion exacerbates social inequality and marginalization. In the Sa'ada Basin in the north of the country, only wealthy landowners have adapted to the drying of shallow wells by drilling even deeper wells (Lackner and Al-Eryani 2020). Smallholders had to abandon or sell their land because of the drying up of their wells. In other parts of the country, disenfranchised farmers have often resorted to violence to secure access to the remaining wells (Ward 2014).

Water-related externalities across MENA cost tens of billions of dollars a year and have both environmental and social consequences. Part II of this report examines why institutions in MENA struggle to manage water sustainably or contain the related negative externalities.

Figure 5.8 Deaths caused by diarrhea in children younger than age five, 2017

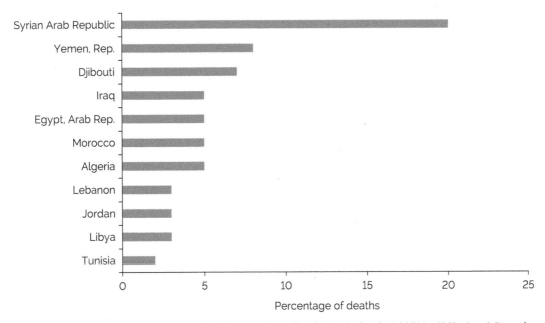

Percentage of deaths

Source: WHO and Maternal and Child Epidemiology Estimation Group (http://data.unicef.org/topic/child-health/diarrhoeal-disease/).
Note: Data were not available for Djibouti or West Bank and Gaza.

NOTES

1. Water-related ecosystems consist of five categories: (1) vegetated wetlands, (2) rivers and estuaries, (3) lakes, (4) aquifers, and (5) artificial waterbodies.

2. Using Food and Agriculture Organization AQUASTAT data on total water withdrawals (2013–17).

3. To study the role of these factors in groundwater depletion, Turner et al. (2019) employ a global data set that specifies that cost of groundwater extraction as a function of depletion.

4. Produced water is the groundwater brought to the surface as part of oil and gas extraction processes and that needs to be safely disposed of.

REFERENCES

Abdel-Satar, A. M., M. H. Ali, and M. E. Goher. 2017. "Indices of Water Quality and Metal Pollution of Nile River, Egypt." *Egyptian Journal of Aquatic Research* 43 (1): 21–29.

Abdunaser, K. 2020. "Spatio-Temporal Analysis of Oil Lake and Oil-Polluted Surfaces from Remote Sensing Data in One of the Libyan Oil Fields." *Scientific Reports* 10: 20174. https://doi.org/10.1038/s41598-020-76992-5.

Abulibdeh, A., T. Al-Awadhi, N. Al Nasiri, A. Al-Buloshi, and M. Abdelghani. 2021. "Spatiotemporal Mapping of Groundwater Salinity in Al-Batinah, Oman." *Groundwater for Sustainable Development* 12: 100551. https://doi.org/10.1016/j.gsd.2021.100551.

AbuZeid, K., A. Wagdy, M. Ibrahim, CEDARE (Center for the Environment and Development for the Arab Region and Europe), and Arab Water Council. 2019. *3rd State of the Water Report for the Arab Region 2015.* Water Resources Management Program. Cairo, Egypt: CEDARE and Arab Water Council. ISSN: 2357 0318.

Al-Mudaffar Fawzi, N., K. P. Goodwin, B. A. Mahdi, and M. L. Stevens. 2016. "Effects of Mesopotamian Marsh (Iraq) Desiccation on the Cultural Knowledge and Livelihood of Marsh Arab Women." *Ecosystem Health and Sustainability* 2 (3): e01207. https://doi.org/10.1002/ehs2.1207.

Amin Al Manmi, D. A. M., T. O. Abdullah, P. M. Al-Jaf, and N. Al-Ansari. 2019. "Soil and Groundwater Pollution Assessment and Delineation of Intensity Risk Map in Sulaymaniyah City, NE of Iraq." *Water* 11 (10): 2158. https://doi.org/10.3390/w11102158.

Aw-Hassan, A., F. Rida, R. Telleria, and A. Bruggeman. 2014. "The Impact of Food and Agricultural Policies on Groundwater Use in Syria." *Journal of Hydrology* 513: 204–15. 10.1016/j.jhydrol.2014.03.043.

Benabdelfadel, A. 2012. "Plan d'action: Protection des ressources en eau souterraines au Maroc (Contrat de nappe)." PowerPoint presentation, Secrétariat d'Etat auprès du Ministère de l'Energie, des Mines, de l'Eau et de l'Environnement, Charge de l'Eau et de l'Environnement, Département de l'Eau, Royaume du Maroc. https://www.slideserve.com/kayo/p-rotection-des-ressources-en-eau-souterraines-au-maroc-contrat-de-nappe.

Bierkens, M. F. P., and Y. Wada. 2019. "Non-renewable Groundwater Use and Groundwater Depletion: A Review." *Environmental Research Letters* 14 (6): 063002. https://iopscience.iop.org/article/10.1088/1748-9326/ab1a5f/meta.

Camacho, A., M. Bouhenia, R. Alyusfi, A. Alkohlani, M. A. M. Naji, X. de Radiguès, A. M. Abubakar, et al. 2018. "Cholera Epidemic in Yemen, 2016–18: An Analysis of Surveillance Data." *Lancet Global Health* 6 (6): e680–90. https://doi.org/10.1016/S2214-109X(18)30230-4.

Campos, E. J. D., F. Vieira, G. Cavalcante, B. Kjerfve, M. Abouleish, S. Shariar, R. Mohamed, and A. L. Gordon. 2020. "Impacts of Brine Disposal from Water Desalination Plants on the Physical Environment in the Persian/Arabian Gulf." *Environmental Research Communications* 2 (12): 125003. https://doi.org/10.1088/2515-7620/abd0ed.

Closas, A., and K. G. Villholth. 2016. *Aquifer Contracts: A Means to Solving Groundwater Over-exploitation in Morocco?* Groundwater Solutions Initiative for Policy and Practice Case Profile Series 1. Colombo, Sri Lanka: International Water Management Institute.

Cox, N., N. García, I. J. Harrison, and M. F. Tognelli. 2015. *The Status and Distribution of Freshwater Biodiversity in the Arabian Peninsula.* IUCN Red List of Threatened Species—Regional Assessment. Gland, Switzerland: International Union for the Conservation of Nature. https://doi.org/10.2305-IUCN.CH.2015.MRA.4.en.

Damania, R., S. Desbureaux, M. Hyland, A. Islam, S. Moore, A.-S. Rodella, J. Russ, and E. Zaveri. 2017. *Uncharted Waters: The New Economics of Water Scarcity and Variability.* Washington, DC: World Bank. https://openknowledge.worldbank.org/handle/10986/28096.

Damania, R., S. Desbureaux, P. L. Scandizzo, M. Mikou, D. Gohil, and M. Said. 2019. "*When Good Conservation Becomes Good Economics: Kenya's Vanishing Herds.*" World Bank, Washington, DC. https://openknowledge.worldbank.org/handle/10986/33083.

Damania, R., S. Desbureaux, E. Zaveri, 2020. "Does Rainfall Matter for Economic Growth? Evidence from Global Sub-National Data (1990–2014)." *Journal of Environmental Economics and Management* 102:102335. ISSN 0095-0696. https://doi.org/10.1016/j.jeem.2020.102335.

Daoudy, M. 2020. *The Origins of the Syrian Conflict: Climate Change and Human Security.* Cambridge: Cambridge University Press. doi:10.1017/9781108567053.

Darwall, W. R. T., S. Carrizo, C. Numa, V. Barrios, J. Freyhof, and K. Smith. 2014. "Freshwater Key Biodiversity Areas in the Mediterranean Basin Hotspot: Informing Species Conservation and Development Planning in Freshwater Ecosystems." Occasional Paper of the IUCN Special Survival Commission, Monographic Series 52. International Union for the Conservation of Nature, Gland, Switzerland. https://doi.org/10.2305/IUCN.CH.2014.SSC-OP.52.en.

Darwish, T., A. Shaban, I. Masih, H. Jaafar, I. Jomaa, and J. P. Simaika. 2021. "Sustaining the Ecological Functions of the Litani River Basin, Lebanon." *International Journal of River Basin Management* (2021): 1–15. https://doi.org/10.1080/15715124.2021.1885421.

EcoPeace Middle East. 2018. "EcoPeace's Vision for Stabilizing the Water Level of the Dead Sea—2018." EcoPeace Middle East, Amman, Jordan. https://old.ecopeaceme.org/wp-content/uploads/2018/03/Dead-Sea-Brief_2018.pdf.

El-Agha, D. E., D. J. Molden, and A. M. Ghanem. 2011. "Performance Assessment of Irrigation Water Management in Old Lands of the Nile Delta of Egypt." *Irrigation and Drainage Systems* 25 (4): 215–36. https://doi.org/10.1007/s10795-011-9116-z.

Ewaid, S. H., S. A. Abed, N. Al-Ansari, and R. M. Salih. 2020. "Development and Evaluation of a Water Quality Index for the Iraqi Rivers." *Hydrology* 7 (3): 67. https://doi.org/10.3390/hydrology7030067.

FAO and IWMI (Food and Agriculture Organization of the United Nations and International Water Management Institute). 2018. "More People, More Food, Worse Water? A Global Review of Water Pollution from Agriculture." FAO, Rome, and IWMI, Colombo, Sri Lanka. http://www.fao.org/3/CA0146EN/ca0146en.pdf.

Faysse, N., T. Hartani, A. Frija, S. Marlet, I. Tazekrit, C. Zairi, C., and A. Challouf. 2011. "Usage agricole des eaux souterraines et initiatives de gestion au Maghreb: défis et opportunités pour un usage durable des aquiféres." Note Economique, African Development Bank (AfDB)-Banque Africaine de Developpement (BAfD), Abidjan, Côte d'Ivoire.

Foster, S., and D. P. Loucks, eds. 2006. *Non-Renewable Groundwater Resources: A Guidebook on Socially-Sustainable Management for Water-Policy Makers.* IHP-VI Series on Groundwater 10. Paris: United Nations Educational, Scientific and Cultural Organization. https://unesdoc.unesco.org/ark:/48223/pf0000146997.

Grafton, R., J. Williams, C. J. Perry, F. Molle, C. Ringler, P. Steduto, B. Udall, S. Wheeler, Y. Wang, D. Garrick, and R. Allen. 2018. "The Paradox of Irrigation Efficiency." *Science.* 361:,748–50. 10.1126/science.aat9314.

Hillel, N., S. Geyer, T. Licha, S. Khayat, J. B. Laronne, and C. Siebert. 2015. "Water Quality and Discharge of the Lower Jordan River." *Journal of Hydrology* 527: 1096–105. https://doi.org/10.1016/j.jhydrol.2015.06.002.

HRW (Human Rights Watch). 2019. "Basra Is Thirsty: Iraq's Failure to Manage the Human Rights Crisis." HRW, New York. https://www.hrw.org/report/2019/07/22/basra-thirsty/iraqs-failure-manage-water-crisis.

Hssaisoune, M., L. Bouchaou, A. Sifeddine, I. Bouimetarhan, and A. Chehbouni. 2020. "Moroccan Groundwater Resources and Evolution with Global Climate Changes." *Geosciences* 10 (2): 81. https://doi.org/10.3390/geosciences10020081.

IOM (International Organization for Migration) and Deltares. 2020. "Water Quantity and Water Quality in Central and South Iraq: A Preliminary Assessment in the Context of Displacement Risk." Baghdad: IOM.

Jones, E., M. Qadir, M. T. H. van Vliet, V. Smakhtin, and S.-m. Kang. 2019. "The State of Desalination and Brine Production: A Global Outlook." *Science of the Total Environment* 657: 1343–56. https://doi.org/10.1016/j.scitotenv.2018.12.076.

Joodaki, G., J. Wahr, and S. Swenson. 2014. "Estimating the Human Contribution to Groundwater Depletion in the Middle East, from GRACE Data, Land Surface Models, and Well Observations." *Water Resources Research* 50 (3): 2679–92. https://doi.org/10.1002/2013WR014633.

Jordan Ministry of Environment. 2017. *A National Green Growth Plan for Jordan.* Amman: Hashemite Kingdom of Jordan.

Kanter, D. R., and T. D. Searchinger. 2018. "A Technology-Forcing Approach to Reduce Nitrogen Pollution." *Nature Sustainability* 1: 544–52. https://doi.org/10.1038/s41893-018-0143-8.

Kenigsberg, C., S. Abramovich, and O. Hyams-Kaphzan. 2020. "The Effect of Long-Term Brine Discharge from Desalination Plants on Benthic Foraminifera." *PLoS ONE* 15 (1): e0227589. https://doi.org/10.1371/journal.pone.0227589.

Lackner, H., and A. Al-Eryani. 2020. "Yemen's Environmental Crisis Is the Biggest Risk for Its Future." Century Foundation, New York. https://tcf.org/content/report/yemens-environmental-crisis-biggest-risk-future/.

Leberger, R., I. R. Geijzendorffer, E. Gaget, A. Gwelmami, T. Galewski, H. M. Pereira, and C. A. Guerra. 2020. "Mediterranean Wetland Conservation in the Context of Climate and Land Cover Change." *Regional Environmental Change* 20: 67. https://doi.org/10.1007/s10113-020-01655-0.

Liptrot, T., and H. Hussein. 2020. "Between Regulation and Targeted Expropriation: Rural-to-Urban Groundwater Reallocation in Jordan." *Water Alternatives* 13 (3): 864–65.

Molle, F., and O. Tanouti. 2017. "Squaring the Circle: Agricultural Intensification vs. Water Conservation in Morocco." *Agricultural Water Management* 192: 170–79. https://doi.org/10.1016/j.agwat.2017.07.009.

Mukhopadhyay, A., M. Quinn, A. Al-Haddad, A. Al-Khalid, H. Al-Qallaf, T. Rashed, H. Bhandary, et al. 2017. "Pollution of Fresh Groundwater from Damaged Oil Wells, North Kuwait." *Environmental Earth Sciences* 76 (4): 145. https://doi.org/10.1007/s12665-017-6457-4.

MWI (Ministry of Water and Irrigation, Jordan). 2017. MWI Portal. MWI, Amman, Jordan. https://www.mwi.gov.jo/ebv4.0/root_storage/ar/eb_list_page/-2017_وارقام_حقائق_المياه_قطاع.pdf.

Othman, A., and A. Z. Abotalib. 2019. "Land Subsidence Triggered by Groundwater Withdrawal under Hyper-arid Conditions: Case Study from Central Saudi Arabia." *Environmental Earth Sciences* 78 (7): 243. https://doi.org/10.1007/s12665-019-8254-8.

Ouda, M., D. Kadadou, B. Swaidan, A. Al-Othman, S. Al-Asheh, F. Banat, and S. W. Hasan. 2021. "Emerging Contaminants in the Water Bodies of the Middle East and North Africa (MENA): A Critical Review." *Science of the Total Environment* 754: 142177. https://doi.org/10.1016/j.scitotenv.2020.142177.

Ouda, O. K. M. 2014. "Impacts of Agricultural Policy on Irrigation Water Demand: A Case Study of Saudi Arabia." *International Journal of Water Resources Development* 30 (2): 282–92. https://doi.org/10.1080/07900627.2013.876330.

Petersen, K. L., H. Frank, A. Paytan, and E. Bar-Zeev. 2018. "Impacts of Seawater Desalination on Coastal Environments." In *Sustainable Desalination Handbook: Plant Selection, Design and Implementation*, edited by V. G. Gude, 437–63. Oxford, UK: Butterworth-Heinemann. https://doi.org/10.1016/B978-0-12-809240-8 .00011-3.

Petersen, K. L., A. Paytan, E. Rahav, O. Levy, J. Silverman, O. Barzel, D. Potts, and E. Bar-Zeev. 2018. "Impact of Brine and Antiscalants on Reef-Building Corals in the Gulf of Aqaba—Potential Effects from Desalination Plants." *Water Research* 144: 183–91. https://doi.org/10.1016/j.watres.2018.07.009.

Piña, B., J. M. Bayona, A. Christou, D. Fatta-Kassinos, E. Guillon, D. Lambropoulou, C. Michael, F. Polesel, and S. Sayen. 2020. "On the Contribution of Reclaimed Wastewater Irrigation to the Potential Exposure of Humans to Antibiotics, Antibiotic Resistant Bacteria and Antibiotic Resistance Genes—NEREUS COST Action ES1403 Position Paper." *Journal of Environmental Chemical Engineering* 8 (1): 102131. https://doi .org/10.1016/j.jece.2018.01.011.

Prüss, A., M. Neira, and R. Bos. 2016. *Preventing Disease through Healthy Environments: A Global Assessment of the Burden of Disease from Environmental Risks*. Geneva: World Health Organization. file:///C:/Users /wb321759/Downloads/9789241565196_eng.pdf.

Rahi, K., and T. Halihan. 2018. "Salinity Evolution of the Tigris River." *Regional Environmental Change* 18: 1–11. 10.1007/s10113-018-1344-4.

Richey, A. S., B. F. Thomas, M.-H. Lo, J. S. Famiglietti, S. Swenson, and M. Rodell. 2015. "Uncertainty in Global Groundwater Storage Estimates in a Total Groundwater Stress Framework." *Water Resources Research* 51 (7): 5198–216. https://doi.org/10.1002/2015WR017351.

Rodell, M., J. S. Famiglietti, D. N. Wiese, J. T. Reager, H. K. Beaudoing, F. W. Landerer, and M.-H. Lo. 2018. "Emerging Trends in Global Freshwater Availability." *Nature* 557: 651–59. https://doi.org/10.1038/s41586-018 -0123-1.

Sadoff, C. W., J. W. Hall, D. Grey, J. C. J. H. Aerts, M. Ait-Kadi, C. Brown, A. Cox, S. Dadson, D. Garrick, J. Kelman, P. McCornick, C. Ringler, M. Rosegrant, D. Whittington, and D. Wiberg. 2015. *Securing Water, Sustaining Growth: Report of the GWP/OECD Task Force on Water Security and Sustainable Growth*. Oxford, U.K.: University of Oxford.

Schyns, J. F., A. Hamaideh, A. Y. Hoekstra, M. M. Mekonnen, and M. Schyns. 2015. "Mitigating the Risk of Extreme Water Scarcity and Dependency: The Case of Jordan." *Water* 7 (10): 5705–30. https://doi.org/10.3390 /w7105705.

Sultan, M., N. C. Sturchio, S. Alsefry, M. K. Emil, M. Ahmed, K. Abdelmohsen, M. M. AbuAbdullah, et al. 2019. "Assessment of Age, Origin, and Sustainability of Fossil Aquifers: A Geochemical and Remote Sensing-Based Approach." *Journal of Hydrology*, 576, pp. 325-341. ISSN 0022-1694. https://doi.org/10.1016/j.jhydrol .2019.06.017.

Sun, J., X. Dai, Q. Wang, M. C. M. van Loosdrecht, and B.-J. Ni. 2019. "Microplastics in Wastewater Treatment Plants: Detection, Occurrence and Removal." *Water Research* 152: 21–37. https://doi.org/10.1016/j .watres.2018.12.050.

Taheripour, F., W. E. Tyner, E. Sajedinia, A. Anguiar, M. Chepeliev, E. L. Corong, C. Z. de Lima, and I. Haqiqi. 2020. "Water in the Balance: The Economic Impacts of Climate Change and Water Scarcity in the Middle East." World Bank, Washington, DC.

Turner, S. W. D., M. Hejazi, C. Yonkofski, S. H. Kim, and P. Kyle. 2019. "Influence of Groundwater Extraction Costs and Resource Depletion Limits on Simulated Global Nonrenewable Water Withdrawals over the Twenty-First Century." *Earth's Future* 7 (2): 123–35. https://doi.org/10.1029/2018EF001105.

UN-Habitat and WHO (United Nations Human Settlements Programme and World Health Organization). 2021. "Progress on Wastewater Treatment: Global Status and Acceleration Needs for SDG Indicator 6.3.1." UN-Habitat and WHO, Geneva. https://unhabitat.org/progress-on-wastewater-treatment-%E2%80%93 -2021-update.

UNEP (United Nations Environment Programme). 2001. *The Mesopotamian Marshlands: Demise of an Ecosystem.* Early Warning and Assessment Technical Report. Nairobi, Kenya: UNEP.

UNEP (United Nations Environment Programme) 2020. *State of Environment and Outlook Report for the Occupied Palestinian Territory 2020.* Nairobi, Kenya: UNEP.

USGS (U.S. Geological Survey). 2014. "Groundwater Depletion." USGS, Reston, VA. https://water.usgs.gov/edu/gwdepletion.html.

Voss, K. A., J. S. Famiglietti, M. Lo, C. de Linage, M. Rodell, and S. C. Swenson. 2013. "Groundwater Depletion in the Middle East from GRACE with Implications for Transboundary Water Management in the Tigris-Euphrates-Western Iran Region." *Water Resources Research* 49 (2): 904–14. https://doi.org/10.1002/wrcr.20078.

Wada, Y., and F. Bierkens. 2014. "Sustainability of Global Water Use: Past Reconstruction and Future Projections." *Environmental Research Letters* 9: 104003. http://dx.doi.org/10.1088/1748-9326/9/10/104003.

Wada, Y., and L. Heinrich. 2013. "Assessment of Transboundary Aquifers of the World—Vulnerability Arising from Human Water Use." *Environmental Research Letters* 8 (2): 024003. https://doi.org/10.1088/1748-9326/8/2/024003.

Ward, C. 2014. *The Water Crisis in Yemen: Managing Extreme Water Scarcity in the Middle East.* London: Bloomsbury Publishing.

Ward, C., and S. Ruckstuhl. 2017. *Water Scarcity, Climate Change and Conflict in the Middle East: Securing Livelihoods, Building Peace.* New York: Bloomsbury.

World Bank. 2018. *Beyond Scarcity: Water Security in the Middle East and North Africa.* MENA Development Series. World Bank, Washington, DC.

World Bank 2019. "The Role of Desalination in an Increasingly Water-Scarce World." Technical Paper, Water Global Practice, World Bank, Washington, DC. https://openknowledge.worldbank.org/handle/10986/31416.

Wurtsbaugh, W. A., C. Miller, S. E. Null, R. J. DeRose, P. Wilcock, M. Hahnenberger, F. Howe, and J. Morre. 2017. "Decline of the World's Saline Lakes." *Nature Geoscience* 10 (11): 816–21. https://doi.org/10.1038/ngeo3052.

Zhang, X., E. A. Davidson, D. L. Mauzerall, T. D. Searchinger, P. Dumas, and Y. Shen. 2015. "Managing Nitrogen for Sustainable Development." *Nature* 528: 51–59. https://doi.org/10.1038/nature15743.

PART II

Understanding Why Status Quo Institutions Produce Outcomes That Endanger Water Security and Well-Being

This part of the report provides answers to the following questions:

- Why have governments relied excessively on supply-side investments and not addressed the negative externalities in the demand for water through price and quantity regulations?
- Why are utilities unable to raise the financing needed to cover their operations and investments for reliable water services?
- Why are utilities suffering from large leakages and losses of water?

Using an economic framework of "principal-agent" relationships, it shows how the answers can be found in the incentives and norms (beliefs and expectations about how others behave, and therefore how one should too) of a variety of actors along the chain of water supply and demand.

CHAPTER 6

Economic Framework to Understand How State Institutions Function in Allocating, Managing, and Investing in Water

INTRODUCTION

States in the Middle East and North Africa (MENA) have been managing all aspects of water through the public sector. National investments in dams, desalination, and wastewater treatment plants enable powerful national ministries to exercise control (within natural and physical constraints, of course) over where and how water flows. National laws are established for the regulation of water resources. Public ownership of water and irrigation utilities is the norm in the region, with few examples of private concessions or private ownership; even when partnerships with the private sector exist, state agencies ultimately regulate tariffs and the rules of service delivery.

To understand any outcome of water resource management or service delivery, it is thus necessary to understand how state institutions function. This chapter lays out an economic framework of logic that can be applied to understand the functioning of state institutions in any country context, with tailoring for the specifics of each unique setting. This framework builds on an established body of economic theory of complex organizations, which the current research frontier is extending to understand the particularities of organizations in the sphere of government or the public sector (Dal Bo and Finan 2016; Estache 2016; Khemani 2019; Somanathan 2020; World Bank 2016, 2017).

The purpose of this chapter and part II of the report is to explain and understand outcomes as they are, a so-called positive analysis. The logic of the framework is then used to derive normative policy ideas to offer to reform leaders and their external partners. These policy ideas are developed and presented in part III, which is rooted in the framework of this chapter, using it first for a better understanding of the problem and then deriving pathways from the problem toward improved outcomes.

As the chapter shows, political economy and a "behavioral" view of norms, such as beliefs and expectations of how others behave, are integral pieces of this framework. The analysis thus progresses on the path laid out for the future by past work in the water sector. For example, Mumssen, Saltiel, and Kingdom (2018, ix) write the following: "New thinking that draws not only on infrastructure economics but also on the understanding of political, behavioral, and institutional economics is needed." (See also Garrick et al. 2019; Goksu et al. 2019; Waalewijn et al. 2019.)

THE FRAMEWORK

Economic theory provides a framework to examine water sector outcomes by understanding the behaviors and interactions between millions of actors, from citizens and society to political and national leaders, to senior managers of public utilities, to frontline staff engaged in managing water resources and water service delivery. Insights emerge from structuring the behaviors and actions of these different types of actors into interdependent "principal-agent" problems in which one type of actor, the agent, takes actions on behalf of or at the behest of another, the principal. The state selects and implements public policies, including water policies, within the following principal-agent relationships, which are illustrated in figure 6.1: (1) between citizens, or society, or the sovereign in a MENA context and political leaders; (2) between political leaders and public officials who lead government agencies; and (3) between public officials and frontline providers. These principal-agent relationships are a formal way of thinking about the metaphor of a "social contract" between citizens and the state.[1]

This framework builds on *World Development Report 2004: Making Services Work for Poor People* (World Bank 2004) and updates it using the learning about governance and accountability in the years since its publication. *World Development Report 2004* was one of the first major World Bank reports to include analysis of political incentives. It spawned policy innovations and a rich research agenda on accountability and governance, going beyond capacity building alone. Yet the bulk of the work on governance that followed was silent on the so-called long route of accountability, which goes through

Figure 6.1 Principal-agent relationships of government

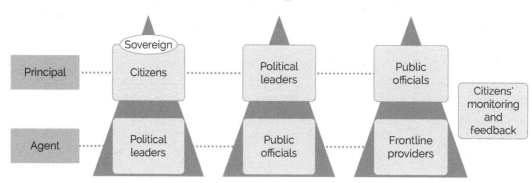

Source: World Bank 2016, 103.

political institutions, in favor of a so-called short route by which citizens might directly solve local problems of service delivery.

That is, at the same time that it made the discussion of political incentives and accountability more acceptable, *World Development Report 2004* appears to have inadvertently contributed to popularizing the idea that politics, when a problem, can be bypassed.[2] It has subsequently been clarified that the only short route is the market (Devarajan 2014). This chapter shows how for commodities such as water, where standard market mechanisms fail and state intervention is needed, there is no short route solution to fixing service provision—whether through citizen engagement or switching to market mechanisms in certain segments of water services, such as bottled water or tanker trucks.

The "short route" is a misnomer when it comes to solving problems of accountability in the public sector, creating a false impression that it is easier for citizens to organize local collective action to improve local services directly than to use political pressure on leaders to make the state serve citizens better. Furthermore, well-intentioned leaders are often constrained by prevailing beliefs and perceptions among citizens that make it difficult to win their trust and compliance with reforms. That is, some public policy problems, such as those of managing the scarce resource of water, are problems not only of accountability of leaders to citizens but also of building a societal consensus on the appropriate public policies. The framework offered here allows for examining the role of leaders in communicating issues to citizens to build legitimacy and trust (box 6.1).

In specific examples from MENA, the following sections show how legitimacy and trust constitute key informal institutions that matter for water investments and management; how formal institutional reforms, copied from other places, can be ineffective because informal institutions have not changed; and how informal institutions are the route through which societies transition to better outcomes, adopting the formal institutions that work in their contexts.

APPLYING THE FRAMEWORK TO UNDERSTAND THE STATE'S TARIFF AND REVENUE-RAISING CAPACITY TO INVEST IN WATER

Consider the example of the Arab Republic of Egypt and its government's plans for substantially increasing the country's supply of water through the construction of desalination plants. A market study produced by the World Bank and International Finance Corporation reports that more than 70 percent of the financing for desalination investments in Egypt has come from the national budget, with external financing coming only from one bilateral agency, the Kuwait Fund for Arab Economic Development (World Bank and IFC 2020). Going forward, the government of Egypt plans to increase its water capital expenditure from US$890.0 million at present to more than US$2.0 billion in 2022 and approximately US$4.3 billion by 2037. Operational expenditures will likely increase from US$222.0 million for the present capacity to more than US$1.0 billion by 2037. During 2022, the operational expenditures of desalination investments are expected to increase to about 25 percent of the total operation and maintenance costs for the government of Egypt's holding company for water and wastewater and its subsidiaries.

The World Bank and International Finance Corporation market study shows that Egypt will not be able to attract private sector financing without substantial increases in water tariffs. Such increases present a challenge for a country that has historically had one of the lowest water tariffs in the world. Despite an increase in tariffs of 47 percent in 2017, revenues from tariffs in Egypt remain below cost-covering levels (World Bank and IFC 2020). To invest in water, Egypt thus needs to persuade its citizens and society to contribute to state revenues, through tariffs, other fiscal instruments, or a combination of the two.

Box 6.1 Definitions of "legitimacy" and "trust" from economics and game theory research

Legitimacy is the ability of leaders to win compliance with new laws or public orders because people share a widespread belief that everyone is complying. Recent work on law and economics reexamines the puzzle of why developing countries have laws on paper that are not effectively implemented (World Bank 2017). Instead of relying on explanations about weak governance, low capacity, and perverse political incentives, Basu and Cordella (2018) argue that a conceptually clearer way of thinking about compliance with a new law is whether the new law changes people's beliefs about how others are behaving, and thus legitimizes compliance. Legitimacy depends on beliefs—or focal points, in the language of game theory—about how others are behaving in political and bureaucratic institutions (Garrick et al. 2019; Goksu et al. 2019; Waalewijn et al. 2019). For example, whether farmers and households comply with reforms in irrigation and water supply and sanitation policies, such as tariff increases, depends on the legitimacy of those policies, viewed as beliefs about how others are likely to behave. This view provides new ideas for using transparency and local political contestation to shift beliefs toward greater legitimacy.

Trust has also been broken down in research to the fundamental elements of game theory—beliefs about how others are behaving in a particular game of life, society, or politics (Alesina and Giuliano 2015; Algan and Cahuc 2014). High levels of trust are equated with beliefs that others are playing the game in cooperative ways that enhance the payoffs to all, whereas low levels of trust are equated with beliefs that others are playing the game in noncooperative ways, with worse outcomes for all players. Within this large body of research on different types of trust, the segment that is most relevant for understanding governance issues in water examines trust, or lack thereof, in public institutions. Corruption or rent seeking is one manifestation of lack of trust. If people believe that others are likely to be extracting rents in the public sector, they are likely to behave in the same way, yielding an equilibrium of high corruption and low trust. Trust can also be examined in the water sector as the strength (or weakness) of professional norms among the multiple principals and agents involved in the sector. If agents believe that others are likely to behave unprofessionally, by holding up decisions or not performing their assigned tasks on time or effectively, then they may be more inclined to behave the same way, yielding an equilibrium of weak professional norms and low trust. This view of trust provides new ideas for improving the performance of utilities through management reforms that use greater autonomy along with communication among peers to build peer-to-peer monitoring and accountability, or professional norms.

Sources: Dal Bo and Finan 2016; Estache 2016l Khemani 2019; Somanathan 2020; World Bank 2016, 2017.

Technical economic analysis of how much a country should invest in a public good yields the classical characterization that the marginal benefit or value to society from the investment should equal the marginal cost of the investment. However, technical economic analysis is silent on the normative question of preferences over the public good, which is a political choice problem of the first principal-agent relationship in figure 6.1—between citizens and the state, as represented by its political leaders.[3] Recent economic research on understanding the emergence of the fiscal capacity of states in the developed world—to be able to tax their citizens—concludes that intangible phenomena like "civic culture" and "legitimacy" are at the heart of fiscal capacity (Besley 2020; Besley and Persson 2009; Fergusson, Molina, and Robinson 2022). These concepts relate to the beliefs or views citizens hold about the state and its leaders, and the expectations citizens have about how others, their fellow citizens, are behaving toward the state (which then shape their own behavior).

Evidence from the World Values Survey shows that people in MENA believe that a key role of government should be to keep prices down, there is widespread concern about governments "raising prices," and states in MENA face protests following tariff increases.[4] This evidence explains why governments are reluctant to raise tariffs because of the risk of widespread protests and political instability. Instead of avoiding this problem as "politically sensitive," this report argues that reform leaders and their external partners can tackle the problem through a combination of policy instruments that take seriously the role of beliefs and expectations. Prior political economy work on subsidy reforms has tried to address this issue and generally pointed to the important (or "essential") role of communication. This report builds on prior efforts and brings in economic research on institutional change. The resulting ideas can be powerful to shift societywide beliefs and expectations in the direction of increasing the state's ability to win citizens' compliance with advancing critical reforms. Local institutions of political contestation—such as municipal or district-level elections for leadership positions in local government—can play a key role, as discussed further in chapter 9, in part III of the report.

APPLYING THE FRAMEWORK TO UNDERSTAND QUANTITY REGULATIONS TO CONSERVE WATER AS A RESOURCE

Regulations on the quantity of groundwater that can be abstracted and the number of wells that can be dug are prevalent across MENA. Case studies in Morocco show how overabstraction depleted aquifers and whole farming communities faced an existential threat, leading the government to respond by bringing in surface water from elsewhere (Talbi et al., forthcoming). To avoid this cycle—of first depleting groundwater and then deploying emergency efforts to save the people affected—the government of Morocco has been trying to strengthen a regime of licensing wells and restricting the quantity of water withdrawals so that groundwater has a chance to replenish before it is depleted. However, "illegal" wells abound. This outcome, logically, must be the result of a combination of the following: (1) lack of legitimacy of water regulation (farmers are not complying); (2) government agencies charged with implementing the regulations are not performing their task effectively; and (3) the regulations are badly designed from an administrative perspective, making it technically difficult for agencies to implement them.

The first factor—lack of legitimacy of water regulations—is part of the first principal-agent relationship between citizens and the state. The case study from Morocco (Talbi et al., forthcoming) suggests that beliefs among farmers are that the state does not have the right to impose on their use of water, and expectations are that other farmers are flouting the regulations, with no qualms about social disapproval. That is, once again, beliefs and expectations among citizens—farmers—affected by state policies shape the effectiveness of those policies in managing water. In Jordan, there are examples of communities of farmers threatening frontline public officials with violence when the officials tried to enforce regulations (Hussein 2016).

The Moroccan case study also suggests that the other two factors play a role. The second principal-agent relationship—how political leaders delegate the responsibilities of designing policies such as water regulations—shapes the administrative quality of the policy. The third principal-agent relationship—how frontline officials, who monitor and enforce the regulations, are managed—shapes their performance in implementing the regulation policy. The next section illustrates the application of these two principal-agent relationships to understand the performance of water utilities.

APPLYING THE FRAMEWORK TO UNDERSTAND THE PERFORMANCE OF WATER UTILITIES

Governments and their development partners have long been concerned about the financial stability and service delivery performance of state-owned water utilities, not just in MENA but across the developing world. Along with other market-oriented economic reforms during the 1990s, the solutions to the problem of public water utilities were thought to lie in private sector participation, corporatization, and establishment of regulatory authorities that are autonomous and independent of ministries. These solution areas can be examined through the lens of principal-agent relationships in utilities, shedding light on why these reform efforts may have failed, where they may have succeeded, and why.[5]

The underlying assumption behind the proposed reforms of the 1990s was that political incentives negatively interfered with and were therefore inimical to high-quality service delivery. State-owned utilities were thought to perform poorly because state ownership could not promote the entrepreneurship and ingenuity needed for organizations to succeed, like organizations in the private sector that are driven by the forces of market competition. In the language of principal-agent relationships, public officials appointed as leaders or managers of state-owned companies (the second relationship) were thought to suffer from weak incentives and perhaps nonmeritocratic selection, being political appointees. These political appointments of the leaders or managers of utilities, in turn, would affect how they manage the staff within their organization (the third relationship). It was expected that political patronage appointments in the public sector would directly affect the quality and incentives of lower-level staff, in addition to the appointment of senior staff in managerial positions. In some contexts, these political patronage appointments are referred to as "wasta" (Brixi, Lust, and Woolcock 2015).

In the early 2000s, following limited success with privatization in the water sector, reform efforts downplayed privatization in favor of corporatization of water utilities or corporatization with private sector participation—which was expected to insulate the technical day-to-day management of utilities from political interference. Corporatization and new public management reforms were expected to improve outcomes by changing incentives and promoting performance- and competence-based selection of staff from the top-most levels down to the frontlines. Although these mechanisms of incentives and selection in principal-agent economics may not have been identified as such in the general discussion of market-oriented reforms in the 1990s, they are the mechanisms underpinning the expectations of those reforms. Recent research has added formal analysis of a third mechanism, which may have been intuitively regarded in the 1990s—the culture or norms within an organization (Khemani 2019). Corporatized management and private sector participation are thought to promote a performance-oriented culture, going beyond individual incentives to synergies between individuals who each believe that others are motivated or incentivized to perform well. To summarize, the following three mechanisms, rooted in the economics of principal-agent relationships, are at the heart of any reform that is expected to improve the performance of utilities:

1. *Incentives.* The reform would be expected to change the extent to which personnel are rewarded (punished/disciplined) for good (bad) performance or high (low) effort.
2. *Selection.* The reform would be expected to change the extent to which competence and intrinsic motivation (attraction to the job) matter for recruitment/appointments of personnel.
3. *Norms or culture.* The reform would be expected to change what individuals believe or expect about how their peers are behaving (such as through stronger incentives or better selection), adding additional motivation to change how they interact with others, or how effectively they work in teams.[6]

Once it is boiled down to these fundamental mechanisms, reforming formal institutions—through establishing laws for corporatization or entering into a public-private partnership—is not sufficient to improve outcomes. Water utilities, regardless of their ownership structure, operate in the context of a natural monopoly, in which forces of market competition are limited by the technological characteristics of the infrastructure needed to deliver water and sanitation services (as discussed in chapter 1). Various reviews of public-private partnerships in the sphere of natural monopolies have concluded that privatization per se does not have a clear record of success (Engel, Fischer, and Galetovic 2014). In a well-documented case in Argentina, frequent renegotiations between the private firms and public regulators and local politicians appear to have been necessary to ensure "fairness" in pricing and equity in the reach or coverage of water services, without which the positive impact of privatization on child health outcomes might not have happened (Galiani, Gertler, and Schargrodsky 2005).

Chapter 8 discusses in further detail how the principal-agent framework can help in understanding the performance of utilities in MENA. Chapter 10 continues the discussion, offering new ideas for management reforms that address the three fundamental mechanisms—incentives, selection, and norms—of utility performance. Together, these chapters show how the "political economy" of reforms to improve the performance of utilities is about strengthening incentives, selection, and norms in state agencies that directly provide utility services or regulate natural monopolies.

A set of outcomes in MENA, examined in chapter 4, of households increasing their reliance on private tankers and the purchase of bottled water, even as access to piped water from public utilities grows, suggests significant scope for improving service delivery and tapping the "willingness to pay" for water. The framework here could be applied to explain these outcomes as a "lose-lose" situation and a vicious cycle: citizens pay more for poor-quality water from tankers than they pay public utilities, and public utilities are unable to increase own revenues, such as through tariff reforms, to improve infrastructure and enhance service delivery. The reform ideas offered in part III, using the framework laid out in this chapter, can help to break this cycle. These ideas involve strengthening incentives, intrinsic motivation, and professional norms in utilities and empowering utility staff to engage in outreach and communication with citizens.

RELATIONSHIP BETWEEN LEGITIMACY AND TRUST: APPLYING THE LINK ACROSS THE THREE PRINCIPAL-AGENT RELATIONSHIPS

One way of thinking about the relationship between legitimacy and trust has been that trustworthy government institutions, which earn trust by government performance in service delivery, is at the root of the legitimacy of the state (Besley 2020; Levi, Sacks, and Tyler 2009; World Bank 2011). Building trust in government institutions is thus analytically equivalent, in this view, to strengthening incentives, improving selection, and establishing performance-oriented norms in government agencies.

Legitimacy can also be distinguished from trust in the new game theory approach as described in box 6.1. Beliefs about how others are behaving are key in this view of legitimacy, opening up possibilities to create compliance with new laws and regulations even in contexts where trust is low at the start.[7] Legitimacy depends on beliefs, or focal points in the language of game theory, about how others are behaving in political and bureaucratic institutions. Ideas for building the legitimacy of new water regulations, when legitimacy and overall trust in society and government are low, proceed along the following logical frame:

- Legitimacy of new rules can be purposively built, and in the short run, by thinking through the problem as one of "shocking" the beliefs held by people, or the different players in the game of public policy in water.
- Institutional contexts of low levels of pre-shock trust in government can nevertheless allow a high level of initial legitimacy to be established if the "shock" persuades people that the urgency of the problem is so great that many others are choosing to change their behavior, so they should too. That is, the "shock" needs to create a new focal point for behavior.

- Credible information about the nature of the water crisis can help to shock beliefs, and it is one of the building blocks in the idea proposed here.
- The other building blocks come from the nature of local political contestation, which has lower barriers to entry for new types of leaders who can use credible information for communication and persuasion to shift the focal point.

These ideas about the role of credible information and local political contestation would not follow from other ways of analyzing legitimacy. For example, political science has analyzed the legitimacy of governments as a whole, by examining cases of protests and resistance against a government, rather than rule-specific attributes (Weatherford 1992). Furthermore, the political science literature has focused on theories of whether democratic institutions, which enable broad-based participation of citizens in selecting their government, and participatory processes of decision-making are more likely to confer legitimacy (Ackerman and Fishkin 2004; Fishkin 1991; Lind and Tyler 1988). Another prominent analysis of legitimacy, in the World Development Report on conflict (World Bank 2011), examines it as a bundle of complex attributes of government, politics, economies, and societies, which are far more likely to be present in rich than in poor countries.[8] That approach to legitimacy is thus as complex as the overall question of development—how do poor countries become rich? It also creates a dilemma—if services need to be delivered to build legitimacy, but lack of legitimacy is constraining governments from delivering services, how will governments deliver services to build legitimacy? The expectation of the report is that these ideas will be tried going forward and evaluated rigorously, to learn from both success and failure.

NOTES

1. This figure also shows citizen engagement to monitor frontline providers and participate in service delivery. Public officials in leadership positions can engage the help of citizens to pressure service delivery cadres to perform better.

2. One of the authors of the *World Development Report 2004* subsequently clarified his thinking that the short route pertains to market-based transactions and the long route applies every time there is a government intervention to solve a market failure (Devarajan 2014; Devarajan, Khemani, and Walton 2014).

3. The second two principal-agent relationships shape the ability of the state to lower the costs of construction and operations and maintenance of water infrastructure, which also matters for the quantum of financing a state would need to raise. The following sections address this cost side.

4. See chapter 9 and the World Values Survey website (https://www.worldvaluessurvey.org/wvs.jsp).

5. Estache (2016) provides a review of the experience with privatization of water utilities.

6. An early economics paper comparing the sources of productivity in Japanese versus U.S. automobile firms pointed out that peer-to-peer interaction, or norms, can be a powerful force in certain contexts (Kandel and Lazear 1992). This line of research is being developed at the frontiers of economic research on the productivity of organizations (Akerlof 2017; Besley and Ghatak 2018; see review in Khemani 2019).

7. For example, Akerlof (2017) models how the legitimacy of an authority in any complex organization can enable the authority to get agents to follow rules simply by announcing them. This is because agents incur costs—such as social sanctions from peers—if they do not comply with rules announced by legitimate authorities, whereas they face no such costs if they do not comply with rules announced by authorities who lack legitimacy. Akerlof (2017) links his economic modeling of legitimacy to insights in the sociology and political science literature. He cites Blau (1964) as arguing that, in the absence of legitimacy, rules will be disobeyed because coercive power alone can lead to resistance. He quotes from Ostrom (1990) that "the legitimacy of rules...will reduce the costs of monitoring, and [its] absence will increase [the] costs."

8. *World Development Report 2011: Conflict, Security and Development* (World Bank 2011, xvi) offers the following definition:

Legitimacy—Normatively, this term denotes a broad-based belief that social, economic, or political arrangements and outcomes are proper and just. The concept is typically applied to institutions. Legitimacy is acquired by building trust and confidence among various parties. Forms of legitimacy include process legitimacy (which relates to the way in which decisions are made), performance legitimacy (which relates to action, including the delivery of public goods), and international legitimacy (which relates to the discharge of values and responsibilities that international law view as the responsibility of states).

REFERENCES

Ackerman, B. A., and J. S. Fishkin. 2004. *Deliberation Day*. New Haven, CT: Yale University Press.

Akerlof, R. 2017. "The Importance of Legitimacy." *World Bank Economic Review* 30 (S1): S157–65. https://doi .org/10.1093/wber/lhw009.

Alesina, A., and P. Giuliano. 2015. "Culture and Institutions." *Journal of Economic Literature* 53 (4): 898–944. https://doi.org/10.1257/jel.53.4.898.

Algan, Y., and P. Cahuc. 2014. "Trust, Growth, and Well-Being: New Evidence and Policy Implications." In *Handbook of Economic Growth*, volume 2, edited by P. Aghion and S. N. Durlauf, 49–120. Amsterdam: Elsevier.

Basu, K., and T. Cordella, eds. 2018. *Institutions, Governance and the Control of Corruption*. International Economic Association Conference Volume No. 157. London: Palgrave Macmillan. https://doi.org/10.1007/978-3-319 -65684-7.

Besley, T. 2020. "State Capacity, Reciprocity, and the Social Contract." *Econometrica* 88 (4): 1307–35. https://doi .org/10.3982/ECTA16863.

Besley, T., and M. Ghatak. 2018. "Prosocial Motivation and Incentives." *Annual Review of Economics* 10: 411–38. https://doi.org/10.1146/annurev-economics-063016-103739.

Besley, T., and T. Persson. 2009. "The Origins of State Capacity: Property Rights, Taxation, and Politics." *American Economic Review* 99 (4): 1218–44. https://doi.org/10.1257/aer.99.4.1218.

Blau, P. M. 1964. "Justice in Social Exchange." *Social Inquiry* 34 (2): 193–206. https://doi.org/10.1111/j.1475 -682X.1964.tb00583.x.

Brixi, H., E. Lust, and M. Woolcock. 2015. *Trust, Voice, and Incentives: Learning from Local Success Stories in Service Delivery in the Middle East and North Africa*. Washington, DC: World Bank. https://openknowledge .worldbank.org/handle/10986/21607.

Dal Bo, E., and F. Finan. 2016. "At the Intersection: A Review of Institutions in Economic Development." Center for Effective Global Action, University of California, Berkeley, CA. https://escholarship.org/uc/item/3q15n1rq.

Devarajan, S. 2014. "What the 2004 WDR Got Wrong," *World Bank Blogs*, March 11, 2014.

Devarajan, S., S. Khemani, and M. Walton. 2014. "Can Civil Society Overcome Government Failure in Africa?" *World Bank Research Observer* 29 (1): 20–47.

Engel, E., R. D. Fischer, and A. Galetovic. 2014. *The Economics of Public-Private Partnerships: A Basic Guide*. New York: Cambridge University Press.

Estache, A. 2016. "Institutions for Infrastructure in Developing Countries: What We Know … and the Lot We Still Need to Know." Working Paper 2016-27, European Center for Advanced Research in Economics and Statistics, Université Libre de Bruxelles, Brussels. https://ideas.repec.org/p/eca/wpaper/2013-230527.html.

Fergusson, L., C. A. Molina, and J. A. Robinson. 2022. "The Weak State Trap." *Economica* 89 (354): 293–331. https://doi.org/10.1111/ecca.12399.

Fishkin, J. S. 1991. *Democracy and Deliberation: New Directions for Democratic Reform*. New Haven, CT: Yale University Press.

Galiani, S., P. Gertler, and E. Schargrodsky. 2005. "Water for Life: The Impact of the Privatization of Water Services on Child Mortality." *Journal of Political Economy* 113 (1): 83–120. https://doi.org/10.1086/426041.

Garrick, D., L. De Stefano, L. Turley, I. Jorgensen, I. Aguilar-Barajas, B. Schreiner, R. de Souza Leão, E. O'Donnell, and A. Horne. 2019. "Dividing the Water, Sharing the Benefits: Lessons from Rural-to-Urban Water Reallocation." Water Global Practice Discussion Paper, World Bank, Washington, DC. https://openknowledge.worldbank.org/handle/10986/32050.

Goksu, A., A. Bakalian, B. Kingdom, G. Saltiel, Y. Mumssen, G. Soppe, J. Kolker, and V. Delmon. 2019. "Reform and Finance for the Urban Water Supply and Sanitation Sector." Water Global Practice Summary Note, World Bank, Washington, DC. https://openknowledge.worldbank.org/handle/10986/32244.

Hussein, H. 2016. "An Analysis of the Discourse of Water Scarcity and Hydropolitical Dynamics in the Case of Jordan." PhD thesis, University of East Anglia.

Kandel, E., and E. P. Lazear. 1992. "Peer Pressure and Partnerships." *Journal of Political Economy* 100 (4): 801–17. https://www.jstor.org/stable/2138688.

Khemani, S. 2019. "What Is State Capacity?" Policy Research Working Paper 8734, World Bank, Washington, DC. https://openknowledge.worldbank.org/handle/10986/31266.

Levi, M., A. Sacks, and T. Tyler. 2009. "Conceptualizing Legitimacy, Measuring Legitimating Beliefs." *American Behavioral Scientist* 53 (3): 354–75. https://doi.org/10.1177/000276420933879.

Lind, E. A., and T. R. Tyler. 1988. *The Social Psychology of Procedural Justice*. New York: Springer Science & Business Media.

Mumssen, Y., G. Saltiel, and B. Kingdom. 2018. "Aligning Institutions and Incentives for Sustainable Water Supply and Sanitation Services." World Bank, Washington, DC. https://openknowledge.worldbank.org/handle/10986/29795.

Ostrom, E. 1990. *Governing the Commons: The Evolution of Institutions for Collective Action*. Cambridge: Cambridge University Press.

Somanathan, E. 2020. "Institutions, the Environment, and Development." In *Economic Development and Institutions*, edited by J.-M. Baland, F. Bourguignon, J.-P. Platteau, and T. Verdier, chapter 20. Princeton, NJ: Princeton University Press.

Talbi, A., C. Dominguez Torres, S. Bahije, D. de Waal, S. Dahan, R. Trier, H. Benabderrazik, et al. Forthcoming. "The Economics of Tariffs in the Water and Sanitation Sector: Strategies for Improving Pricing Performance." World Bank, Washington, DC.

Waalewijn, P., R. Trier, J. Denison, Y. Siddiqi, J. Vos, E. Amjad, and M. Schulte. 2019. "Governance in Irrigation and Drainage: Concepts, Cases, and Action-Oriented Approaches—A Practitioner's Resource." Water Global Practice, World Bank, Washington, DC. https://openknowledge.worldbank.org/handle/10986/32339.

Weatherford, M. 1992. "Measuring Political Legitimacy." *American Political Science Review* 86 (1): 149–66. https://doi.org/10.2307/1964021.

World Bank. 2004. *World Development Report 2004: Making Services Work for Poor People*. Washington, DC: World Bank. https://openknowledge.worldbank.org/handle/10986/5986.

World Bank. 2011. *World Development Report 2011: Conflict, Security, and Development*. Washington, DC: World Bank. https://openknowledge.worldbank.org/handle/10986/4389.

World Bank. 2016. *Making Politics Work for Development: Harnessing Transparency and Citizen Engagement.* Washington, DC: World Bank.

World Bank. 2017. *World Development Report 2017: Governance and the Law.* Washington, DC: World Bank. https://openknowledge.worldbank.org/handle/10986/25880.

World Bank and IFC (International Finance Corporation). 2020. "Market Study on Desalination in Egypt." Unpublished working paper.

CHAPTER 7

Why Policy Has Focused on Supply-Side Investments and Ignored Demand-Side Problems of Overusing and Polluting Water

INTRODUCTION

Using the economic framework of "principal-agent" relationships, this chapter examines what is holding countries back from pursuing demand-side measures more actively and why governments have struggled to address the negative externalities, particularly the unsustainable use of water resources—the issue of managing the common pool resource problem—described in chapter 5.

To date, policy frameworks across most countries in the Middle East and North Africa (MENA) have directed sector financial flows toward supply-side interventions to maximize agricultural production and provide water for cities. As set out in part I of this report, this practice has been spearheaded by powerful state institutions that have harnessed available conventional freshwater resources drawing on a combination of own fiscal resources, concessional financing, and, more recently, private sector financing. These supply-side interventions have been an integral component of the social contract through the provision of cheap water for both agricultural production and domestic use—and indirectly to keep the cost of staple foods affordable. While there was still opportunity to develop freshwater resources—state-led dam building for surface water storage and state-promoted exploitation of groundwater—there were strong incentives to follow an expansionist path. This path established the widespread belief in societies across MENA that the problem of water scarcity is driven by supply-side constraints. These beliefs enabled leaders to gain political support for large infrastructure investments to increase the supply of water even when those investments were technically unsound or unneeded (Blaydes 2011; Herrera 2019).

As opportunities to develop conventional freshwater resources have plateaued, states have transitioned toward developing nonconventional water resources, including desalination and wastewater reuse. This expansion of nonconventional water resources has put new pressures on, and threatens the financial viability of, the established policy framework that underpins the social contract. Nonconventional water has become the mainstay of the overall water use mix[1] in old water scarce high-income economies, is a major contributor to the water mix in old water scarce middle-income countries, and is being viewed as a solution in new water scarce agrarian economies. The transition to nonconventional water, and the much higher costs of both producing desalinated water and treating wastewater for reuse with present-day technology, poses a fiscal sustainability challenge to all countries in MENA, even high-income oil exporters, when viewed against the backdrop of the global energy transition.

Estimates of future water resource needs in MENA vary widely. Conservative estimates based on a model of global resource stocks and flows using a middle-of-the-road scenario (medium population growth, medium meat consumption, and moderate climate change) indicate that countries across MENA would need an additional 24.8 billion cubic meters of water per year by 2050 (Borgomeo et al. 2018, 35). Much higher estimates exist, including that the gap will increase to 199.0 billion cubic meters of water per year by 2050 (Mualla 2018).

With very limited opportunities for further development of conventional freshwater resources, additional supply to meet the needs of growing populations will no doubt have to come from nonconventional water sources. The conservative estimate of 24.8 billion cubic meters per year required in 2050 would be equivalent to building another 65 desalination plants the size of the Ras Al Khair plant in Saudi Arabia—currently the largest in the world.

Today's leaders in the region are aware that efforts to stem demand for water would push back the need for these costly investments in nonconventional water. Yet managing demand has proved challenging in the context of MENA, where society's established belief is that the state's role is to provide water and that it is not a legitimate role of the state to ask citizens to reduce water consumption or pay higher tariffs. Supply-focused water service provision reflects the broader state-citizen relationship at play in the region, especially before the Arab Spring, characterized by subsidized food and fuel (Yousef 2004). In the face of the possibility of public protest, political leaders have strong incentives to back down from demand-side interventions and default to tackling the problems of water by building new supply-side infrastructure.

The following sections use the principal-agent framework to explore how institutions struggle to resolve two aspects of managing the "common pool resource problem" (figure 7.1). The first, trade-offs among competing uses of water among sectors, examines how conflicting demands that emerge in the first relationship (citizens and political leaders) fail to be resolved by the structure of formal bureaucratic institutions. The second examines how not recognizing assumed water rights undermines attempts to win user compliance for quantity restrictions, particularly in agricultural water management.

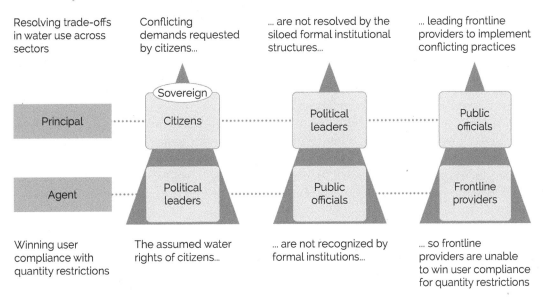

Resolving trade-offs in water use across sectors | Conflicting demands requested by citizens... | ... are not resolved by the siloed formal institutional structures... | ... leading frontline providers to implement conflicting practices

Winning user compliance with quantity restrictions | The assumed water rights of citizens... | ... are not recognized by formal institutions... | ... so frontline providers are unable to win user compliance for quantity restrictions

Source: Based on World Bank 2016, 103.

RESOLVING TRADE-OFFS: HOW FORMAL INSTITUTIONAL SETUPS FAIL TO RESOLVE CITIZENS' CONFLICTING WATER DEMANDS

The dual calls by citizens on political leaders (in the first relationship) both to deliver cheap water to cities and to expand employment through the expansion of irrigated agriculture have led to policy incoherence in the second relationship—that between political leaders and senior public officials. As noted in the previous chapter, technical economic analysis is silent on the normative question of preferences over a public good, which is a political choice problem of the first relationship—as represented by its political leaders.

Because of the formal line ministry structure of many central governments, competing interests that are not resolved in the first relationship are perpetuated at the level of line ministries—particularly the ministries of water, energy, and agriculture—that then pull in different directions. Sectors have separate regulatory and investment planning frameworks to address sector-specific challenges and demands. Typical examples of policy incoherence and ambiguities include the following:

- Encouraging expansion of irrigated agriculture to create more rural jobs while not allowing tariffs for urban water to increase to pay for desalination or reuse (the Arab Republic of Egypt, Iraq, Morocco, and Tunisia)
- Reallocating water from agricultural irrigation schemes to provide water for cities while promoting expansion of agricultural irrigation (Jordan and Morocco)
- Increasing electricity costs for water pumping and treatment while limiting the amount of renewable energy the water sector is allowed to develop, to protect revenues in the energy sector (Jordan)

- Subsidizing the cost of energy to promote the use of groundwater in agriculture while not increasing energy-related costs for domestic water supply (Morocco's butane gas subsidies and the Syrian Arab Republic before the crisis)
- Subsidizing water intensive crop production—such as wheat through guaranteed prices, input subsidies, and import tariffs—rather than promoting virtual water through wheat imports (Egypt and Iraq) (OECD and FAO 2018, 88)

These policy inconsistencies, and their unintended consequences, can also translate into unclear roles and competition among government frontline agencies (the third relationship). In Morocco, for example, when river basin organizations (Hydraulic Basin Agencies) were introduced by the ministry responsible for water, it was agreed that they would grant water use permits. Under the ministry of agriculture, the irrigation agencies (Regional Offices for Agricultural Development) remained responsible for authorizing well drilling. This double line of command made it possible for the irrigation agencies to bypass restrictions linked to unsustainable use of aquifers and promote the drilling of new wells as part of the *Plan Maroc Vert* in contravention of the regulatory objectives and role of the Hydraulic Basin Agencies (Molle 2019, 64).

Proponents of a water-agriculture-energy nexus approach point out the dire risks of policy incoherence, including large-scale depletion of aquifers. They also point to the upsides: that reducing the dependence of the agriculture and energy sectors on water can reduce water scarcity and that transitioning to renewable energy sources could reduce greenhouse gas emissions (Borgomeo et al. 2018).

Aware of these policy inconsistencies and in an effort to adopt the water-agriculture-energy nexus approach, some governments, especially those of old water scarce countries, have tried reorganizing their bureaucracies to better align with incentives. In most of the high-income Gulf Cooperation Council countries, energy and water portfolios have been integrated into single ministries (Bahrain, Kuwait, Qatar, and the United Arab Emirates) because producing desalinated water is so energy intensive. These countries have also integrated water and electricity production within single state-owned enterprises.

In old water scarce countries with significant agricultural output, a single ministry responsible for water and agriculture was formed, such as in Tunisia in 2014. In 2016, the government of Saudi Arabia, concerned about the depletion of aquifers by agriculture, restructured separate ministries responsible for water and agriculture into the Ministry of Environment, Water and Agriculture.

Another approach has been to create cross-sectoral institutions, such as the Water Resource Council in Bahrain, which formulates overall water resource policies and strategies for the country. The institutional framework in Israel takes this cross-sectoral water governance approach a step further. A parliamentary investigation of the water sector found that the division of responsibilities in water management was not clear, resulting in excessive political interference in the day-to-day management of the water sector. In response, the Israeli Water Authority was established in 2007 to formalize the representation of competing water interests around one decision-making table, the National Water Authority Board, which includes the ministries representing water, energy, agriculture, the environment, finance, and the interior, as well as public representatives (Marin et al. 2017). Notably, the ministry responsible for investment in water infrastructure has only one of the seats around the table (figure 7.2).

These cross-government approaches have the advantage that they acknowledge the influence of various sectors on water use and consumption. The Bahrain and Israeli examples of cross-sectoral institutions, although described as independent, are more accurately characterized as institutional mechanisms to bring politics into the heart of water sector decisions (on water allocation and tariff setting) in a transparent and documented way. They bring together the formal institutions that actually

Figure 7.2 National Water Authority Board of Israel

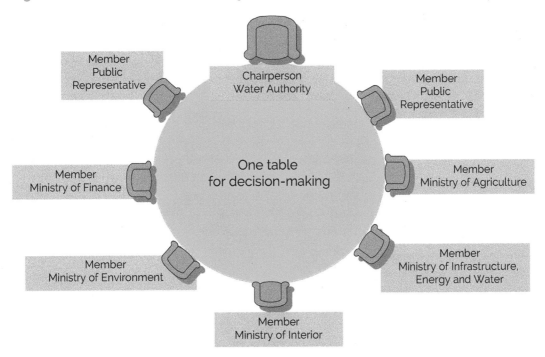

Source: Israeli Water Authority.

allocate water—which are not water institutions but rather the institutions deciding on agricultural policy, trade policy, land tenure, urban planning, public finance, and so forth.

These reorganizations of formal institutions help align incentives and solve principal-agent problems between political leaders and public officials. With the examples of integrated energy and water state-owned enterprises, they may also help better align the incentives in the third relationship between public officials and frontline providers.

Despite their benefits, these reorganizations do little to shift citizens' beliefs about the proper prioritization of water allocation among sectors. Such a shift would rely on building a much broader societal consensus on the role of water in the economy, which many advanced countries are also struggling to reach. For example, a 2015 survey of Organisation for Economic Co-operation and Development countries reported that, despite a clearly established sequence of priority uses in nearly all the water allocation regimes, water for the environment was rarely among the highest priorities. A quarter of the allocation regimes did not secure environmental flows. Only half of the allocation regimes accounted for the potential impacts of climate change in their allocation arrangements (OECD 2015). The point is that the value derived from water uses and the objectives of water allocation change over time, reflecting shifting social preferences. Many countries in the survey have, relatively recently, begun to see water requirements to ensure adequate environmental flows as a legitimate and valuable use of water. It is only once these requirements are seen as such that governments gain public acceptance to secure water flows for the environment in their formal water allocation regimes.

The challenge for countries in MENA is that they must (re)prioritize water for cities, agriculture, and the environment in a context where there is already overallocation and overuse of water conditioned by historical use patterns that trace their roots to previous decades or even centuries. Putting in place the building blocks of water allocation regimes—adjustable limits on abstraction and legally defined volumetric entitlements—is ideally done when water resources are relatively abundant and the risk of shortage is low. In practice, reallocations around the world have been reactive and typically happened in response to droughts (Jorgensen et al. 2021). The urgent policy question for countries in MENA, particularly low- and middle-income countries that cannot spend their way out of scarcity, is whether there are intermediate solutions between administrative reallocations ordered by the state and individual water rights. Such solutions would provide a pathway to transition from countries' current systems (overallocation with legal pluralism) to systems seen as legitimate and fair by those who will forgo current water resource allocations or have to pay more for them.

For example, consultations for this report in Morocco included a discussion about how the National Office of Electricity and Drinking Water (ONEE) is currently the highest-priority recipient of water allocations during times of drought. This priority increasingly creates tension with other users and places the risk of water shortages disproportionally on the agriculture sector and the environment. Participants noted that ONEE provides drinking water, which is considered a high priority, as well as water for other domestic uses (for example, for gardens or swimming pools) and industries that are, in principle, a lower priority. Thus, in dry years, ONEE should receive only the allocation related to drinking water and other essential uses. For technical reasons, however, ONEE cannot separate distribution for essential uses from that for nonessential uses. The technical choices that led to ONEE's inability to separate essential and nonessential uses[2] result in its receiving priority access to water allocation and do not incentivize ONEE to increase efficiency or raise the finance for providing nonessential water from nonconventional water.

Following through on such discussions on a societal scale is an essential part of coming to consensus on sectoral prioritization of water, quotas, and tariffs because allocating water across uses has first-order consequences on economic and social outcomes as well as intergenerational equity. Part III of this report picks up and develops further this thread on building societal consensus through political institutions underpinned by science.

The second half of this chapter examines "principal-agent" problems related to demand-side interventions in irrigation because agriculture uses the lion's share of freshwater and directly impinges on the ability to satisfy supply to cities. Chapter 8 discusses applying the framework to understand why utilities are distressed and households receive poor services.

DEMAND-SIDE INTERVENTIONS IN AGRICULTURAL WATER MANAGEMENT

Political leaders are not necessarily experts in the sectors for which they are responsible. In delegating the priorities articulated in the first relationship (between citizens and political leaders), they rely on senior public officials to set out for them the science and the policy options (the second relationship). They also rely on those same public officials to implement the selected policies through frontline providers (the third relationship).

The quality of the policy advice that senior public officials offer to political leaders can be assessed in two ways: whether the policies lead to the desired outcomes, and whether the policies are possible for frontline providers to implement. This section first briefly examines two long-standing areas of policy dialogue on demand-side interventions that have led to inconsistent advice and messaging: that of pricing of irrigation water, and that of water-saving technologies. It then contrasts water-saving technologies with water-saving policies and discusses the issues of legitimacy and trust involved in the implementation of water-saving policies, both globally and in MENA.

As a key point of context, the relevance of the distinction between water-saving technologies and water-saving policies came into play across MENA as groundwater use in irrigation became widespread through improved and lower-cost water drilling technology in the late 1970s and early 1980s. This period coincided with a drought across many of the countries in the Mediterranean (Talbi et al., forthcoming). Groundwater became the new frontier for irrigated agriculture, complementing diminishing flows from surface water irrigation systems and opening up new areas hitherto not supplied by surface water irrigation systems. Initially, groundwater exploitation was promoted by governments (for example, through subsidies for drilling) that saw it as a way to expand agricultural production and achieve food self-sufficiency ambitions. Although it liberated irrigators from the hierarchical state-controlled surface water irrigation systems and diminished reliance on traditional collective management systems, groundwater exploitation also led to a lessening of state control over agricultural water abstractions. The extensive use of groundwater exposed issues of legal pluralism: the inconsistencies between customary, Islamic, and statutory law over water and land rights. It has also led to externalities, specifically a myriad of examples of overexploitation that have led to diminishing groundwater levels and salinization of aquifers that have affected farming communities, urban water supplies, and natural ecosystems (set out in chapter 5). The costs of mitigating these negative externalities have been significant. For example, in the Guerdane area of the Souss in Morocco, a pipe to transfer water from a dam to an area of 10,000 hectares, where groundwater depletion had dried up orchards and strongly affected the profitability of citrus farms, cost €70 million, half of which was covered by the state (Houdret 2012; Houdret and Bonnet 2016). In West Bank and Gaza, the depletion and salinization of the aquifer has rendered municipal water supplies too salty to drink and required a US$633 million investment program in desalination to compensate (Palestinian Water Authority 2018).

How Misconceptions in Policy Design Can Undermine Demand Management and Lead to Erosion in Trust between Political Leaders and Senior Public Officials

The first area of policy dialogue that has led to misconceptions in policy design is that of water pricing for demand management in agriculture. The extensive literature on water pricing in agriculture puts forward three main objectives: (1) to recover the cost of providing the irrigation service; (2) as a benefit tax on those receiving water services, to provide potential resources for further investment to benefit others in society (equity); and (3) to provide an incentive for efficient use of scarce water resources. The third objective has repeatedly and misguidedly been proposed by senior public officials to political leaders (or vice versa) as a means of demand management—possibly because they conflate the price and value of water.

The main critiques of the use of pricing of irrigation water are levied from the standpoints of demand and supply. Irrigators' elasticity of demand for water is very low within the prevailing ranges of irrigation water charges across MENA. Raising these charges to levels that would result in greater elasticity of demand would effectively lead to considerable income losses for farmers. This outcome would trigger political considerations, because the response of irrigators is usually resistance, and prevent using price as an economic instrument (de Fraiture and Perry 2007). A further problem in applying pricing, especially if only to surface water irrigation sources, is that it would simply drive farmers to use more groundwater. From the supply perspective, in the rare cases where conditions exist to regulate demand through prices—that is, where on-farm volumetric management and on-demand irrigation systems both exist—supply is invariably managed through quotas or water rights. Moreover, Molle and Berkoff (2007, 10) point out that the question of charging for agricultural water has "suffered from an unfortunate lack of distinction between agriculture and the domestic [water] sector."

The second common area of policy design leading to misconceptions is that of water conservation technologies (WCTs) such as drip irrigation. WCTs are often presented as demand-side interventions that can lead to both higher water productivity and less water being consumed by agriculture, thus "freeing" water for other sectors. In a comprehensive review of the theoretical and empirical literature on WCTs from 230 studies around the world, Dionisio Pérez-Blanco, Hrast-Essenfelder, and Perry (2020) conclude that, in the absence of quantity regulation, WCTs lead to increased water consumption by farms and reduced return flows to the environment, reducing water availability for other uses.

The issue common to these two areas of policy design, agricultural water pricing and WCTs, is that, although misplaced, they keep reemerging as options that do not lead to the desired policy outcome of demand management. These policies not only divert energy and resources from other potential "solution spaces" but also, when they do not lead to water savings, lead to an erosion of legitimacy and trust between the political leaders and senior public officials (including development partners) who are the parties in the second principal-agent relationship. The lack of results from these supposed demand-side interventions forces political leaders back to pursuing supply-side interventions.

Water Conservation Policies Rely on Winning the Compliance of Irrigators

Water conservation policies (WCPs) have the expressed aim of achieving water conservation targets (quantity regulation) albeit at the potential expense of reduced agricultural water consumption. They can integrate WCTs to mitigate impacts on agricultural income, which can enhance the acceptability of effective WCPs—but the aim is nevertheless to reduce, or at least regulate, agricultural water consumption. A long-standing hope was that the combination of WCPs and WCTs could provide the basis for pursuing a "soft path" approach to reducing water demand without reducing well-being, but this result has remained elusive (Gleick 2003).

WCPs involve developing a scientific understanding of what levels of abstraction are sustainable, setting limits accordingly, and reforming water rights, especially to manage users without formal rights. These actions are necessary precursors to potential reallocations of water that would better reflect the shifting patterns of supply and demand (for example, between rural and urban areas or to the environment) as well as adjustments to mitigate the impacts of reallocations (figure 7.3).

A spectrum of approaches to limiting water withdrawals exists, from those setting explicit legal "caps" on water use to those that prescribe restrictions on infrastructure development. Explicit "caps" are defined as an "aggregate [limit] on resource extraction" (Heinmiller 2007, 446). They require significant involvement of the central government to establish or reform property rights and enable trade in a manner that adheres to the cap. At the other end of the spectrum, moratoria aim to restrict the drilling or deepening of wells or irrigated acreage. Between explicit legal caps and moratoria, quota-based approaches have been used as a means to pave the way for explicit legal caps. The quota-based approaches represent a "softer" starting point for developing policy on water demand, compared

Figure 7.3 Steps along the pathway to water conservation policies and water reallocation within economies

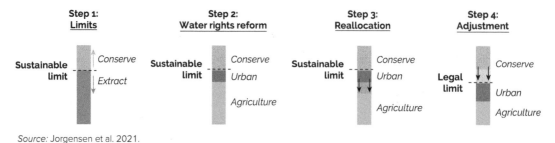

Source: Jorgensen et al. 2021.

to explicit legal caps. Quota-based approaches have tended to be set at the basin level, reflecting aggregate demand and offering authorities greater flexibility of enforcement, particularly when they lack sufficient data for a rigorous scientific assessment of water availability (Jorgensen et al. 2021).

Examples of legal caps set by a central government include the Murray-Darling Basin in Australia and the design of China's "three red lines." The cap on water use in the Murray-Darling Basin, perhaps the most well-known, is set at the basin and subbasin levels (Grafton and Wheeler 2018; Hanemann and Young 2020). The basin-level cap is set by the Murray Darling Basin Authority, and the subbasin-level caps are set through decentralized state recommendations to the Murray Darling Basin Authority based on the best available science.

In China, the "three red lines" refer to the cap on total national water use, national water use efficiency, and national pollution levels (World Bank 2018). The central government sets national caps as future targets, and then jurisdictional authorities propose caps at the basin, province, prefecture, and county levels for central government approval. These caps were built on an earlier system of basin-level quotas introduced throughout the country, making their implementation more amenable.

Although the limits are generally set at the scale of a basin or aquifer (a hydrological or hydrogeological unit), the role of enforcement and accountability for operating within that limit falls to jurisdictions (political/administrative entities) rather than technical or administrative water institutions (table 7.1).

Table 7.1 Global examples of setting limits on water withdrawals: Type, scale, and jurisdictions with authority

Location	Type of limit	Example(s)	Scale of limit	Jurisdiction(s) with authority
Australia	Cap on surface water withdrawals	Murray-Darling Basin	Basin and subbasin	National, subnational, basin
	Cap on environmental flows	Murray-Darling Basin	Basin	National
California, United States	Groundwater caps	Statewide application	Subbasin	Subnational, local
	Individual caps on indoor water use	Statewide application	Individual	Subnational, local
	Interstate cap	State share of Colorado River Basin	State share of basin	National, subnational
	Surface water cap	Imperial Valley, Coachella Valley, Metropolitan Water District	Irrigation district, water district	Subnational
Chile	Temporary moratorium on well drilling	Copiapó Basin	Any recharge zone with groundwater decline	National, local

(table continues on next page)

Table 7.1 Global examples of setting limits on water withdrawals: Type, scale, and jurisdictions with authority *(continued)*

Location	Type of limit	Example(s)	Scale of limit	Jurisdiction(s) with authority
China	Basin-level quotas on surface water use (before 2013)	Shiyang Basin	Province, basin, county	National, subnational
	National three red lines with nested caps	Heihe Basin	National, river basin, province, city/prefecture, county	National, subnational
Colorado, United States	Interstate cap	Colorado River Basin, Rio Grande River Basin	State share of basin	National, subnational
	Moratorium on well drilling	San Luis Valley (Rio Grande)	Subbasin	Subnational, local
Jordan	Transboundary groundwater moratorium on agriculture	Southern Jordan (Disi/Mudawwara area)	Zone confined aquifer	National
	Moratorium on new wells paired with water tariffs	Northern Highlands	National except Jordan Valley (under the Jordan Valley Authority)	National
Mexico	Moratorium-quota system for well drilling	State of Sonora	Basin and irrigation district	National, subnational
	Surface water limits	Lerma-Chapala Basin, Ixtlahuaca Basin	Basin, user	National, subnational, basin, municipalities irrigation district
Oregon, United States	Moratorium on well drilling	Deschutes River Basin	State, basin	Subnational, local
	Penalty caps	None yet	Municipality	Subnational

(table continues on next page)

Location	Type of limit	Example(s)	Scale of limit	Jurisdiction(s) with authority
Spain	Moratorium-quota system for well drilling	Guadiana River Basin	Basin	Local
Texas, United States	Implicit cap	Lower Rio Grande Valley	Basin	Subnational, local
	Explicit cap	Edwards Aquifer	Aquifer	Subnational, local

Source: Jorgensen et al. 2021.

In the Australia and China cases, caps were set for both hydraulic and administrative boundaries. For limit setting, there are hydrological and administrative factors to consider. Subbasin and basin nesting is hydrologically useful because of the relevance of these scales in the hydrologic cycle. In Australia, the autonomy of subnational regions required dividing basins and/or subbasins into their administrative components. For this reason, the Murray-Darling Basin is managed at the basin, state, and then subbasin levels (Hanemann and Young 2020). Setting limits at both hydraulic and administrative boundaries makes political institutions legally accountable for their part of the hydraulic cap. This nested nature of caps also aims to confine regulatory capture to smaller jurisdictions, the theory being that local irrigators may be able to influence the setting of county-level caps but would struggle to influence higher-level caps. However, in Australia, when science-based adjustments to the cap were introduced to protect the environment in 2012, large irrigators lobbied the central government, which led it to "correct" the adjustment. The "correction" meant abolishing the National Water Commission (which had carried out the science) and halving government buybacks of water for the environment (Hanemann and Young 2020). This example illustrates that even science-based, legally binding caps with nested structures are not immune to regulatory capture.

Although Australia and China did not undertake the route of moratoria, various other countries have done so, and this route is very much part of the policy debate in MENA. The global experience in using moratoria to set limits indicates that their effectiveness is impaired by competing interests for economic development if they are not supported by explicit legal caps. For example, in Spain's Guadalquivir River Basin, in 2005, the river basin authority set an administrative moratorium on new irrigated acreage, in response to rapidly expanding irrigated farmland in the late 1990s. At first, the moratorium was highly effective and confined growth to the 10 percent of the basin not under the moratorium, reducing the annual growth rate of irrigated area from 9.0 percent to 0.8 percent. Additionally, large water users' associations began to focus on intensification through the development of more efficient irrigation infrastructure rather than extensification. Despite this success, in 2015, the moratorium was relaxed to allow an additional 20 cubic hectometers for drip irrigation olives, a "priority" crop because of their lucrative nature. This relaxation of the administrative moratorium will likely result in an additional 13,000 hectares being brought under cultivation and a 1.5 percent increase in irrigated area, and it could result in unsustainable water use (Expósito and Berbel 2017a, 2017b). To address these competing interests, a sector-specific approach to the setting of legal limits may be useful.

In Jordan, since 1988, a series of laws have been enacted to regulate the drilling of public and private wells as a means of limiting water abstractions. Among other means, these laws sought to control the number, density, and depth of wells in the Jordanian Highlands to free up supply for Amman. Irrigators nonetheless found ways to evade the regulations. The Ministry of Water and Irrigation enacted a series of creative countermeasures to toughen law enforcement and increase pressure on groundwater users. Direct measures included licensing wells, establishing annual quotas per well, sealing illegal wells (and destroying them with dynamite), licensing and monitoring drilling companies, limiting the number of well licenses to one per plot of land, and banning well drilling for agriculture. Indirect measures included implementing a block tariff pricing system, increasing the water tariff on illegal wells, constraining the granting of labor permits, publishing the names of violators in newspapers, publicizing tough actions on the ground, using satellite imagery to estimate and charge water consumption, and improving interdepartmental coordination to force users to pay water bills. In their detailed review of these measures, Al Naber and Molle (2017, 706) conclude:

> First, direct measures are hard to implement on the ground and often overestimate the power of the state to act on the ground; this is in particular the case for metering which can be replaced by indirect measurement through remote sensing imagery. Second, too big "sticks" (sealing wells or prohibitive water tariffs), while signaling the gravity of the violation, may turn out to be non-credible and even counterproductive (by pushing people into illegal solutions). Third, the creative tools deployed (administrative interconnection, naming and blaming, etc.) may be inspirational for other countries. Fourth, aggressively raising awareness, not only of citizens but also MPs [members of parliament], judges or imams, may well bear fruit over the long term. Last, it is hard to assess the effectiveness of each measure and it is likely that success will depend on both articulating a diversity of tools and the advent of a felicitous mix of leadership and high-level support.

This case study from Jordan raises two key issues. The first is that the process of setting limits forces the state to take a position on who has and who does not have water rights. The second is that direct measures may push people into illegal solutions, do little to win the compliance of water users, and have high transaction costs.

In the context of MENA, where there is de facto overallocation of water, the first point—that setting limits requires taking a position on water rights—is particularly critical because it forces users into those who are considered legal and those who are not (figure 7.4). It is often assumed that the introduction of formal allocation systems also introduces water rights, but informal water use constitutes an informal allocation system with which the formal system must contend (Heinmiller 2009). This situation highlights that there is no blank slate when it comes to water rights and their reform (Jorgensen et al. 2021) and that the introduction of water rights will fundamentally change the social contract—the first principal-agent relationship between citizens and the state. Without renegotiating this aspect of the social contract, the legitimacy of top-down rules defining what is legal (and what is not) will be contested (for example, on the grounds of legal pluralism), making it extremely difficult to delegate the implementation of water rights in the second and third principal-agent relationships along the long route of accountability.

Identifying a path to becoming a legal water user is, therefore, foundational to renegotiation of the social contract (Bruns, Ringler, and Meinzen-Dick 2005). Examining eight case studies from around the world, Garrick and Hahn (2021) illustrate a range of different paths to legal use.

Figure 7.4 The unavoidable process of converting users into legal or illegal users when establishing formal water rights and setting explicit legal limits to withdrawals

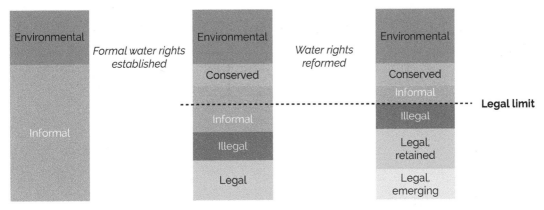

Source: Jorgensen et al. 2021.

Figure 7.5 The spectrum of types of water rights from public to private

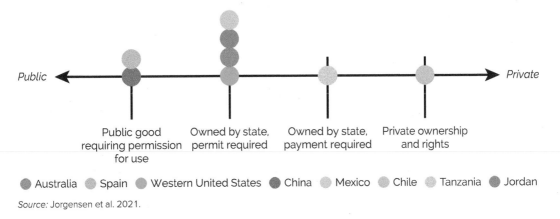

Source: Jorgensen et al. 2021.

Legal use (the destination) ranged from a public good, requiring permission to use, to fully private rights (figure 7.5). Chile is the only country globally where water is fully privatized (Correa-Parra, Vergara-Perucich, and Aguirre-Nuñez 2020). In China and Spain, water is a public good and users must receive permission from the government to use it. Although this policy requires administrative costs to permit users, maintaining water as a public good allows water to be reallocated to priority uses more easily; however, in Chile reallocation is possible only through market transactions between voluntary buyers and sellers.

Having established the spectrum of legal destinations, figure 7.6 illustrates general paths to these destinations. They range from those with low short-term administrative burden (for example, regularization without application) to those with high short-term administrative burden (for example, a universal requirement to apply with strict enforcement). An example of regularization without application is that of California, in the United States, where any rights from before 1914 were simply declared "exempt" and lack regulatory authority (Hanemann and Young 2020). This path has resulted in costly conflict resolution over the long term, however, because many of these rights are unquantified, poorly documented, and

Figure 7.6 Relative administrate burden of legal use regimes established in different countries

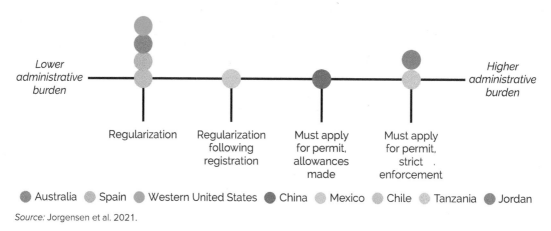

| Lower administrative burden | | Higher administrative burden |

Regularization   Regularization following registration   Must apply for permit, allowances made   Must apply for permit, strict enforcement

● Australia ● Spain ● Western United States ● China ● Mexico ● Chile ● Tanzania ● Jordan

Source: Jorgensen et al. 2021.

often for large volumes of water. For example, the Imperial Irrigation District in California was entitled to 86 percent of California's total 5.4 billion cubic meters Colorado River entitlement and agreed to reduce it to 70 percent only following coercion and litigation (MacDonnell 2013). Sliding down the scale is Mexico, which regularized informal users and registered them in a public register on the basis of self-reporting of water use (Reis 2014). The consequence has been overallocation, basin closure, and the emergence of a black market for water rights that has caused high levels of regulatory capture and rent-seeking behavior.

In some cases, informal users have been required to apply formally for legal water rights. These cases can be further divided into those that have made allowances versus those that have strictly upheld this requirement. China represents the former group, with users required since 2006 to register their use (Calow, Howarth, and Wang 2009). However, in many southern basins, where water is less scarce, irrigation districts operate without permits. Instead, they have developed an informal agreement with the relevant basin authority on their entitlement and priority, reducing enforcement costs in a context where the environmental and social cost of noncompliance is low because withdrawals are far below natural limits and competition is low. Conversely, Tanzania has discursively pledged to enforce water laws strictly and reduce illegal use to improve cost recovery and reduce basin scarcity (Van Koppen et al. 2007). This commitment has been largely unmet, likely because of the prevalence of customary, informal water use in rural areas where water users' associations lack the legitimacy to enforce water rights.

In the Jordan case described earlier, penalties, including fines and prison time, were imposed for drilling illegal wells or violating water use permit conditions. However, the country also implemented a gradual transition process to account for preexisting illegal wells, making the process of becoming a legal user more forgiving than in Tanzania (Van Koppen et al. 2007). Nevertheless, by 2014, enforcement in Jordan was strengthened and permit applications were mandated.

These case studies highlight both the range of costs involved in establishing water rights and the importance of providing users, especially informal users, a path to establishing a legal right to use water. Without a clear pathway, resistance and/or black markets are likely to emerge.

This chapter has used the principal-agent framework to explore how institutions in countries across MENA have struggled to resolve two aspects of managing the "common pool resource problem."

The first concerns how trade-offs among competing uses of water among sectors are resolved (or not) in the formal institutions of government. The second is how the introduction of quantity restrictions involves building trust and legitimacy to win the compliance of users by providing a pathway from assumed water rights to legal use of water.

Managing the trade-offs among competing demands for water has been shown to be hampered by the siloed nature of formal ministerial structures. Trade-offs are more likely to be resolved in cross-sectoral governance institutions. These institutions cannot resolve water allocations through economic analysis alone because some aspects of allocation decisions require coming to political agreement in a transparent way. Resolving these competing demands helps align incentives in the second and third relationships and thus avoids inconsistencies in policy design and implementation.

Quantity regulation, the second key aspect of managing the common pool resource problem, involves the state adopting a science-based understanding of sustainable levels of withdrawals and setting limits on water use. The setting of water use limits is closely linked to the process of defining legal use. In the MENA context of overallocation and legal plurality, setting water use limits forces users into those users considered legal and those not. Without renegotiating this aspect of the social contract, which is foundational to the first relationship, the legitimacy of limits will be contested. Such dispute would make implementation of quantity restrictions difficult for public officials and their frontline staff, as well as lead to the likely emergence of black markets. Global experience points to the importance of defining pathways for water users, especially informal users, to establish a legal right to use water. In conjunction with promoting the adoption of water-saving technologies to mitigate losses of income, particularly in agriculture, doing so can help win compliance with quantity restrictions.

Progress on quantity regulation can in turn free up water for reallocation in the first aspect of the common pool resource problem. The institutional options for making allocation trade-offs—and sharing the benefits gained by those receiving additional water allocations with those giving up allocations—are discussed further in chapter 10.

NOTES

1. The term "water mix" is used here in a way analogous to "energy mix" and refers to the proportion of conventional versus nonconventional water in a particular country.

2. For example, through monitoring and enforcing that only essential uses are being met in times of drought.

REFERENCES

Al Naber, M., and F. Molle. 2017. "Controlling Groundwater over Abstraction: State Policies vs. Local Practices in the Jordan Highlands." *Water Policy* 19 (4): 692–708. https://doi.org/10.2166/wp.2017.127.

Blaydes, L. 2011. *Elections and Distributive Politics in Mubarak's Egypt*. Cambridge, UK: Cambridge University Press. https://doi.org/10.1017/CBO9780511976469.

Borgomeo, E., A. Jägerskog, A. Talbi, M. Wijnen, M. Hejazi, and F. Miralles-Wilhelm. 2018. "The Water-Energy-Food Nexus in the Middle East and North Africa: Scenarios for a Sustainable Future." World Bank, Washington, DC. https://openknowledge.worldbank.org/handle/10986/29957.

Bruns, B. R., C. Ringler, and R. Meinzen-Dick. 2005. "Reforming Water Rights: Governance, Tenure, and Transfers." In *Water Rights Reform: Lessons for Institutional Design*, edited by B. R. Bruns, C. Ringler, and R. S. Meinzen-Dick, 281–308. Washington, DC: International Food Policy Research Institute.

Calow, R. C., S. E. Howarth, and J. Wang. 2009. "Irrigation Development and Water Rights Reform in China." *International Journal of Water Resources Development* 25 (2): 227–48. https://doi.org/10.1080/07900620902868653.

Correa-Parra, J., J. F. Vergara-Perucich, and C. Aguirre-Nuñez. 2020. "Water Privatization and Inequality: Gini Coefficient for Water Resources in Chile." *Water* 12 (12): 3369. https://doi.org/10.3390/w12123369.

de Fraiture and Perry. 2007. "Why Is Agricultural Water Demand Unresponsive at Low Price Ranges?" *Irrigation Water Pricing: The Gap between Theory and Practice*, edited by F. Molle and J. Berkoff, 94–107. Wallingford, UK: Centre for Agriculture and Bioscience International.

Dionisio Pérez-Blanco, C., A. Hrast-Essenfelder, and C. Perry. 2020. "Irrigation Technology and Water Conservation: A Review of the Theory and Evidence." *Review of Environmental Economics and Policy* 14 (2): 216–39.

Expósito, A., and J. Berbel. 2017a. "Agricultural Irrigation Water Use in a Closed Basin and the Impacts on Water Productivity: The Case of the Guadalquivir River Basin (Southern Spain)." *Water* 9 (2): 136. https://doi.org/10.3390/w9020136.

Expósito, A., and J. Berbel. 2017b. "Sustainability Implications of Deficit Irrigation in a Mature Water Economy: A Case Study in Southern Spain." *Sustainability* 9 (7): 1–13.

Garrick, D. E., and R. W. Hahn. 2021. "An Economic Perspective on Water Security." *Review of Environmental Economics and Policy* 15 (1). https://doi.org/10.1086/713102.

Gleick, P. H. 2003. "Global Freshwater Resources: Soft-Path Solutions for the 21st Century." *Science* 302 (5650). https://doi.org/10.1126/science.1089967.

Grafton, R. Q., and S. A. Wheeler. 2018. "Economics of Water Recovery in the Murray-Darling Basin, Australia." *Annual Review of Resource Economics* 10 (1): 487–510.

Hanemann, M., and M. Young. 2020. "Water Rights Reform and Water Marketing: Australia vs the US West." *Oxford Review of Economic Policy* 36 (1): 108–31. https://EconPapers.repec.org/RePEc:oup:oxford:v:36:y:2020:i:1:p:108-131.

Heinmiller, T. 2007. "The Politics of Cap and Trade Policies." *Natural Resources Journal* 47 (2): 445–68.

Heinmiller, T. 2009. "Path Dependency and Collective Action in Common Pool Governance." *International Journal of the Commons* 3 (1). https://doi.org/10.18352/ijc.79.

Herrera, V. 2019. "Reconciling Global Aspirations and Local Realities: Challenges Facing the Sustainable Development Goals for Water and Sanitation." *World Development* 118: 106–17. https://doi.org/10.1016/j.worlddev.2019.02.009.

Houdret, A. 2012. "The Water Connection: Irrigation, Water Grabbing and Politics in Southern Morocco." *Water Alternatives* 5 (2): 284–303.

Houdret, A., and S. Bonnet. 2016. "Le premier partenariat public-privé pour l'irrigation au Maroc: durable pour tous?" *Cahiers de l'Agriculture* 25 (2).

Jorgensen, I., D. Garrick, H. Hussein, and S. Erfurth. 2021. "Pathways to Water Reallocation." Background paper for *The Economics of Water Scarcity in the Middle East and North Africa: Institutional Solutions*. World Bank, Washington, DC.

MacDonnell, L. 2013. "Arizona v. California: Its Meaning and Significance for the Colorado River and beyond after Fifty Years." *Arizona Journal of Environmental Law and Policy* 4 (1): 88–129.

Marin, P., S. Tal, J. Yeres, and K. Ringskog. 2017. "Water Management in Israel: Key Innovations and Lessons Learned for Water-Scarce Countries." World Bank, Washington, DC. https://openknowledge.worldbank.org/handle/10986/2809.

Molle, F. 2019. "Morocco." In *Irrigation in the Mediterranean*, edited by F. Molle, C. Sanchis-Ibor, and L. Avellà-Reus, 51–88. Cham, Switzerland: Springer. https://doi.org/10.1007/978-3-030-03698-0_9.

Molle, F., and J. Berkoff, eds. 2007. *Irrigation Water Pricing: The Gap between Theory and Practice*. Wallingford, UK: Centre for Agriculture and Bioscience International.

Mualla, W. 2018. "Water Demand Management Is a Must in MENA Countries... But Is It Enough?" *Journal of Geological Resource and Engineering* 6 (2). https://doi.org/10.17265/2328-2193/2018.02.002.

OECD (Organisation for Economic Co-operation and Development). 2015. *Water Resources Allocation: Sharing Risks and Opportunities.* OECD Studies on Water. Paris: OECD Publishing. http://dx.doi.org /10.1787/9789264229631-en.

OECD (Organisation for Economic Co-operation and Development) and FAO (Food and Agriculture Organization). 2018. *OECD-FAO Agricultural Outlook 2018–2027.* Paris: OECD Publishing and Rome: FAO. https://doi .org/10.1787/agr_outlook-2018-en.

Palestinian Water Authority. 2018. *Gaza Central Desalination Plant and Associated Works Program: Donor Information Handbook.* Ramallah, West Bank and Gaza: Palestinian Water Authority.

Reis, N. 2014. "Coyotes, Concessions and Construction Companies: Illegal Water Markets and Legally Constructed Water Scarcity in Central Mexico." *Water Alternatives* 7 (3): 542–60.

Talbi A., C. Dominguez Torres, S. Bahije, D. de Waal, S. Dahan, R. Trier, H. Benabderrazik, et al. Forthcoming. "The New Normal of Allocating Water Scarcity: Adapting Water Resources Management and Services to the Changing Future." World Bank, Washington, DC.

Van Koppen, B., C. S. Sokile, B. A. Lankford, N. Hatibu, H. Mahoo, and P. Z. Yanda. 2007. "Water Rights and Water Fees in Rural Tanzania." In *Irrigation Water Pricing: The Gap between Theory and Practice*, edited by F. Molle and J. Berkoff, 143–63. Wallingford, UK: Centre for Agriculture and Bioscience International.

World Bank. 2016. *Making Politics Work for Development: Harnessing Transparency and Citizen Engagement.* Washington, DC: World Bank.

———. 2018. "Watershed: A New Era of Water Governance in China—Synthesis Report." World Bank, Washington, DC. https://openknowledge.worldbank.org/handle/10986/31928 License: CC BY 3.0 IGOPolicy https://pub docs.worldbank.org/en/999601541495579766/China-Water-Policy-Brief-EN.pdf.

Yousef, T . M. 2004. "Development, Growth and Policy Reform in the Middle East and North Africa since 1950." *Journal of Economic Perspectives* 18 (3): 91–116.

CHAPTER 8

Applying the Framework to Understand Why Utilities Are Distressed and Households Receive Poor Service

INTRODUCTION

This chapter applies the principal-agent framework of the report, laid out in chapter 6, to understand the political and economic incentives of water and sanitation utilities. It shows how the problems of utilities' financial distress and poor performance, as reflected in high rates of water losses (nonrevenue water) or poor-quality service delivery, can be understood not only as a problem of lack of resources but also in how utility managers and staff work within existing resource constraints

The principal-agent model is a powerful tool for understanding the long route of accountability in which water utilities operate. A utility (or firm) providing a public service like urban water supply and sanitation (WSS)—for which laissez-faire approaches are ill suited[1]—faces two proximate principal-agent relationships: the external relationship with political leaders and the internal relationship between top management and frontline workers (figure 8.1). The relationship between citizens and political leaders (the social contract) sets the context within which political leaders maneuver in this cascade of "games" between principals and agents. The following are examples:

- With informed citizens, there would be a request for WSS utilities to be properly funded and therefore conditions of sound regulation would be in place.

Figure 8.1 Principal-agent relationships of water supply and sanitation utilities

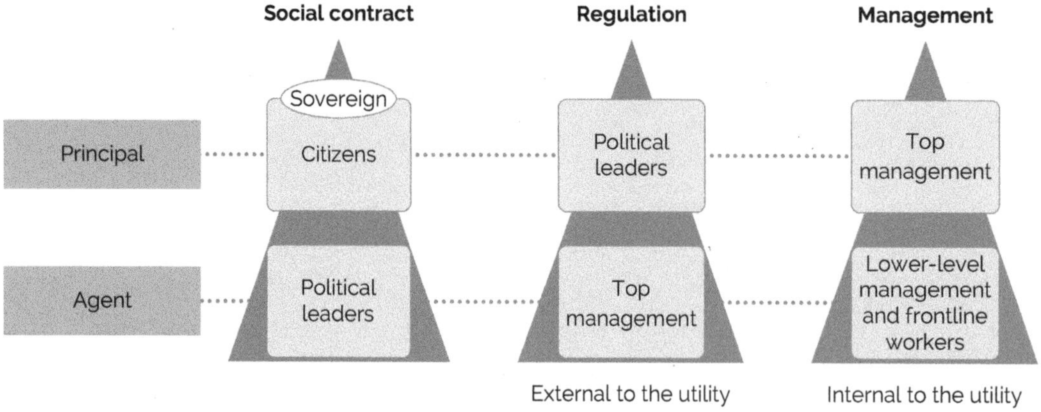

Source: Based on World Bank 2016, 103.

- With uninformed citizens, the immediate benefit of cheap water would push investment and maintenance to the future, so that it is not possible to put sound regulation in place.

The regulatory problem is external to the utility. The "principal" is the political leader (central or local) who wants to provide WSS services to the population. The "agent" is the top management of the utility and organizes production. The agent makes decisions (on prices, quality of service, investment levels, cost structure, and so forth) on behalf of the principal, or implements the principal's decisions. The existence of imperfect information does not allow the politician to observe all the actions performed by top managers; therefore, the politician defines the regulatory framework of the sector (with respect to ownership structure, legal form, allocation of decision power, and so forth) to minimize the possible misalignment of incentives for the preferred actions to be undertaken. Such a principal-agent relationship is general and emerges irrespective of the ownership structure of the water utility or the specific legal form adopted. Depending on the country, utilities could belong to the public or private sector. In the first case, they could be directly part of the public administration or have the status of a state-owned enterprise. Conversely, when private participation is allowed, a large variety of models could be followed, from full private ownership to the range of possible forms of public-private partnership (PPP) (Engel, Fischer, and Galetovic 2014). All these institutional details will ultimately influence the outcome of the external principal-agent relationship, but not its existence: even fully private firms are subject to significant public policy constraints.[2]

The management problem is internal to the water utility and related to the managerial practices adopted. The existence of various levels of management naturally creates a principal-agent structure between the higher and lower ranks. In this context, delegation of authority and decision power to improve overall performance becomes the focus of interest.

The relevant theoretical concepts for the analysis of principal-agent relationships are derived from the "theory of incentives," which studies how the objectives of economic subjects with differing interests can be aligned in situations when cooperation is necessary to achieve a common goal but information about the actions taken by each of the individuals is imperfectly observed by the others.[3] As pointed out by Arrow (1968, 538), "by definition the agent has been selected for his specialized knowledge and therefore the principal can never hope to completely check the agent's performance." The theory of incentives provides answers to how this difficulty can be mitigated to control as much as possible the potentially conflicting interests of principals and agents.

This chapter first discusses the relationship between political leaders and utility managers, including how it is framed by the relationship between citizens (or the sovereign) and political leaders. The chapter then discusses the internal management within a utility.

REGULATORY RELATIONSHIP BETWEEN THE STATE AND WSS UTILITIES

First, as described in part I of the report, in the WSS sector, fixed and sunk costs constitute the overwhelming proportion of the total cost of supply compared to variable costs. Second, water consumption by an agent can generate substantial negative externalities on other users, especially at the local level. These two characteristics give rise to significant market failures that justify public intervention.

Subproblems of Regulation: "Commitment" and "Capture"

The high entry barriers constituted by high infrastructure investments to build a network in most circumstances lead to natural monopolies in the WSS sector. Inevitably this situation creates the regulatory risks of monopolistic pricing and excessively low service quality, which are two sides of the same coin. Insufficient competition creates market power that can be exploited to earn rents by driving a wedge between the price and average cost of production. In addition, production efficiency suffers because few incentives would be in place to keep costs under control. As chapters 3 and 4 demonstrated, this latter aspect is of particular relevance for the Middle East and North Africa (MENA), where prices are low, but also the quality of service is often low.

Although the possibility to earn monopolistic rents (in the form of excess pricing and/or lax management) can be attractive to private investors, once they have built the water infrastructure, they are vulnerable to the risk of expropriation by public authorities or that public authorities forbid them to charge prices that allow the recovery of the incurred capital costs. The incentives for public authorities to expropriate infrastructure or to forbid the private investor to recover costs in the WSS sector are substantial because, given the extremely long life of the water assets, current users face only a tiny fraction of the discounted present value of the problems that underfunded networks will create in the distant future, while immediately benefiting from the cheap tariffs. Private utilities would anticipate such behavior and therefore would immediately reduce investments (the so-called hold-up problem) and defer maintenance expenditures. These problems make purely private provision difficult in the WSS sector, and public production is widespread in most countries, fully through administrative offices or public enterprises, or partially through PPPs. At the same time, public provision does not guarantee that water utilities are sufficiently capitalized to remain viable. Politicians could decide to underinvest in WSS infrastructure and use the resources saved for other projects. In this case, the costs of a collapsing network will be borne in the future, whereas the political benefits from the alternative projects would be immediate.

Irrespective of the (public, private, or hybrid) model of provision chosen, public authorities face the so-called commitment problem, the need to find institutional mechanisms that enable the utility to recover its long-run capital costs (through tariffs or transfers from the state's general budget). They do so through the establishment of a regulatory framework that reduces political influence over the funding of WSS utilities. At the same time, the opposite risk must also be minimized, namely, that corrupt (public or private) utilities are allowed to charge for their capital costs (or receive public money) but use such revenues for private benefits and not to carry out the necessary expansion, repair, and replacement investments. This situation is an example of the problem of "capture," which occurs when the utility is able to manipulate sectoral regulation to its own advantage.

Ultimately, in both cases (lack of commitment and capture), the outcome would be that the necessary infrastructure would never be built or, if it is built by the public sector or an overoptimistic[4] private company, it would ultimately collapse because of prolonged underfunding during its operational life.

The state—or political leaders as principals of utilities—needs to balance this tension between the problem of commitment and capture. In essence, it is a problem of how much funding from state budgets and autonomy to give to utility managers. In contexts where political leaders have made the decision to invite private sector participation to operate utilities, the policy decisions pertain to the regulatory contract, which includes the structure of tariffs/prices that the utility will be allowed to charge customers and the fiscal transfers the utility would receive from the state. The decision to invite privatization can be understood as a decision to give managerial autonomy to a private firm for management decisions within the utility, within the "budget constraints" of the contract with the state.

The reason why utilities in MENA are financially distressed therefore boils down to the problem of the insufficient credibility of states in MENA to provide steady and sufficient returns to capital through a variety of domestic and/or global financiers. Chapter 3 showed that both a lack of transparency in financial reporting and a lack of financial viability exist across the vast majority of utilities across MENA. This lack of transparency and creditworthiness, the basis for trust between financiers and the state in MENA, in turn, is rooted in the principal-agent relationship between citizens and their political leaders (the first triangle in figure 8.1), which determines by how much a state can raise domestic revenues—through tariff structures for services provided or through taxation.

Neither the existence of a regulator nor private sector participation offers simple answers to solving the problem of financially distressed utilities in MENA because it depends on solving the underlying problem of generating sufficient revenues to service financing.

Across the region, only four economies have WSS utility regulatory agencies, and these agencies focus mainly on monitoring key performance indicators.[5] The regulatory agencies are supported by statutory funding mechanisms in only two economies. In the other two economies, the regulatory agencies were supported by donors in their start-up phase and then insufficiently funded through statutory mechanisms to guarantee their independence thereafter. Except in one economy, the United Arab Emirates, these regulators are not in a position to regulate contracts with private service providers, and none of the economies makes independent tariff determinations. The "capture" and "commitment" problems are therefore two areas of regulation not covered by most formal WSS utility regulators, let alone in countries that have no formal regulators.

Most PPPs in the water sector across the region are regulated by contracts, the terms of which are not public, and they are potentially subject to regulatory capture. To improve the quality of service delivery and financial sustainability of WSS utilities, countries have been encouraged to pursue PPPs. The World Bank's Private Participation in Infrastructure database reports US$4.3 billion of water sector PPP transactions in the region, the majority of which were put in place between 2000 and 2010 (figure 8.2).

Three features of these PPPs stand out. First, they exist in a context where tariffs do not cover WSS operation and maintenance costs. Second, they are only for horizontal parts/phases of WSS systems (bulk water, distribution, or wastewater) but never vertically integrated. Third, the contracts are not in the public domain; therefore it can only be assumed that the PPPs are meant to be profitable enclaves in a loss-making system, and they are on more favorable terms than the remaining public sector elements of the system. Furthermore, without the routine use of public sector comparators or fiscal commitment and contingent liabilities analysis in country PPP procurement processes, it is not known whether the viability gap financing is a burden on the overall system. In other words, there is a lack of scrutiny of the regulatory "capture" problem.

Figure 8.2 Public-private partnership investment projects in water and sanitation services, 1990–2020

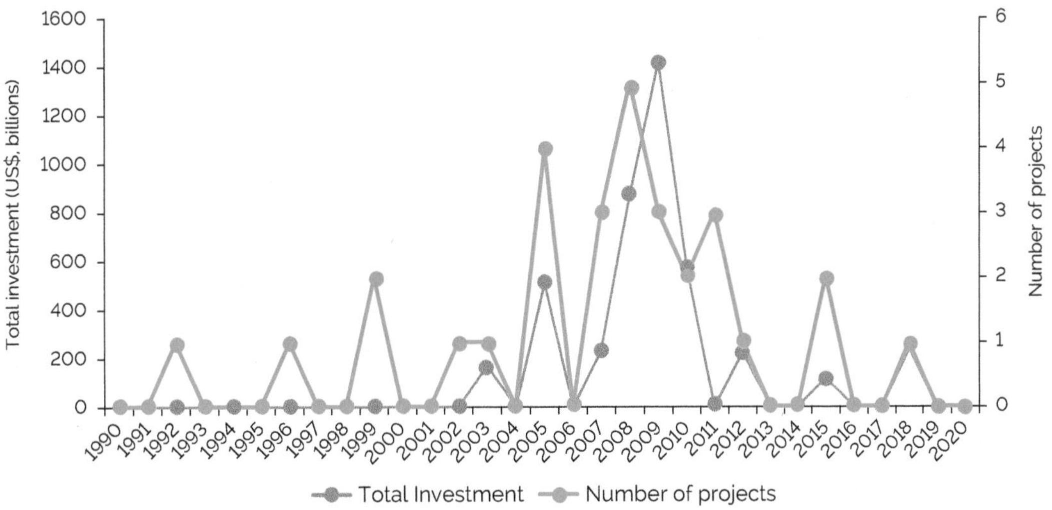

Source: World Bank, Sector Snapshots (https://ppi.worldbank.org/en/snapshots/sector/water-and-sewerage).

This subsection has shown how the principal-agent relationship between citizens and political leaders governing the state shapes the ability of utilities to raise own financing through tariffs or receive financing from government budgets (through general taxation). The reason utilities in MENA are financially distressed can thus be traced to the politics of raising tariffs and allocating public spending, regardless of the ownership structure of the utilities, whether private or public. The next subsection delves into why pricing water is politically difficult.

Economics and Politics of Water Tariffs

This subsection argues that utilities are financially distressed in MENA because economic practice has not taken sufficient and legitimate account of the politics of pricing water.

Traditional Economics of Pricing Water

Efficient tariffs are prices that allow the utility to recover all its costs while ensuring that allocative distortions are minimized.[6] When the cost structure entails a fixed component, full cost recovery and allocative efficiency cannot be jointly reached with simple volumetric charges, and more complex pricing schedules are necessary. Allocative efficiency would require a price per unit that corresponds to the marginal cost of supply. However, this price would not generate any revenue to pay for the utility cost components that do not depend on the quantities consumed.

Inevitably, if the sectoral regulations mandate linear pricing schedules, allowing the utility to break even requires creating a wedge between price and marginal cost. This wedge would automatically generate allocative distortions because users with intermediate valuations between price and marginal cost are excluded from consumption. In such a constrained environment, if it includes different classes of users with different valuations of the service (for example, residential and business users), to minimize the deadweight losses, so-called Ramsey-Boiteaux pricing[7] would suggest differentiating the price according to the demand elasticity. The group with a lower demand elasticity would face a higher price compared to the other consumers, allowing for minimizing the overall reduction in consumed quantities compared to the first best.

Achieving the dual objectives of allocative efficiency and full cost recovery is instead possible with two-part tariffs, which, as the name reveals, contain two elements. The fixed part, an access charge, is independent of the actual amount consumed and would pay for establishing the water and sewer connections.[8] The second part would instead be a volumetric usage price, which could potentially vary during the year if water availability is subject to seasonality.[9] With these two instruments, a regulator could equate the variable unit price to the marginal cost of supply and define the amount of the access charge to generate sufficient resources for the utility to cover all its fixed expenditures. Assuming that every consumer can pay the fixed charge, no deadweight losses would be generated because everyone with valuation above marginal cost would purchase the desired quantities, and the fixed component would simply act as a lump sum tax. Moreover, no overconsumption would be induced because the prices would reflect the costs of provision.

In the above discussion, we implicitly considered only the industrial costs of water provision. The negative externalities generated by water consumption can be easily incorporated into the optimal tariff simply by adding their associated marginal cost to the volumetric charge. This consideration is important for countries in the MENA region because in water scarce environments the price of the externality tends to constitute the largest proportion of the optimal volumetric price component.

Politics of Pricing Water

In principle, the optimal water tariff structure allows solving the commitment problem by permitting water utilities to fund both their capital and operational expenditures over the decades, to recover the investments in the network. This requirement does not necessarily lead to the imposition of full cost tariffs on users.

The optimality of the two-part tariff rests on the assumption that all users can pay the access fee. In reality, however, this fee might be prohibitively high for poorer households.[10] In that case, universal coverage and affordability cannot be reached, so the pursuit of these additional objectives requires the politician to enlarge the policy toolbox by creating subsidy mechanisms for the poorest and most vulnerable parts of the population. These mechanisms are funded through general taxation, which inevitably generates its own distortions (Stiglitz and Rosengard 2015). Therefore, subsidies are worthwhile only if the expected improvements in social welfare are larger than the subsidies. Given the importance of good-quality water for human health, subsidizing connections for the poor can have a solid justification to reach affordable universal coverage.

To increase the affordability of water, often the volumetric charge is also adjusted. In particular, the volumetric charge is composed of several blocks with rising marginal cost—and in some cases, it is adjusted for family size or geographic location—the so-called increasing block tariff.[11] The first block is usually well below the marginal cost of production and in some places even free. Consumption beyond the first block is instead charged at progressively higher levels. Therefore, the first block corresponds to the social tariff and could possibly be set below the marginal cost of provision. The subsidy given through the social tariff[12] is then recouped by charging the levels of consumption above the minimum necessary marginal price that is higher than the marginal cost. If the consumption thresholds of the different blocks are set appropriately, every household would be able to afford the quantity necessary for a decent living standard irrespective of its income, ensuring that the welfare gains generated by the subsidization scheme exceed its cost.

The above discussion has shown that politics is an inherent part of the classical economic approach to pricing water. In the economic approach, as laid out in Joskow (2007) and Laffont (1994), "optimal" quantities of production are determined through a "social welfare function," and "optimal" financing also involves a political decision on how to finance (the combination of tariffs and generalized taxation) the optimal quantity that society desires. It can also be described using the terminology of a "social contract" over water. The reason water utilities in MENA are persistently distressed is that the principal-agent relationship between citizens and politicians has not found a stable social contract over how much to invest in water and sanitation services and how to pay for it. This situation is hardly surprising because in MENA utilities have very limited information on the social status of customers, such as their income level, family size, or the number of households using a connection. Customer typologies are generally split only between domestic and business. In some countries, the size of the house (floor area or number of rooms) is used as a basis for deciding which tariff to apply. In some Gulf Cooperation Council countries, a distinction is made between citizens and noncitizens.

Part III of this report offers ideas to reform leaders on how they can build the social contract through a three-pronged approach—strategic communication, empowerment of locally elected government leaders, and greater delegation and autonomy to utility managers. Before that, the following section takes up the problem of why utilities are underperforming.

PROBLEM OF PERFORMANCE OF WSS UTILITIES

To deliver the service, the water utility top management must delegate some tasks to the middle management. This act creates a principal-agent relationship between the upper and lower ranks of the utility decision structure, with the latter enjoying some degree of private information because it is closer to the actual operations. The information asymmetries can be of two types: adverse selection and moral hazard. The first situation occurs when the agent knows something that is unobserved by the principal and is relevant for the production process of interest, such as the agent's intrinsic ability or the true cost of performing specific activities. The second situation happens when the principal cannot perfectly observe the actions undertaken by the agent, for example with reference to the effort and diligence employed in the agent's work. Naturally, the first case is also known as a problem of "hidden knowledge," whereas the second is a problem of "hidden action."

Broadly speaking, these informational problems prevent the water utility from achieving the most efficient production outcome that would correspond to the level at which the marginal productivity of the action taken by the middle management equals the marginal cost it sustains in performing it.[13] The intuition for this divergence (and the associated allocative inefficiency) lies in the fact that the agent has the incentive to use their superior knowledge to extract higher compensation from the principal. For example, in the water sector, to improve their utility (monetary or nonmonetary) in the context of adverse selection, the middle manager could claim that a given activity is more costly than it truly is (for example, in the WSS industry, the time and cost required by maintenance activities) or—in a moral hazard situation—that the middle manager is exerting the maximum possible effort when instead they are spending time on wasteful activities.[14]

In these contexts, the principal reacts by adjusting the performance it requires from the agent so that it induces the latter to engage in behaviors that reveal at least in part the "hidden information," or that make it also in the agent's interest to exert additional attention and care in the job.[15] By doing so, the top-level management tries to minimize the overall cost of production, which equals the technological cost and the information rent that must be given to the agent.[16] The latter is also known as agency costs, which are a specific type of transaction cost (see Williamson 1975).

A rich literature exists on incentives, and some of its results are particularly useful for characterizing the optimal compensation scheme and appropriate degree of delegation for middle managers in complex organizations like water utilities. The following subsections discuss specific features of the agency relationship that are relevant in the WSS sector: (1) the power of the incentives given to the agent, (2) the likely multidimensionality of the asymmetries of information, (3) the intertemporal dimension, (4) the existence of monitoring tools that could help the principal to improve their information set, (5) channels that can increase the agent's motivation, and (6) the risks of collusion between the different levels of management.

Power of Incentives

The power of the incentives given to middle management is determined by how much of their compensation depends on their performance.[17] The larger the proportion is of the monetary benefits that are tied to output, the higher the power of the incentive given to the agent. A fixed remuneration corresponds to the case of no power because, in the absence of intrinsic motivation or other nonmonetary benefits,[18] the agent has no reason to behave in a manner that is different from simply exerting the minimum effort compatible with the preservation of the relationship with the principal.

The optimal level of power that should be embedded in an incentive contract between the upper and lower managerial levels depends on various factors. Two results are worth emphasizing. First, the larger the information asymmetry is, the less powerful the remuneration scheme of the agent should be. For example, in the case of moral hazard, a weak connection between effort and output means that it is better to limit the amount of variable compensation. By reducing the risk borne by the agent, it is possible to lower the risk premium that the agent requires to participate in the relationship with the principal. This result hinges on the assumption that the agent is risk averse, which is reasonable given that in most settings the agent has limited ability to diversify risk.[19]

The second result links the power of the incentive scheme to the degree of risk aversion of the parties involved. It can be shown that the more risk averse the agent is, the lower the power of the contractual arrangement should be (to avoid paying excessively high risk premia) (see Holmström and Milgrom 1987). The opposite occurs with the risk aversion of the principal: the higher it is, the more weight the principal puts on the desired outcome (and therefore the more powerful are the incentives) despite that doing so raises the risk premium the principal needs to offer the agent.

The following are areas of information asymmetries, in order from lower to higher information asymmetries: (1) nonrevenue water, (2) the degree of customer satisfaction, (3) pollution of the environment from lack of wastewater treatment, and (4) illegal connections.

On risk premiums, the problem WSS middle management and frontline workers face in MENA is that they do not have the tools and equipment (or funds) to address the various types of risks in positive ways, so they may extract rents from customers instead.

Multidimensional Asymmetries

In most real-world situations, and certainly in the context of water utilities, asymmetric information exists about many aspects of the production process and the actions taken by middle management. For example, the top management might be uncertain about the true level of many fixed or variable cost components, the allocation of common costs across different types of customers (like households or businesses), or geographies (for example, the neighborhoods in a city). Moreover, middle managers perform actions that differently affect the various dimensions of performance that matter to the top management, like the quantity and quality of the service provided, or its affordability for different classes of users. Such multiple dimensions (of information, effort, and outcomes) interact in subtle and complex ways, and no general theory has yet been fully developed to capture all of them. Some useful insights are nevertheless available.

In the context of moral hazard, in which different actions are associated with different dimensions of the output of interest for the principal, the impact on the power of the incentives provided to the agent depends crucially on whether such actions are substitutes or complements in the latter's cost function (see Holmström and Milgrom 1990, 1991). If they are substitutes, it means that increasing the effort made in one action raises the marginal cost of performing the other; conversely, when they are complements, synergies occur among actions and the performance of one reduces the cost of undertaking the other. Intuitively, in the first case, it is better to have relatively low-powered incentives; in the second case, it is efficient to have stronger incentives. The reason is straightforward: in the case of a substitution relationship, the principal fears that the agent would focus on the most rewarded action and neglect the other that is associated with a dimension of outcome that the principal also cares about. Instead, in the case of complementary actions, this danger is not incurred because focusing on one action does not excessively reduce the other action since it becomes "cheaper" to undertake.

An important application in the context of water sector regulation occurs when service quality levels are not perfectly observable but are costly to provide. Middle managers offered high-powered contracts that reward their contributions to the financial performance of the utility might be tempted to skimp on investments in maintenance because deterioration of the assets will not be immediately apparent. Therefore, lower-powered incentives are warranted when important aspects of performance cannot be precisely defined and measured. In the context of the water sector, this would avoid potentially serious negative effects, like waterborne diseases that could occur, when the quality of the service is allowed to deteriorate significantly because of excessive cost-cutting efforts.[20]

Intertemporal Dimension

The relationship between the various managerial levels usually develops over time, giving the principal the opportunity to observe the agent's performance in different periods and potentially alleviating information asymmetries. For example, in some moral hazard contexts, the actions undertaken by the agent are observable with a delay. In such cases, it is optimal for the principal to devise a payment mechanism for the agent that allows for punishments for past actions. Such a mechanism provides incentives for good behavior, given that the punishment in such cases is not constrained by limited liability clauses or the possibility that the agent will quit the job in advance. In the latter situations, the principal must instead act on the reward side and keep it slightly above the level necessary to provide high quality, as long as the agent is not discovered cheating. The stream of information rents accruing to the agent eliminates the temptation to cheat.[21] In the WSS context, the bad behavior could involve skimping on maintenance, which leads over time to the degradation of the quality of the service.

Monitoring Tools

Given the costs incurred because of asymmetric information, the utility's top management has an incentive to devise tools that mitigate these costs.[22] Competition among several agents has often been advocated as a potent tool for improving performance, provided that collusion among them can be prevented.[23] Specifically, forms of yardstick competition could be put in place so that the performance of different middle managers is appropriately compared, to elicit information about technology and effort.[24] Even imperfect comparisons are valuable as long as they reduce the principal's uncertainties.[25]

Alternatively, the principal could perform costly audits on what the agent claims about the economic context in which the agent operated or the actions the agent undertook. Obviously, it is optimal to audit only a sample of such claims. The minimization of the audit cost for the utility's top management imposes straightforward optimality conditions. First, agents reporting outcomes that are worse for them should not be audited, because they are clearly telling the truth. Second, the more favorable the report is to the agent, the higher that agent's probability of being audited should be. Third, if the audit confirms the agent's report, the agent should be given a reward; alternatively, in case of cheating, the agent should be punished (see Mookherjee and Png 1989; Townsend 1979).

In MENA, the widespread lack of routine monitoring of basic service parameters (for example, nonrevenue water), regular nationally representative household surveys, and basic financial transparency means that the region has particularly large information asymmetries compared to other regions. For example, although data on nonrevenue water are widely quoted, little of this information is founded on a solid evidence base. Senior and midlevel managers responsible for reduction of nonrevenue water in utilities are often in the uncomfortable position of having to provide formal reports against public budget releases on progress without having the equipment, staff, or budgets to provide the underlying data.[26] Economic theory suggests that a significant investment in filling this information gap and transparency deficit would be needed before it is possible to introduce incentives that have higher power.

Increasing the Intrinsic Motivation of the Agent

Agents' intrinsic motivation helps to mitigate the information problems of adverse selection and moral hazard. Various channels for increasing motivation have been highlighted in the literature and are relevant in the water sector.

The first channel is the possibility that agents derive utility from nonmonetary aspects of their relationship with the principal. For example, agents and the principal share the mission and goals of the organization in which they work, which gives them pride. Recognition from peers and individuals outside the agency relationship may provide the agents status and respect in the society at large. This factor is especially important in public organizations[27] that generally have a smaller capacity than the private sector to provide explicit monetary incentives.[28]

A second channel is the possibility that career concerns induce the desire to perform well and put in effort. The agent may want to build a solid reputation of effectiveness because doing so will allow the agent to obtain better opportunities in the future, in the same organization or elsewhere.[29] The agent's desire to perform well reduces the need for the principal to provide explicit incentives and reduces the agency costs incurred because of asymmetric information. The magnitude of the effects will depend crucially on the length of the agent's remaining work life. Intrinsic effort naturally declines with seniority; therefore, explicit incentives need to be sharpened later in the career to induce the agent to remain engaged in the job.

The difference between the "ethical push" of intrinsic motivation and that produced by career concerns is that in the first case observability of actions and outcomes is not a problem, whereas the second case requires verifiability to be effective because agents must be able to prove their abilities and the results they obtained earlier in their career (see Dewatripont, Jewitt, and Tirole 1999).

Risks of Collusion between Principal and Agent

In a situation of consecutive hierarchical agency relationships, in which the principal is an agent in a higher-level agency relationship, collusion could emerge in the lower tiers of the organization's overall structure. This is precisely the context of water utilities, because the top management is the agent of the political leadership. Therefore, upper and lower levels of management may decide jointly to take advantage of the asymmetries of information that the government faces for delivering water services.

Politicians should be aware of this danger and design compensation schemes accordingly. An interesting result, as shown by Laffont and Tirole (1993),[30] is that the solution lies in reducing the power of the incentives given at the lower agency level (midlevel management in the WSS context considered here). The intuition is that limiting the incentives for performance inside the water utility reduces the size of the rents that can be appropriated through collusion, which in turn limits the temptation to collude in the first place.

In sum, this chapter has shown that, in the absence of effective regulation, the existence of natural monopolies in the WSS sector creates the double risk of monopolistic pricing and excessively low service quality regardless of the ownership model. Across most of MENA, the central problem of excessively low service quality occurs because governments have not solved the "commitment problem" that establishes the sectoral rules that allow utilities to recover their long-run costs. Intervening to solve this regulatory problem is necessary but insufficient without also addressing the politics of the social contract (the relationship between citizens and political leaders) and the management problem (the relationship between utility management and frontline workers).

The social contract is foundational for ensuring sufficient financing for the sector so as to avoid a structural mismatch between revenues and costs. Communicating the higher cost implications of water scarcity and the transition from conventional to nonconventional water is a first step in readjusting citizens' expectations and adjusting the social contract to solve the "commitment problem." The cost of water will inevitably rise and must be paid from taxes or tariffs.

Acting on the management problem, in turn, will increase the efficiency of service delivery. The nature of the "tasks" that need to be performed at the utility level is such that agents have specialized technical knowledge that "principals" cannot elicit. The logic of principal-agent theory shows that, for agents to have incentives or motivation to perform these tasks well, principals could alternatively rely on peer pressure, monitoring, and professional norms. In the MENA region, for the most part, utilities are not managed this way—they are not trusted to perform and, in turn, are not trustworthy—leading to a low-level equilibrium of low expectations and poor performance.

Utility staff are not empowered or encouraged to explore ways of increasing revenues through reducing losses, such as nonrevenue water, through better management of frontline staff within the organization. In turn, utility staff are not motivated to improve operating efficiency because they do not expect any rewards (punishments) for (not) exerting greater effort in their jobs. Utility staff are heavily circumscribed by the overall policy environment and lack autonomy and discretion. In the language of game theory, government leaders, from the highest levels down to midtier and frontline utility staff, lack *trust* that others in the system are exerting effort to improve performance. Instead, there are widespread beliefs that many are engaging in corruption and rent seeking, which can lead to "bandwagon" behavior (of also engaging in rent seeking because everyone is doing it anyway) or demoralization and resignation (why try to improve if no one else is).

Chapter 9 offers ideas for reform leaders on how to try alternative contracts with utility managers and staff, which provide greater autonomy and strengthen expectations and peer pressure to perform.

NOTES

1. This is the short route of accountability as represented by true market approaches.

2. As noted in the early contribution of Helm (1994, 17) with reference to the British experience of utility reform: "The demands for intervention have not decreased with privatization: they have, in fact, probably increased."

3. One of the leading textbooks is by Laffont and Martimort (2002). According to those authors, incentive theory encompasses "contract theory, principal-agent theory, agency theory and mechanism design" (Laffont and Martimort 2002, 13).

4. That is, it is overoptimistic about its ability to recoup the full cost of its investment.

5. The Arab Republic of Egypt, Malta, the United Arab Emirates, and West Bank and Gaza.

6. A useful discussion is provided in Joskow (2007, section 6).

7. The original contributions for this result are by Ramsey (1927) and Boiteux (1956).

8. If a maximum water allowance per billing period is also set, the fixed component is defined as a "capacity charge."

9. The drier periods might require higher volumetric charges if higher cost water sources must be exploited.

10. See Komives et al. (2008) for an early analysis of the problem and the potential role of connection subsidies in the sector.

11. The size of the blocks increases with the number of household members.

12. This is justified because of health externalities and on fairness grounds.

13. This is the first best level that can be achieved when both the principal and the agent know all the information necessary for the production process (in technical terms, all the information is "common knowledge").

14. Of course, the two types of asymmetric information could be present at the same time, further complicating the principal's problem. For a discussion of mixed models, see Laffont and Martimort (2002, chapter 7).

15. In technical terms, the agent's compensation scheme respects the agent's incentive constraint (the agent is maximizing utility) and the agent's participation constraint (the agent obtains a level of utility that matches what the agent would obtain in another occupation).

16. Therefore, the fact that the first best is not attainable is not a sign of inefficiency. The second best that the principal seeks to reach is the solution to a constrained optimization problem.

17. An early definition can be traced back to Williamson (1985). For a critical discussion, see Lazear (2000).

18. See the subsection on monitoring tools.

19. It can be easily shown that with risk neutrality the first best can be achieved most of the time, provided that the institutional framework does not impose forms of limited liability that limit the losses the agent should sustain in case of low effort (in the context of moral hazard) or a bad state of the world (with adverse selection). See Laffont and Martimort (2002), chapter 3, for adverse selection models, and chapter 4, for moral hazard models.

20. See Hart, Shleifer, and Vishny (1997) for a discussion of how these problems also explain the allocation of tasks between the public and private sectors.

21. This mechanism is analogous to that described in labor economics with reference to "efficiency wages." See Shapiro and Stiglitz (1984).

22. In the literature, these tools are known as verification schemes that provide "informative signals."

23. The subsection on risks of collusion between principal and agent briefly discusses the case when this is part of a set of consecutive hierarchical agency relationships (precisely what is seen in the context of water utilities).

24. The seminal paper is Shleifer (1985).

25. That the principal should use all the informative signals follows from Holmström's (1979) Sufficient Statistic Theorem.

26. Performance-based budgeting in countries such as Jordan lacks the underlying monitoring tools.

27. Wilson (1989) provides an extensive treatment of the incentive structures found in bureaucracies and complex public organizations. He offers an interesting classification between craft organizations (those in which the actions of the agents are not observable, but the outcomes are), procedural organizations (in which the actions of the agents are observable, but not the outcomes), and coping organizations (in which neither the actions nor the outcomes are observable). Dixit (2002) instead provides a summary description of incentives in public organizations, explicitly using the principal-agent framework.

28. Although private firms have more tools at their disposal to motivate their staff (for example, managers can be given stock options), peer pressure also has an important role in explaining the emergence of professional norms in specific private sector contexts. See Kandel and Lazear (1992).

29. The pioneering study is Holmström (1982/1999). Later research also shows that this effect could be limited by the presence of so-called ratchet effects, which discourage agents from revealing information or putting in effort because they fear that reducing the information asymmetry with the principal will excessively weaken their bargaining power in future periods. See Laffont and Tirole (1993, chapter 9) and Meyer and Vickers (1997).

30. See chapters 11 and 12 of this report.

REFERENCES

Arrow, K. 1968. "The Economics of Moral Hazard: Further Comment." *American Economic Review* 58 (3): 537–39.

Boiteux, M. 1956. "Sur la gestion des Monopoles Publics astreints à l'équilibre budgétaire." *Econometrica* 24 (1): 22–40. https://doi.org/10.2307/1905256.

Dewatripont, M., I. Jewitt, and J. Tirole. 1999. "The Economics of Career Concerns, Part II: Application to Missions and Accountability of Government Agencies." *Review of Economic Studies* 66 (1): 199–217. https://www.jstor.org/stable/2566956.

Dixit, A. 2002. "Incentives and Organizations in the Public Sector: An Interpretative Review." *Journal of Human Resources* 37 (4): 696–727. https://doi.org/10.2307/3069614.

Engel, E., R. D. Fischer, and A. Galetovic. 2014. *The Economics of Public-Private Partnerships: A Basic Guide.* New York: Cambridge University Press.

Hart, O., A. Shleifer, and R. W. Vishny. 1997. "The Proper Scope of Government: Theory and an Application to Prisons." *Quarterly Journal of Economics* 112 (4): 1127–61. https://www.jstor.org/stable/2951268.

Helm, D. 1994. "British Utility Regulation: Theory, Practice, and Reform." *Oxford Review of Economic Policy* 10 (3): 17–39. https://doi.org/10.1093/oxrep/10.3.17.

Holmström, B. 1979. "Moral Hazard and Observability." *Bell Journal of Economics* 10 (1): 74–91. https://doi.org/10.2307/3003320.

Holmström, B. 1982/1999. "Managerial Incentive Problems: A Dynamic Perspective." In *Essays in Economics and Management in Honor of Lars Wahlbeck,* Swedish School of Economics, Helsinki. Reprinted in *Review of Economic Studies* 66 (1): 169–82. https://www.jstor.org/stable/2566954.

Holmström, B., and P. Milgrom. 1987. "Aggregation and Linearity in the Provision of Intertemporal Incentives." *Econometrica* 55 (2): 303–28. https://doi.org/10.2307/1913238.

Holmström, B., and P. Milgrom. 1990. "Regulating Trade among Agents." *Journal of Institutional and Theoretical Economics* 146 (1): 85–105. https://www.jstor.org/stable/40751306.

Holmström, B., and P. Milgrom. 1991. "Multitask Principal-Agent Analysis: Incentive Contracts, Asset Ownership, and Job Design." Special issue, *Journal of Law, Economics, and Organization* 7: 24–52. https://doi.org/10.1093/jleo/7.special_issue.24.

Joskow, P. L. 2007. "Regulation of Natural Monopoly." In *Handbook of Law and Economics*, vol. 2, edited by A. M. Polinsky and S. Shavell, 1227–348. Amsterdam: Elsevier. https://doi.org/10.1016/S1574-0730(07)02016-6.

Kandel, E., and E. P. Lazear. 1992. "Peer Pressure and Partnerships." *Journal of Political Economy* 100 (4): 801–17. http://dx.doi.org/10.1086/261840.

Komives, K., V. Foster, J. Halpern, Q. Wodon, and R. Abdullah. 2008. "Water, Electricity, and the Poor: Who Benefits from Utility Subsidies?" Water P-Notes 20, World Bank, Washington, DC. https://openknowledge.worldbank.org/handle/10986/11745.

Laffont, J.-J. 1994. "The New Economics of Regulation Ten Years After." *Econometrica* 62 (3): 507–37. https://doi.org/10.2307/2951658.

Laffont, J.-J., and D. Martimort. 2002. *The Theory of Incentives: The Principal-Agent Model.* Princeton, NJ: Princeton University Press.

Laffont, J.-J. and J. Tirole. 1993. *A Theory of Incentives in Procurement and Regulation.* Cambridge, MA: MIT Press.

Lazear, E. P. 2000. "Performance Pay and Productivity." *American Economic Review* 90 (5): 1346–61. https://www.jstor.org/stable/2677854.

Meyer, M. A., and J. Vickers. 1997. "Performance Comparisons and Dynamic Incentives." *Journal of Political Economy* 105 (3): 547–81. https://doi.org/10.1086/262082.

Mookherjee, D., and I. Png. 1989. "Optimal Auditing, Insurance, and Redistribution." *Quarterly Journal of Economics* 104 (2): 399–415. https://doi.org/10.2307/2937855.

Ramsey, F. P. 1927. "A Contribution to the Theory of Taxation." *Economic Journal* 37: 47–61. https://doi.org/10.2307/2222721.

Shapiro, C., and J. E. Stiglitz. 1984. "Equilibrium Unemployment as a Worker Discipline Device." *American Economic Review* 74 (3): 433–44. https://www.jstor.org/stable/1804018.

Shleifer, A. 1985. "A Theory of Yardstick Competition." *RAND Journal of Economics* 16 (3): 319–27. https://doi.org/10.2307/2555560.

Stiglitz, J. E., and J. K. Rosengard. 2015. *Economics of the Public Sector*. 4th ed. New York: Norton.

Townsend, R. M. 1979. "Optimal Contracts and Competitive Markets with Costly State Verification." *Journal of Economic Theory* 22 (2): 265–93. https://doi.org/10.1016/0022-0531(79)90031-0.

Williamson, O. E. 1975. *Markets and Hierarchies: Analysis and Antitrust Implications: A Study in the Economics of International Organization*. New York: Free Press.

Williamson, O. E. 1985. *The Economic Institutions of Capitalism*. New York: Free Press.

Wilson, J. Q. 1989. *Bureaucracy: What Government Agencies Do and Why They Do It*. New York: Basic Books.

World Bank. 2016. *Making Politics Work for Development: Harnessing Transparency and Citizen Engagement*. Washington, DC: World Bank.

Policy Ideas for the Leaders and People of MENA to Defuse Water Crises and Transform Their Economies

This part of the report presents policy ideas distilled from the economic analysis of how state institutions function in managing water, and how transition happens from a low-trust/low-legitimacy to a higher-trust/higher-legitimacy equilibrium.

CHAPTER 9

The Fundamental Importance of Informal Institutions of Legitimacy and Trust

INTRODUCTION

This chapter lays out policy principles that emerge from the economic analysis of water scarcity in the Middle East and North Africa (MENA). It argues that formal institutional reforms, such as, for example, public-private partnerships, will not work without addressing the informal institutions of legitimacy and trust. Furthermore, independent of any formal reform, policy efforts to build legitimacy and trust are essential for MENA to be able to attract long-term financing to invest in sustainable infrastructure for water security. The following chapters offer ideas for reform leaders and their external development partners on how to build trust and legitimacy through greater autonomy and empowerment of water utilities and an enhanced role for local governments in managing water, combined with strategic communication about water.

The leaders and people of MENA have consistently received policy advice or solutions in the following areas to address persistent and increasingly urgent problems of water scarcity in MENA:

- To improve the quality of service delivery and financial sustainability of water supply and sanitation utilities, countries have been encouraged to pursue private sector partnerships (PSPs), corporatization, and establishment of autonomous regulatory agencies that are independent of political representatives.

- Removal or reduction of subsidies for water and agriculture has been a constant feature of the policy dialogue, with substantial prior and ongoing work measuring subsidies, demonstrating the fiscal and environmental burden, and arguing that the benefit incidence of these subsidies is not as progressive as alternative ways of delivering assistance to the poor.
- To improve water resource management, countries have been advised to establish agencies—typically at the river basin scale—to assess and monitor the water balance and regulate the use of water, through quantity restrictions or quotas.
- To improve irrigation service delivery, decentralized water management systems and establishment of water user associations, representing farmers, have been promoted to accompany the rehabilitation and modernization of irrigation infrastructure as well as to increase water productivity in agriculture.
- Macro-fiscal stability and tariff reforms have been outlined for countries to receive external financing to build water infrastructure—to lower the wastage of water in the course of service delivery and increase the supply of water resources through wastewater treatment and reuse, on the one hand, and desalination, on the other.

These proximate solutions have both tried to insulate service delivery from political influence and laid blame for the failings of the water sector on the lack of political will to address them. Chapters 1 and 6 this report set out the economic theory to show that politics must be at the heart of decision-making in the water sector, precisely because political decisions are an inherent part of the classical economic approach to resource allocation and water pricing.

The economic lens brought to the problems of water in MENA—as outlined in chapters 1 and 6—yields the following insights on these "solution spaces":

- Formal reforms or efforts toward PSPs, corporatization, and independent regulation will not succeed unless the underlying informal institutions of legitimacy of water tariffs—and whether citizens comply with them—are in place. The lack of such legitimacy—as exemplified by protests over tariffs or non-payment of tariffs—undermines formal reforms.
- Tax and tariff revenues from the current generation of customers and residents are unlikely to be sufficient to cover the infrastructure needs of the water sector, particularly given the increased share of nonconventional water in the overall water mix. The state and its political institutions are key to building credibility for long-term debt financing and attracting private investors. Legitimacy of the state to gain the compliance of citizens to cover their share of the costs, generation after generation, is a key institution for building credibility to attract financing for the enormous infrastructure needs of MENA, the world's most water scarce region.
- Countries need more focused advice on how to design tariffs and how/whether to combine revenues from tariffs with general budget transfers for the financial sustainability of utilities (regardless of whether they are operated by private partners, by corporate structures, or as arms of government ministries).
- Countries need also more focused advice on how to improve the technical performance of utilities—whether through private sector management, corporatization, or existing forms of state ownership in which ministerial power is exercised over utilities.
- The focused advice referred to above can be developed through country context–specific projects, using the tools of economics to help reform leaders and their external partners design policies, try out reforms, evaluate impact, and iterate toward those reforms that show evidence of success. This is how other sectors—such as health, education, and social protection—have been building new, concrete policies for improved outcomes.
- Survey evidence on citizens' attitudes toward tariffs and the impact of outreach on willingness to pay is needed for policy breakthroughs. Investing in such survey evidence is not research for research's

- sake but rather the kind of work that the corporate sector does to improve profitability. Such research is needed because no one yet knows the answers.
- Survey evidence on utility managers and staff is needed to help design contracts with utility management and staff that improve their incentives and professional norms, building trust among staff and managers that each person is working to improve utility performance. Again, these kinds of surveys are not research for research's sake but what a variety of complex organizations in the private and public sectors across the world regularly undertake, especially when they worry that they have a management or performance problem.
- External support is more likely to help countries if it provides budget support accompanied by focused policy advice on how to reform tariffs, what tariff structures to use, how to combine tariffs with general budget transfers, and how to improve the technical performance of utilities. This type of support contrasts with the construction of water infrastructure the countries—currently not covering operation and maintenance costs—likely cannot afford or manage because the underlying problems of legitimacy and trust have not been addressed through infrastructure construction.
- On the management of water as a resource or a public good, a problem that has been revealed is that institutions are weak and inadequate even in the most advanced contexts of the world, where institutions, such as of law and property rights, are generally strong. Designing institutions that can address problems of the public good—such as the climate, environment, and water—requires new thinking. There are no old solutions. The questions are wide open and likely to require country context–specific answers. For example, what agencies should be assigned what tasks toward the sustainable management of water? Chapter 11 of this report begins to provide some answers or, rather, a way of thinking about the problem that can help countries to develop policy regimes for managing water that work in their context.
- Strategic communication is a crucial instrument to use to complement all reforms. Communication has been identified as the means to transition from situations of low trust in society to higher levels of trust, albeit in a variety of forms. Chapter 12 of the report begins to provide some answers for how countries might use communication, in the context of their political and bureaucratic institutions, to build trust around the issues of water, which are so significant to the people of MENA.

This chapter examines the first principal-agent relationship, that between citizens and political leaders. It first examines the evidence on links between prices for service delivery and protests. It then examines whether local political contestability could be a potential basis for renegotiating the social contract on water pricing and quantity regulation.

LEGITIMACY OF TARIFFS

Increases in prices or tariffs, or reductions in subsidies, as a result of state policy actions have been met with widespread protests and social unrest not only in MENA but across the world, including in developed countries. An initiative of the International Monetary Fund to measure social unrest and its drivers shows how subsidy reforms contribute to spikes in protests in MENA, even though the region has several other political sources of instability (such as international armed conflict) (Barrett et al. 2020). In Jordan, for example, the International Monetary Fund measure of social unrest spiked in 2012 over fuel prices and in 2018 over general austerity measures (Barrett et al. 2020, online annex figure 1.1). Another source of data on protests, ACLED (the Armed Conflict Location & Event Data Project), shows that the 2018 spike in protests in Jordan can be linked specifically to water tariffs (figure 9.1).[1] This phenomenon of realized and potential protests is, by definition, a phenomenon of lack of legitimacy of tariff increases, meaning that citizens are unwilling to comply voluntarily with tariff increases. The wider implications of protests for political stability thus make

Figure 9.1 Social unrest in Jordan, 2016–21

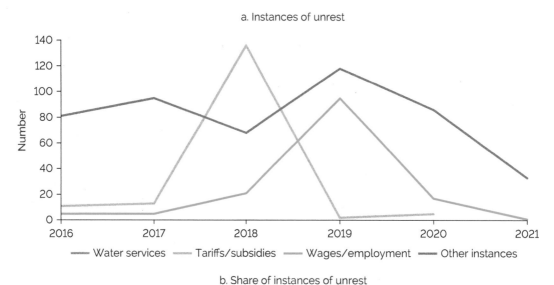

a. Instances of unrest

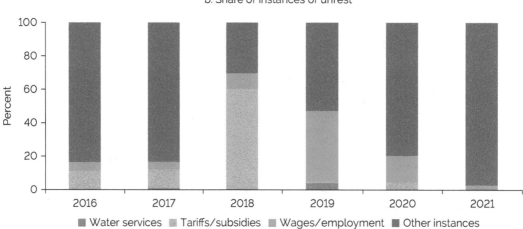

b. Share of instances of unrest

Source: Calculations based on data from Haerpfer et al. 2022.

governments in MENA wary of policy measures that would increase water tariffs. This underlying political fear of raising tariffs in turn hobbles the financing of water utilities—whether owned by the public sector or open to partnerships with the private sector.

Efforts to put PSPs in place can also be met with protests, because citizens fear that PSPs could be a means of raising prices or laying off workers employed in the public sector.[2] In the past, large-scale protests occurred across countries as diverse as Bolivia, India, Ireland, Morocco, the Philippines, and South Africa when governments tried to bring in PSPs, or after PSPs had been in operation for some years (Food & Water Watch 2010). That is, the underlying (lack of) legitimacy of water tariffs would not be removed simply through formal reforms that bring in PSPs, which are often subject to renegotiations (Guasch et al. 2014).

More evidence comes from the World Values Survey (WVS) that people in MENA are particularly concerned about rising prices and especially critical of what they regard as the role of government to keep prices down. Two sets of questions in the most recent data available from the WVS (wave 7, undertaken over 2017–21) include "prices." The first one asks respondents to choose the first and

Figure 9.2 People in MENA say that "fighting rising prices" is among their top two priorities

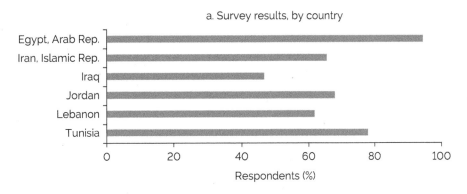

a. Survey results, by country

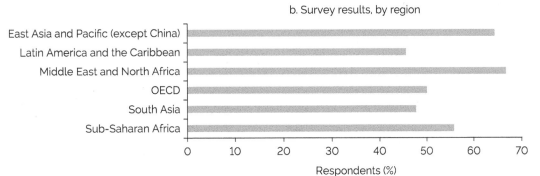

b. Survey results, by region

Source: Calculations based on data from Haerpfer et al. 2022.
Note: OECD = Organisation for Economic Co-operation and Development.

second most important items from the following list: (1) maintaining order in the nation, (2) giving people more say in important government decisions, (3) fighting rising prices, and (4) protecting freedom of speech. Figure 9.2 shows that more than 60 percent of the respondents in MENA chose "fighting rising prices" among the top two priorities, the highest response rate for this category across regions. Among the six MENA countries in which the survey was conducted, the Arab Republic of Egypt stands out as the place where more than 90 percent of the respondents selected "fighting rising prices." Tunisia is a close second—with almost 80 percent choosing this item. Iraq is the only country where a majority of the respondents selected "maintaining order in the nation."

Another set of questions on how people evaluate government performance was included in a MENA-specific module of the WVS and administered in four countries—Egypt, Iraq, Jordan, and Lebanon. Figure 9.3 shows that "controlling prices" is the area of government performance that elicits the highest disapproval from the largest percentage of citizens in three of the four MENA countries where these questions were asked.

In contrast to the lack of legitimacy of increasing prices or tariffs, generalized taxation by the state appears to enjoy legitimacy among MENA's citizens, at levels higher than or comparable to those in other regions of the world. One question in the WVS asks respondents to rate whether cheating on taxes is justifiable, on a scale of 1 to 10, with 1 representing "never justifiable" and 10 representing "always justifiable." Figure 9.4 shows that the vast majority of respondents respond "never justifiable" or close to it (between 1 and 4 on the scale) in every country. Jordan and Lebanon have the highest rates of responses toward the "justifiable" spectrum of the scale (between 5 and 10). This is unlikely to be a trivial

Figure 9.3 Respondents saying that government performance is "very bad," the highest category of disapproval

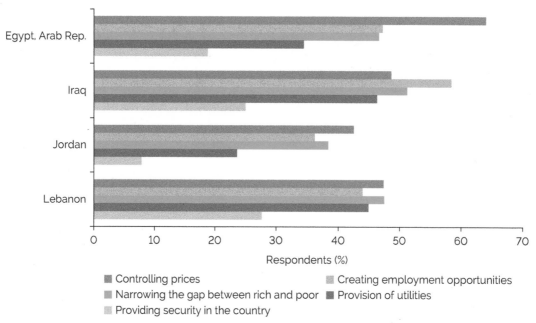

Source: Calculations based on data from Haerpfer et al. 2022.

Figure 9.4 People's responses to a question about whether cheating on taxes is justifiable

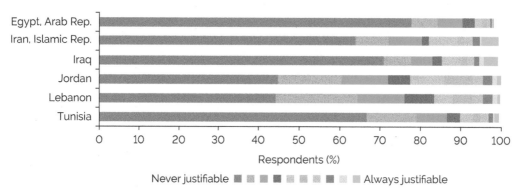

Source: Calculations based on data from Haerpfer et al. 2022.

result driven by fear or social desirability because respondents are willing to answer toward the higher spectrum of justifiability for other sensitive questions, such as "claiming government benefits to which you are not entitled" and "avoiding a fare on public transport." Figure 9.5 shows that only 4 percent of the respondents in MENA say that cheating on taxes is justifiable, compared to 10 percent who say this for "claiming government benefits to which you are not entitled."

As chapter 8 showed, many options exist for designing water tariffs and financing utilities through a combination of tariffs, fiscal transfers, and debt/equity, which can reconcile both the economic

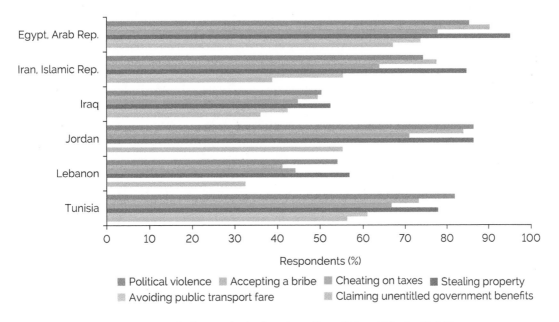

a. Respondents choosing "never justified" in MENA countries

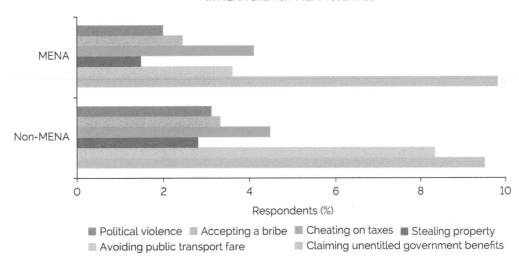

b. Respondents choosing ratings 8, 9, or 10 for justifiability,
in MENA and non-MENA countries

Source: Calculations based on data from Haerpfer et al. 2022.
Note: MENA = Middle East and North Africa.

imperative to cover costs and the political demands of citizens. There is scope for tariff reforms, along with predictable and planned use of general budget transfers, to finance water and sanitation utilities. More focused policy advice is needed, tailored to specific country contexts, on how to design tariffs, using survey evidence on citizens' attitudes and views of tariffs. As noted earlier, such surveys are not research for research's sake, but rather part of concrete policy making and tools that private sector companies regularly use to understand market conditions. There is considerable scope to explore progressive taxation, and general budget transfers, as a way of financing water utilities in the current stage of development of MENA countries. For example, in Jordan, property taxes are used partly to finance the water sector, just as they were in New York City in the late 1800s, where urban property taxes were used to finance connections because poor tenants were not willing to pay the connection charge and continued using water from wells (Ashraf, Glaeser, and Ponzetto 2016).

Tax and tariff revenues from the *current* generation of customers and residents are unlikely to be sufficient to cover the enormous infrastructure needs of the water sector in MENA—particularly given the growing share of nonconventional water in the overall water mix. As climate change ravages the already scarce water resources of the most water stressed region in the world, the governments and people of MENA are asking for external debt and grant financing to secure water as a human right and for global political stability. To access such external financing, however, states in MENA need to be able to demonstrate that they can manage the resources effectively, provide water services to their citizens, and provide returns to external investors by tapping into their societies' willingness to pay for better quality public goods. Legitimacy of the state to gain the compliance of citizens to cover their share of the costs, generation after generation, is a key institution for building credibility to attract financing for water infrastructure in MENA.

TRUST IN PUBLIC UTILITIES AND REGULATORY AGENCIES

Evidence of failing public utilities was used to push for privatization in the 1990s, an era when evidence of market-driven economic growth had created a strong ideology for privatization as a solution. However, the subsequent experience with privatization of water has revealed that water is special and different from other infrastructure sectors, such as telecommunications, in that privatization and even corporatization have not delivered the promised results or attracted sufficient interest from private firms (Estache 2020). Even in the most advanced market economies in the world, such as the United States, water remains largely in the public sector (Lyon, Montgomery, and Zhao 2017).

What countries need is more focused advice on how to improve the technical performance of public utilities, which remain the most common mode of service delivery not just in MENA but across the world. In cases of privatization, more focused advice is needed on how to establish regulatory agencies, which are critical to the success of privatized utilities—ensuring both that costs are covered and that the interests of citizens are well represented. In each case—publicly owned water utilities and regulatory agencies—the problem of performance can be boiled down to the role of trust as an informal institution. As shown in chapters 6 and 8, the role of trust in public sector organizations has come to the fore through applying principal-agent relationships to deliver on multiple complex tasks and requiring agents' specialized private knowledge and technical expertise. Intrinsic motivation and professional norms can matter for the productivity of such organizations, beyond the basic incentive of doing a job for pay. Chapter 10 takes up these issues.

Evidence from the database documenting instances of protests (ACLED) shows that a major source of unrest in MENA is the conditions of employment: wages and job security. For example, figure 9.6 shows that in Egypt and Morocco unrest has grown because of labor market conditions. It provides a simple illustration of what "trust" means in the economies of MENA—these protests can be interpreted as lack of trust between workers and employers.

Although the problem of labor protests is much bigger (encompassing the private sector) and deeper (rooted in age-old class divisions) than the problem of performance of water utilities, the fact that it is widespread and prevalent in MENA suggests the need for careful thinking about the management of utility staff. Top-down and high-powered incentives—such as dismissing workers who are not performing, or making wage increases conditional on performance indicators—may backfire as has happened in

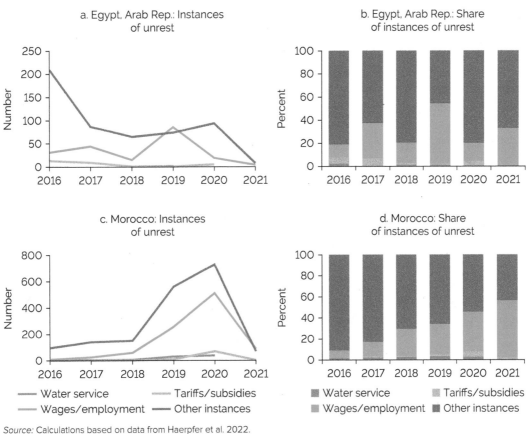

Figure 9.6 How labor market conditions feature in social unrest in the Arab Republic of Egypt and Morocco, 2016–21

a. Egypt, Arab Rep.: Instances of unrest

b. Egypt, Arab Rep.: Share of instances of unrest

c. Morocco: Instances of unrest

d. Morocco: Share of instances of unrest

— Water service ⋯ Tariffs/subsidies
— Wages/employment — Other instances

■ Water service ■ Tariffs/subsidies
■ Wages/employment ■ Other instances

Source: Calculations based on data from Haerpfer et al. 2022.

other sectors, such as public health clinics (Banerjee, Glennerster, and Duflo 2008). The health and education sectors have been building a body of research to examine how to improve the performance of public sector health clinics and schools. The findings show that, although powering up incentives—such as paying bonuses conditional on performance indicators or docking pay conditional on absenteeism—can improve the indicators on which the incentives are concentrated, they can displace bad behavior to other actions that are unmonitored (Dhaliwal and Hanna 2017). Furthermore, there is ample scope for pursuing other policy ideas that would rely on intrinsic motivation, peer-to-peer monitoring, and professional norms, in essence building trust within organizations so that everyone is exerting greater effort to achieve goals that are in the public interest.

Addressing the problem of poorly performing public water utilities thus requires more carefully designed policies that are evaluated through a process of "learning-by-doing." That is, policy actions and projects do not need to "wait" until research and knowledge become available, but rather they should use projects to try out reforms tailored to country-specific contexts, evaluate impact, and iterate toward those reforms that show evidence of success. This process is how other sectors—such as health, education, and social protection—have been building new, concrete policies for improved outcomes. Survey evidence on utility managers and staff is needed to help design contracts with utility management and staff that improve their professional norms, building trust among staff and managers that each person is working to improve utility performance. Again, these kinds of surveys are not research for research's sake; they are what a variety of complex organizations in the private and public sectors across the world regularly undertake, especially when they worry about management or performance problems.

ROLE OF LOCAL POLITICAL CONTESTATION

For managing water as a public resource or a public good, the importance of political institutions is inescapable. Linked to this need is the acute competition for scarce water between the needs of irrigation in agriculture, life in rapidly growing urban centers, the environment, and water's may other uses. Political institutions also mediate this conflict, even in contexts with market mechanisms in place for trading water between cities and farmers. For example, in drought-prone areas in the United States, despite individual property rights over water, mutually beneficial exchange between farmers and cities is thwarted by institutions that give farmers veto rights over such transactions (Bretsen and Hill 2006; Libecap 2008). These farmer institutions were established at a time in the past when water scarcity was not an issue but rather agricultural productivity was the focus for the structural transformation of modern economies.

Designing institutions to address the problems of public goods of our times—public health (in these pandemic times), climate, environment, and water—requires understanding the functioning of political institutions across different contexts. Legitimacy and trust are inescapable issues for political institutions to tackle these problems.[3] But these problems have no off-the-shelf and ready solutions. Chapter 11 offers ideas for empowering local governments in MENA for various tasks in water management. To provide further context to explore these policy ideas, this section uses the WVS to show that (1) people participate in local elections, which are happening, even in a context like MENA's where national political systems are classified as "autocracies" rather than democracies; (2) people participate in elections although they themselves report problems with elections; (3) the vast majority express a belief that having honest elections is important for their country's growth; and (4) confidence in political parties and the national parliament is especially low. Taken together, these patterns suggest that scope exists for trying out an expanded and augmented role for local governments in MENA in managing water.

The WVS asks respondents whether they vote in elections, separately for local and national elections, with response categories including "always," "usually," "never," and "not allowed to vote." Figure 9.7 shows that, although the percentage of respondents in MENA indicating participation in elections ("always" or "usually" responses) is lower than in other regions, the reported participation rates are nevertheless high (more than half of the citizens report participating). Furthermore, in some countries in MENA, such as Jordan and Tunisia, citizens report participating in local elections at the same rate as in national elections. Broadly, this survey evidence shows that local elections are happening. They could be happening in ways that are not conducive to good economic outcomes—what a World Bank (2016) report termed "unhealthy political engagement"—but the question is whether/how policy makers can use and change them, seeking to build legitimacy and trust.

Despite evidence of electoral malpractice, people nonetheless report that they believe that honest elections are important for their lives. In wave after wave of the WVS, more than 80 percent of the respondents across the world and in MENA report that elections are "very" or "rather" important for their lives.[4] Figure 9.8 shows the responses from the latest WVS wave of 2017–21. More substantively, however, research on the impact and role of elections shows that, in places where they are flawed and characterized by glaring malpractice, such as ethnic favoritism, violence, and vote-buying, other nonelectoral political institutions are likely to suffer from the same underlying maladies.[5] In some cases, such as Kenya, concrete evidence shows

Figure 9.7 Participation in local and national elections

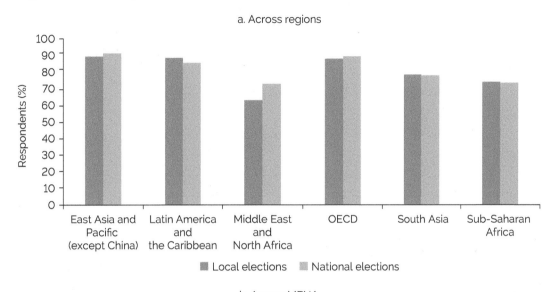

a. Across regions

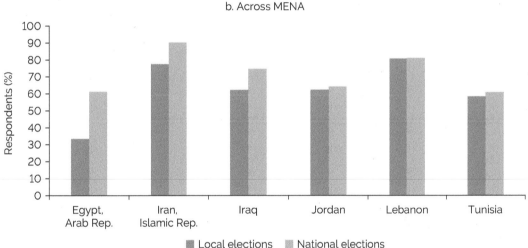

b. Across MENA

Source: Calculations based on data from Haerpfer et al. 2022.
Note: MENA = Middle East and North Africa; OECD = Organisation for Economic Co-operation and Development.

that the incentives created by instituting competitive elections reduced ethnic favoritism and promoted the delivery of broader public goods compared to ethnicity-based patronage under autocratic regimes (Burgess et al. 2015).

Citizens in MENA report various forms of malpractice in the conduct of elections, with voter bribing or vote buying the most widely reported malpractice (figure 9.9). Overall, citizens' reported confidence in elections as they are currently run is low (figure 9.10).

A message from the survey responses—beliefs in the importance of honest elections (figure 9.8) along with low confidence in elections as they are (figure 9.10)—is the *potential* for improving elections so that political leaders have better incentives and motivation to pursue public good policies (World Bank 2016). Local elections may offer fertile ground for policy efforts to improve how elections function in addressing the public good problem of water. For one, national parliaments and the political parties that contest national elections enjoy the lowest confidence among all public institutions in MENA (figure 9.11). More substantially, local elections provide a space with greater information about

Figure 9.8 People's views of the importance of honest elections

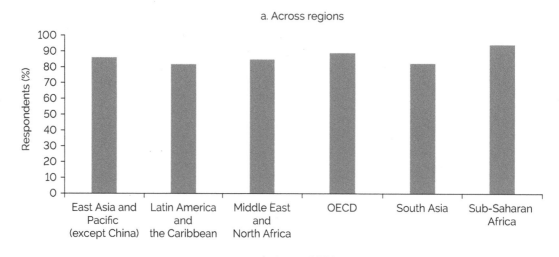

a. Across regions

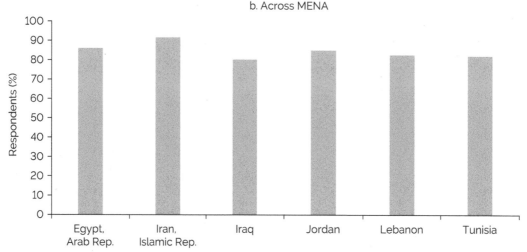

b. Across MENA

Source: Calculations based on data from Haerpfer et al. 2022.
Note: MENA = Middle East and North Africa; OECD = Organisation for Economic Co-operation and Development.

local concerns, greater means of communication, and lower barriers to the entry of new types of local leaders who are motivated to serve the public interest (Casey 2015; Habyarimana, Khemani, and Scot 2018). Local elections also offer the scope to address problems of legitimacy and accountability while maintaining the stability of national regimes (Bardhan and Mookherjee 2006; Cheema, Khwaja, and Qadir 2005; Egorov, Guriev, and Sonin 2009). For conflict-ridden environments in MENA, others have argued that local elections provide possibly the only means to building stable and peaceful state institutions (Myerson 2009).

Local governments as institutions of citizen representation might also address the difficult problem of reconciling the competing claims on water of agriculture and cities. Prior water sector reports have provided persuasive evidence that the rate at which water—surface or ground—is being used for irrigated agriculture is not sustainable. Part I of this report provided further evidence. Countries already face and will continue to grapple with diminishing water availability, depriving whole communities of their traditional livelihoods. Other reports document migration to urban centers as a result of disappearing rural livelihoods (Borgomeo et al. 2021).

Figure 9.9 Malpractice in elections: Respondents answering that bad practices occur during elections "very often" or "fairly often"

a. Across regions

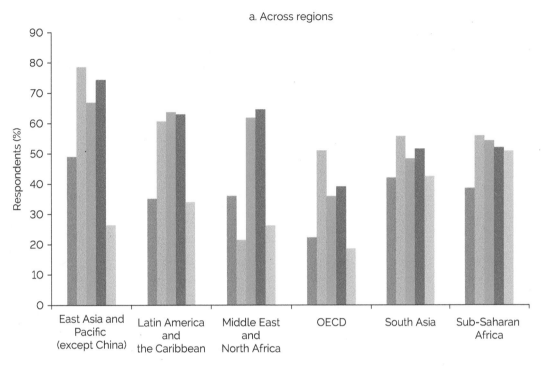

b. Across MENA

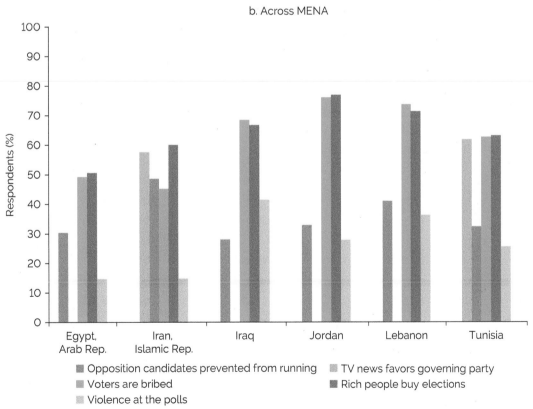

■ Opposition candidates prevented from running   ■ TV news favors governing party
■ Voters are bribed   ■ Rich people buy elections
■ Violence at the polls

Source: Calculations based on data from Haerpfer et al. 2022.
Note: MENA = Middle East and North Africa; OECD = Organisation for Economic Co-operation and Development.

Figure 9.10 Confidence in elections

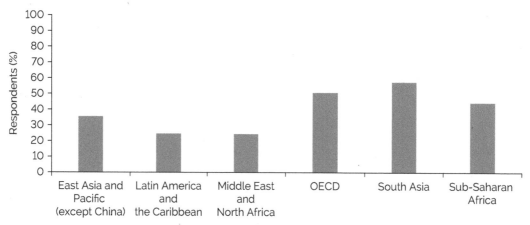

Source: Calculations based on data from Haerpfer et al. 2022.
Note: OECD = Organisation for Economic Co-operation and Development.

Figure 9.11 Rates of low confidence in public institutions

a. Across regions

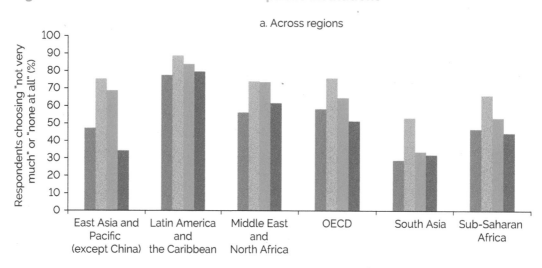

b. Across MENA

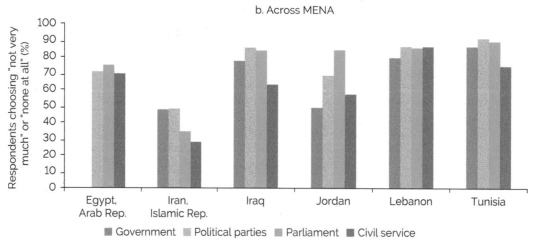

■ Government ■ Political parties ■ Parliament ■ Civil service

Source: Calculations based on data from Haerpfer et al. 2022.
Note: MENA = Middle East and North Africa; OECD = Organisation for Economic Co-operation and Development.

To summarize, this chapter has focused on two policy principles for water resource management. The first is the problem of water in agriculture, and the report shows the importance of quantity regulations (as part of water resource management).[6] The second is the importance of the legitimacy of these water regulations and how it can be built through a combination of national and local strategic communication, delegating the management of "caps" to local governments that represent both farmers and nonfarmers in communities, and that can win legitimacy through the local political process. Addressing these problems would allow farmers to exit agriculture with dignity and by choice, before being forced out by the sudden disappearance of water resources as scarcity accelerates in the region.

The economics of price versus quantity regulation is applied to the case of the "externality" or "common pool" problem of water to show how the quantity regulation tool is a more direct policy instrument than price incentives (subsidies) to change what crops farmers grow. To address the problem of legitimacy of quantity restrictions—or voluntary compliance by farmers and other water users—the chapter shows how research on legitimacy points to a role for strategic communication and local political contestation. Local governments can build this legitimacy because of the communication that happens in communities through the process of local political contestation for leadership positions. Outside the scope of the report, but linked to the general point about the untapped potential of local government, are policy instruments to implement social protection and agricultural extension services, which national governments can also explore as part of the services they use to win legitimacy more broadly.

NOTES

1. Data compiled and analyzed for this report by Luke Hart Gates.

2. The next section takes up this point—about unrest due to labor market conditions.

3. Khemani (2020) provides a review.

4. World Bank (2016) reports results for earlier survey waves.

5. World Bank (2016) reviews the evidence.

6. In contrast to the focus on quantity regulation in this report, prior policy dialogues have focused on price subsidies in agriculture.

REFERENCES

Ashraf, N., E. L. Glaeser, and G. A. M. Ponzetto. 2016. "Infrastructure, Incentives, and Institutions." *American Economic Review* 106 (5): 77–82. https://doi.org/10.1257/aer.p20161095.

Banerjee, A. V., R. Glennerster, and E. Duflo. 2008. "Putting a Band-Aid on a Corpse: Incentives for Nurses in the Indian Public Health Care System." *Journal of the European Economic Association* 6 (2–3): 487–500.

Bardhan, P. K., and D. Mookherjee, eds. 2006. *Decentralization and Local Governance in Developing Countries: A Comparative Perspective.* Cambridge, MA: MIT Press.

Barrett, P., M. Appendino, K. Nguyen, and J. de Leon Miranda. 2020. "Measuring Social Unrest Using Media Reports." IMF Working Paper 20/129, International Monetary Fund, Washington, DC.

Borgomeo, E., A. Jägerskog, E. Zaveri, J. Russ, A. Khan, and R. Damania. 2021. *Ebb and Flow, Volume 2: Water in the Shadow of Conflict in the Middle East and North Africa.* Washington, DC: World Bank. https://openknowledge.worldbank.org/handle/10986/36090.

Bretsen, S. N., and P. J. Hill. 2006. "Irrigation Institutions in the American West." *UCLA Journal of Environmental Law and Policy* 25 (2): 283–331. https://doi.org/10.5070/L5252019544.

Burgess, R., R. Jedwab, E. Miguel, A. Morjaria, and G. Padró i Miquel. 2015. "The Value of Democracy: Evidence from Road Building in Kenya." *American Economic Review* 105 (6): 1817–51. https://doi.org/10.1257/aer.20131031.

Casey, K. 2015. "Crossing Party Lines: The Effects of Information on Redistributive Politics." *American Economic Review* 105 (8): 2410–48. https://www.jstor.org/stable/43821345.

Cheema, A., A. I. Khwaja, and A. Qadir. 2005. "Decentralization in Pakistan: Context, Content and Causes." KSG Faculty Research Working Paper Series RWP05-034, John F. Kennedy School of Government, Harvard University, Cambridge, MA. https://www.hks.harvard.edu/publications/decentralization-pakistan-context-content-and-causes.

Dhaliwal, I., and R. Hanna. 2017. "The Devil Is in the Details: The Successes and Limitations of Bureaucratic Reform in India." *Journal of Development Economics* 124: 1–21. https://doi.org/10.1016/j.jdeveco.2016.08.008.

Egorov, G., S. Guriev, and K. Sonin. 2009. "Why Resource-Poor Dictators Allow Freer Media: A Theory and Evidence from Panel Data." *American Political Science Review* 103 (4): 645–68. https://doi.org/10.1017/S0003055409990219.

Estache, A. 2020. "Institutions for Infrastructure in Developing Countries: What We Know . . . and the Lot We Still Need to Know." In *The Handbook of Economic Development and Institutions*, edited by J.-M. Baland, F. Bourguignon, J.-P. Platteau, and T. Verdier, 634–88. Princeton, NJ: Princeton University Press.

Food & Water Watch. 2010. *Trends in Water Privatization: The Post-recession Economy and the Fight for Public Water in the United States*. Washington, DC: Food & Water Watch.

Guasch, J. L., D. Benitez, I. Portabales, and L. Flor. 2014. "The Renegotiation of PPP Contracts: An Overview of Its Recent Evolution in Latin America." International Transport Forum Discussion Paper 2014/18, Organisation for Economic Co-operation and Development Publishing, Paris. https://doi.org/10.1787/5jrw2xxlks8v-en.

Habyarimana, J. P., S. Khemani, and T. Scot. 2018. "Political Selection and Bureaucratic Productivity." Policy Research Working Paper WPS 8673, World Bank, Washington, DC. http://documents.worldbank.org/curated/en/573111544664789517/Political-Selection-and-Bureaucratic-Productivity.

Haerpfer, C., R. Inglehart, A. Moreno, C. Welzel, K. Kizilova, J. Diez-Medrano, M. Lagos, P. Norris, E. Ponarin, and B. Puranen (eds.). 2022. *World Values Survey: Round Seven – Country-Pooled Datafile Version 4.0*. Madrid, Spain & Vienna, Austria: JD Systems Institute & WVSA Secretariat. https://www.worldvaluessurvey.org/WVSDocumentationWV7.jsp.

Khemani, S. 2020. "An Opportunity to Build Legitimacy and Trust in Public Institutions in the Time of COVID-19." Research and Policy Brief 32, World Bank, Washington, DC. https://openknowledge.worldbank.org/handle/10986/33715.

Libecap, G. D. 2008. "Open-Access Losses and Delay in the Assignment of Property Rights." *Arizona Law Review* 50: 379–408. https://arizonalawreview.org/libecap/.

Lyon, T. P., A. W. Montgomery, and D. Zhao. 2017. "A Change Would Do You Good: Privatization, Municipalization, and Drinking Water Quality." In *Academy of Management Annual Meeting Proceedings: Atlanta 2017*, edited by Sonia Taneja, 10499–501. Briarcliff Manor, NY: Academy of Management. https://doi.org/10.5465/AMBPP.2017.19.

Myerson, R. B. 2009. "A Field Manual for the Cradle of Civilization: Theory of Leadership and Lessons of Iraq." *Journal of Conflict Resolution* 53 (3): 470-82. https://doi.org/10.1177/0022002709333356.

World Bank. 2016. *Making Politics Work for Development: Harnessing Transparency and Citizen Engagement*. Policy Research Report. Washington, DC: World Bank. https://openknowledge.worldbank.org/handle/10986/24461.

CHAPTER 10

Building Trusted and Creditworthy Utilities That Deliver Services and Attract Long-Term Financing

INTRODUCTION

This chapter provides ideas for reform leaders in the Middle East and North Africa (MENA), and their external development partners, to improve the performance of public sector utilities by strengthening the incentives, intrinsic motivation, and professional norms of the personnel. These are the three mechanisms through which the actions and behaviors of the myriad staff, who constitute the human resources that manage and run utilities on a daily basis, shape utility performance. The chapter shows how human resource management reforms aimed at these three mechanisms—incentives, intrinsic motivation, and norms—are not just "soft" options but essential for enabling "hard" investments in water infrastructure. The details, or design, of these reforms would need to be tailored to specific country contexts and evaluated using data and rigorous empirical methods, so that reform leaders in countries can be assured of impact in building public utilities that can effectively deliver services and possibly also attract private sector long-term financing resources (through outright privatization or public-private partnerships [PPPs]).

Part I of the report laid out the evidence of inefficiencies in the functioning of water utilities in MENA, such as large losses of water (nonrevenue water) in the process of service delivery. Further, it laid out the evidence that utilities in MENA are financially distressed and perennially struggling to find the resources to spend on capital investments and infrastructure maintenance. Part II provided a framework to understand how these problems are rooted in weak incentives, motivation, and professional norms among utility staff, and the leaders who wield power over them, to manage existing resources effectively and be trusted with greater resources. This chapter uses the framework to distill reform ideas to build trusted and creditworthy utilities.

The chapter lays out general policy ideas for

- Delegating greater autonomy and discretionary power to utility managers and staff, and
- Structuring water tariffs for households in ways that address social preferences for water as a human right, while increasing and regularizing utility revenues.

These ideas will also be shown to apply to policy decisions of PPP water utilities and principles of public regulation of private utilities or PPPs that have monopoly power. As noted in chapter 8, the policy decision to invite private sector participation in running water utilities can be understood as one that provides greater managerial autonomy to the utility. This chapter lays out the experience with privatization and regulation in MENA and shows how successful PPPs involve the same elements of improved management and ability to raise water tariffs in ways that satisfy social objectives.

The chapter discusses how these general policy principles can work, with detailed designs tailored to specific country contexts, by building trust and creditworthiness. Greater autonomy for public sector utility management, combined with strategic communication about organizational performance, can build trust among utility staff to work together and use their specialized knowledge to solve problems (such as the problem of nonrevenue water). Outreach by utility staff around restructured tariffs can build trust among citizens that tariffs are fair and just, and thus win their compliance (rather than their protests). The chapter also lays out principles of regulation of private firms, showing how tariff regulation is central to successful PPPs, and how regulators need to build trust with firms so that their investments will bear fruit, and trust with citizens that they are looking out for their interests. In the case of PPPs, the issues of incentives, intrinsic motivation, and norms do not disappear—they are simply refocused on the regulatory agency. The public policy question with private utilities becomes how to build a *regulatory agency* that is trusted and trustworthy.

RELATIONSHIP BETWEEN "HARD" INFRASTRUCTURE AND "SOFT" MANAGEMENT POLICIES

The proximate solutions to a problem such as wastage or loss of water during the process of taking it from its source to the customer are engineering solutions: how to build the pipes that convey water, how to monitor the infrastructure and identify breakages, where to install meters for monitoring, and so forth. These engineering solutions, however, are applied by human personnel. For example, identifying breakages in the pipes that need to be repaired to prevent water from leaking out requires frontline staff who vigilantly monitor the pipes. It is difficult for a supervisor to find out whether a pipe breakage could have been identified earlier and to condition wages or employment security on the speed with which the frontline staff identify and report breakages. Frontline staff would thus have weak incentives to be vigilant. However, they may be intrinsically motivated to do their job well, thinking it their duty to perform the assigned tasks to the best of their ability because it is their job (feelings of reciprocity). Furthermore, they may be motivated to perform well because they care about the public service of conserving water and efficiently providing it to their people, especially in water scarce societies. Even intrinsically motivated people, however, can become demoralized and disillusioned if the pervading norms among their peers or in their organization are such that they see many others not doing their job, or worse, using opportunities to extract private gains from public resources (corruption). In utilities with widespread shirking and corruption among frontline personnel, engineering solutions will not be applied effectively.

What if we could circumvent the problem of shirking and corruption among human personnel by building more sophisticated hard infrastructure that does not rely as much on human actions? Such sophisticated infrastructure would need financing to build, and financing in turn would depend on the ability of utilities, or the country in the case of publicly owned and general revenue–financed utilities, to raise the revenues to service that financing. Whether sophisticated infrastructure indeed "works" in reducing water losses and is worth the financing costs, regardless of human incentives, motivation, and norms, is an empirical question. If costly infrastructure is not cost-effective, financing such infrastructure can lead to future problems of debt sustainability or take valuable public spending from other sectors that need spending for economic growth, human development, or social protection. Relying on human personnel who are motivated to be vigilant and effective in finding and fixing sources of water losses can be a lower-cost alternative to hard engineering solutions.

The above is an illustration of the inescapable role of human personnel even in a sector like water that requires engineering solutions. Further, the illustration highlights the following aspects of the human tasks involved in managing and implementing the engineering of water systems:

- Tasks involve private knowledge and professional expertise of agents at the frontline, which are difficult/costly to monitor and condition incentives on (so-called high-powered incentives, such as when a frontline engineer's wages depend on water losses monitored at the site where they work).
- Strengthening intrinsic motivation is an alternative to powering up incentives.
- If a utility has weak prevailing norms—if it has widespread shirking and corruption to start—*any* reform will struggle to improve utility performance *unless* the reform also changes the norms (toward hard work and integrity). That is, if staff working within the utility do not trust that others are working hard and honestly, and for good reason (others are not trustworthy, as evidenced by direct observations of shirking and corruption that peers are in a position to make), they can become unmotivated or motivated to follow suit (shirk and seek rents).

This illustration is rooted in a substantial body of economic theory on how complex organizations work, starting with private sector firms in which the increasing complexity of production systems meant that managers needed to rely on agents who had private knowledge and professional expertise.[1] Comparisons of the management practices in Japanese versus U.S. automobile firms showed that different organizations could pursue greater productivity through different types of contracts with their workers, depending on the prevailing culture or institutions in their societies (Kandel and Lazear 1992). The cutting edge of research on the productivity of organizations identifies management practices in firms as a crucial source of differences in productivity and performance (Bloom et al. 2010; Bloom et al. 2019).

Insights from economic research can be applied to provide ideas for reform leaders in MENA to build trusted and creditworthy utilities. Case studies of the general importance of these ideas—of management and motivation within organizations—abound; however, the details are complicated (Dhaliwal and Hanna 2017). For example, do some wage structures work better than others in incentivizing frontline utility staff? Can communication interventions be as powerful in practice as game theory suggests they can be when it comes to shifting norms?[2] How can existing efforts on key performance indicators use economic insights to leverage these indicators for internal communication within utilities to strengthen performance norms? The argument in this chapter is that it is essential to use reforms that address incentives, motivation, and norms in public sector water utilities, and that there are good starting points from economic theory to consider for such reforms. Empirical evidence to back up these ideas can be generated only if the ideas are tried, tested, and refined, learning from both successes and failures.

Rigorous evidence is needed on the impacts of various designs so that MENA countries can confidently move forward with policies that work.

DELEGATION OF GREATER AUTONOMY AND DISCRETION TO UTILITY MANAGERS AND STAFF

A starting point for reforms is the general principle of delegating greater autonomy and discretion to utility managers and staff, within the ambits of their roles and responsibilities. A growing body of economic research has found that indicators of greater autonomy are associated with better performance of public sector organizations (Kala 2020; Rasul, Rogger, and Williams 2017). This evidence is consistent with two insights that emerge from economic theory on how to structure principal-agent relationships in government agencies:

- Reduced role of high-powered incentives and greater role for recruiting intrinsically motivated agents
- Reduced role for top-down hierarchical monitoring and greater role for autonomy and peer-to-peer professional norms

In practice, bureaucracies across the world tend to use flat and above-market wages, presumably to attract talented and public service–motivated workers (Finan, Olken, and Pande 2015). In many striking cases, these arrangements also work. For example, the success of one of the highest-performing education systems in the world, the Finnish public education system, has been attributed to the meritocratic recruitment of highly trained teachers, imbued with strong professional norms and autonomy in their classrooms (World Bank 2018). Incentives are also strong in that teacher salaries are high, to attract highly competent individuals into the profession, and teachers can be let go by school administrators (who also exercise autonomy in how they manage schools). The incentives are not high powered in that salary structures are flat rather than consisting of bonus components contingent on students' test scores. The Republic of Korea's high-performing education system shares with Finland these characteristics of the management of public school teachers (World Bank 2018).

At the same time, however, critics of bureaucracies argue that federal workers are overpaid and underworked (Johnson and Libecap 1994). These arguments are difficult to assess because the studies cannot address the counterfactual of what the outcomes would be in the absence of an overpaid and underworked bureaucracy. Moreover, the studies focus mainly on advanced countries such as the United States. The value or economic contribution of these bureaucracies to keeping markets well-functioning may justify above-market wages and below-market working hours. Rauch and Evans (1999), for example, find a robust cross-country correlation between indicators of meritocratic bureaucracy and economic growth. Yet, if there is scope to make bureaucracies more efficient, or to find management systems that work better in improving the quality of public goods and policies delivered by those bureaucracies, the research literature provides little information about it, even for the United States. Most of the available work on U.S. bureaucracies is qualitative. The classic work by Wilson (1989) makes the point that well-functioning public agencies, be they schools, prisons, or armies, are characterized by having good-quality leaders who create a sense of "mission" in the organization to perform at high levels. Beyond these general attributes, which resonate with the two insights listed earlier from economic theory, no blueprint exists for the formal structure of state agencies that would promote the sense of mission, professionalism, and leadership that Wilson describes.

The crucial difference between developed and developing countries that comes out in the literature is that state personnel in the former tend to have stronger professional norms and basic incentives (for example, to show up to work) compared to state personnel in poorer countries. In developing countries, the organization of public sector agencies has allowed private rent-seeking and lacked sanctions, both formal and informal, against poor performance. One study finds that the same doctor performs worse in a public sector clinic than in his own private practice (Das et al. 2015); another study finds rampant absenteeism among public sector teachers and health workers (Chaudhury et al. 2006); and yet another study finds that those who cheat in a lab game are more likely to express interest in a public sector career (Hanna and Wang 2013). Other studies document widespread corruption and bribe-taking behavior. Furthermore, several randomized controlled trials of implementing high-powered incentives in the public sector find that these incentives work—performance improves significantly (Mohanan, Hay, and More 2016; Muralidharan and Sundararaman 2011; Singh and Masters 2017)— which might appear contrary to the lessons from theory.

It is unsurprising although perhaps encouraging that a well-implemented randomized controlled trial that changes incentives yields improvements in performance in contexts with weak initial incentives. Even when such trials show that the new incentives work, scaling up and sustaining those incentives requires considerable resources and state capacity (Muralidharan and Sundararaman 2011). Banerjee, Duflo, and Glennerster (2008) discuss how such reforms are sabotaged and repealed. Dhaliwal and Hanna (2014) discuss possible inadvertent side effects of incentive interventions that displace rent-seeking to other areas. At the same time, support for the role of nonpecuniary or intrinsic motivation has begun to emerge: Finan, Olken, and Pande (2015) review the evidence. For example, Ashraf, Glaeser, and Ponzetto (2016) find evidence in Zambia that selection of different types of agents into the public sector matters beyond incentives.

The evidence on what types of policy tools or interventions can strengthen peer-to-peer monitoring, professional norms, and motivation is particularly lacking, even as the idea has gained traction. Economic theory points to the potential of norms evolving over time through interaction among workers at the workplace (Besley and Ghatak 2017, 2018). Historical case studies of how the problems of water and sanitation were tackled in the currently advanced market economies of the world have pointed to the importance of professional norms in public water utilities (Ashraf, Glaeser, and Ponzetto 2016). Case study accounts of water utility turnarounds in developing countries have focused on management reforms that brought about performance orientation.[3] A recent initiative at the World Bank has developed "Field-Level Leadership" (FLL) interventions that can be operationalized through projects in the water sector to build intrinsic motivation and peer-to-peer professional norms among the ranks of water sector organizations (World Bank 2020). Instead of focusing on the senior leadership group, the FLL approach aims to develop broad-based, decentralized leadership that engages the entire institution. It is based on the premise that champions may be in the minority but are not rare, exist at all levels of the organizational hierarchy, can be systematically identified, and have potential that can be reliably tapped for positive change. Building on these research insights and ongoing policy initiatives, this chapter suggests three concrete additions:

1. Rigorous empirical evaluation of the kind that exists for policy reforms in other sectors of public service delivery, such as health and education
2. Complementarities between wage structures and communication interventions
3. Complementarities between and within utility communications and outside utility communications to strengthen incentives in local political markets to pursue the public good

The first point is a general approach to identifying policy instruments that work. Empirical methods and building research capacity in developing countries and through external partnerships have made it feasible and cost-effective to gather bespoke and purposeful data for impact evaluation.[4] This approach and capacity are being put to use in other sectors of public service delivery, such as health and education. Rigorous impact evaluation matters because in its absence reformers will not be able to build credibility.[5] Rigorous impact evaluation also matters because it helps to refine and even dramatically change interventions depending on the evidence of what worked and what did not. This type of rigorous evidence would also underpin the change management dimension of emerging water sector approaches such as the Utilities of the Future method.[6] Although the general ideas of the importance of professional norms and peer-to-peer motivation make logical sense and could simply be supported with case studies, the details of design and tailoring to specific contexts can make the difference between real success and cosmetics.

The second point is one of the insights that the economic view adds to existing work on motivating water utility staff through FLL interventions. As discussed in chapter 9, the MENA region is one where conditions of employment in public sector organizations are regarded as unsatisfactory, leading to significant protests and instability in some countries. Increasing the wages of public sector employees is a policy area that understandably raises concern among reform leaders because it involves substantial increases in fiscal outlays without sufficient guarantee that the increased spending will translate into concrete results and social stability. The combination of introducing greater flexibility in wage structures and communication interventions within utilities may hold particular promise in many contexts in MENA, where low wages have sparked protests. Whether the impact of communication interventions indeed depends on other accompanying policy measures, such as the wage structure, is an important question that needs rigorous impact evaluation, reenforcing the first point.

The third point is another insight from the economic and game theoretic view of how norms change in the public sector and the crucial role of politics.[7] For example, a case study of the turnaround of water utilities in Uganda in the late 1990s has been updated to show how politics played a role in when and how the turnaround happened, and how utility performance slipped again in recent years because the political incentives changed (Bukenya 2020). Other research in Uganda has found that the characteristics of village-level politics, play a significant role in the performance of bureaucracies and their ability to deliver services (Habyarimana, Khemani, and Scot 2018). The research on the influence of local political characteristics and the role of communication in changing political incentives and political norms suggests that within-utility communication interventions (such as the one outlined in the FLL interim report) could be complemented with outside-utility communication interventions, such as through local media. These issues of strategic communication about water through media and around local processes of political contestation, as complements to water sector reforms, are taken up in chapter 12.

TECHNICAL INDEPENDENCE OF REGULATORS

Thus far, the chapter has focused on reforms in the management of public sector employees of state-owned utilities that deliver water and sanitation services. Similar approaches emerge in the case of private sector partners in the water sector that are regulated by state agencies. The question in the case of PPPs becomes how to build trusted and trustworthy regulators that can represent the public interest vis-à-vis the monopoly powers of water utilities.

The value of autonomy and delegation to a technically competent agency can be traced to the role of intrinsic motivation and professional norms in improving the performance of organizations tasked with technical matters.

As discussed in chapter 8, a technical regulatory agency must also solve the commitment problem and limit the risks of government capture if the country is to be attractive to private sector engagement in water utilities and infrastructure. The regulatory institutional setting must make reneging on the promise of funding water systems (through utility own revenues and fiscal transfers) difficult and costly. This problem is one of credibility or trust. Private investors will invest in water utilities if they trust the government to abide by a contract that assures them steady returns. At a very general level, high standards of rule of law protect (public and private) investors because they can go to independent courts to seek redress in cases when government agencies violate contractual terms or expropriate assets. At the sector level, the existence of autonomous technical agencies that are empowered to make enforcement decisions without undue political interference, but only following the law and the contractual agreement, can help build trust. From an institutional perspective, independent agencies would define the specific pricing rules and quality standards to be followed by the utilities (within the principles established by law) and enforce them subject to judicial review.

A key element of the contractual agreement in a PPP, however, is the pricing of water and sanitation services from the perspective of citizens or consumers. As discussed in chapter 8, the pricing of water is a social or political decision. The only "technical" element in it is the need to cover the costs of utility investments and operations through a combination of utility own revenues (from the price or tariff collected from consumers) and fiscal transfers from the general budget of the state. Communication with society and through political institutions is needed to reach water-pricing decisions that people regard as legitimate. In many countries, independent regulation requires the establishment of procedural transparency, disclosure of relevant information to the public (for example, by publishing annual reports and at least a synthesis of the major enforcement decisions made during the year), and creation of channels through which all stakeholders (the regulated utility, customers, and suppliers) can express their views on the regulatory decisions being made. Across most of MENA, such transparency is far from the case. Of the 45 water supply and sanitation utilities for which data were collected (see chapter 3), only five published annual audited financial statements online and only two had credit ratings with the global agencies. Without greater transparency of accounting data, it is impossible to start a public discourse on the pricing of water, let alone reach consensus decisions on tariffs. A simple and foundational first step toward regulation and transparent water pricing would be for all service providers to publish audited financial statements.

The following section discusses the interplay between social and political objectives and technical considerations in the pricing of water and financing of utilities.

STRUCTURE OF WATER TARIFFS

Volumes have been written on the various technical options available for pricing water services,[8] and various models can be used.[9] Traditional "cost plus" methodologies add a predetermined markup on the investments agreed on between the utility and the public authorities (the so-called regulatory asset base). This "cost plus" method has a negative impact on the incentives to reduce cost because any expenditure will be recovered. To counter such problems, the "price cap" model has been suggested. In particular, it aims at maximizing incentives for efficiency by making the utilities the residual claimants of any cost saving they can obtain. In this approach, cost reviews are done only periodically. The data collected in the process constitute the basis for setting the maximum tariffs the utility can charge and their evolution in the following years until the next cost review is conducted. Therefore, any further cost reduction other than those already incorporated in the regulated price trajectory is retained in full by the regulated entity, which thus has full incentives to exploit its superior information and find additional improvements other than those already predicted by the regulator and included in the price path. This capacity makes such an arrangement a "high-powered" incentive scheme, as opposed to the "cost plus" framework, which is considered to be "low powered." The drawback of the price cap model is that the utility might be induced to skimp on quality dimensions that are unobservable.[10]

The cases of Arizona and California in the United States are instructive on how technical considerations interact with social and political objectives (Hall 2000). In Tucson, Arizona, the entire city council was voted out of office in the election immediately following implementation of new water rates in response to a drought in 1976–77. The changes in the water tariffs were widely regarded as responsible for the electoral defeat. Taking the Tucson experience as a lesson, two successive mayors of Los Angeles, California, sought to move carefully in determining water prices after a six-year drought in the city in 1986–91. One mayor established a Blue Ribbon Committee on Water Rates, and the other reconstituted it after the first set of recommendations met with political protests. In both incarnations of the technical committee, community representatives learned about the technical aspects of designing rates and considering various alternatives. A technical advisory subcommittee was established to focus on devising innovations in pricing that would increase both economic efficiency and the perceived fairness and equity of the water rates. Hall (2000, 211) ends with the following observation:

> The example outlined here required resources and time for disinterested, public-spirited citizens to learn enough to make educated choices. It also is a process that is only invoked infrequently. This leaves us with the question: why infrequently?

This example shows that technical and political considerations in the pricing of water are context specific and require detailed deliberation and substantial efforts toward reaching a design that satisfies both economic efficiency considerations and social objectives in a particular context. Few overarching and general policy recommendations can be made; recommendations to "increase water tariffs" and "reduce subsidies" are not meaningful. Instead, this chapter makes a meta-institutional policy recommendation— to learn from the examples of Arizona and California offered here and constitute bodies of technical experts who work together with political representatives to devise water tariffs and determine how much utility own revenues need to be supplemented with general budget transfers. As Hall notes, despite the experience of success with such committees in the case of California, this type of approach is infrequent even in the United States. The challenge is a political one—do sufficient political incentives exist to recruit intrinsically motivated managers ("disinterested" and "public spirited," in Hall's quote) and provide them autonomy and transparency (communication with citizens) to devise context-specific water rates.

To conclude, this chapter has offered the reform ideas of creating institutions to manage water utilities that consist of human resource personnel who have the intrinsic motivation and professional norms to pursue both technical efficiency and social objectives. This is what it means to have trusted and creditworthy utilities. These "soft" institutions are crucial and fundamental to the success of proximate engineering solutions. Reform leaders would be well advised to focus on building these institutions by using recruitment, management, wage contracts, and communication tools. Devising ways of monitoring and acting on water losses and setting appropriate water tariffs are micro policy decisions that require local knowledge in specific contexts (such as which areas of the city are wealthier or poorer). Meta-institutional reforms that empower local technical experts and utility staff, while holding them accountable, are needed. This chapter has provided ideas for such meta-institutional reforms and laid out a forward-looking agenda by which country leaders and external partners can implement these ideas in a learning-by-doing manner. This approach means the ideas are immediately operationalizable, simply requiring water reforms and projects to take intrinsic motivation and professional norms (or lack thereof) seriously, and using data and impact evaluation to make projects more likely to succeed.

NOTES

1. The following are pioneering contributions that review the economic theory developed for private firms and consider how the conclusions change when they are applied to public sector organizations: Alesina and Tabellini (2007, 2008); Besley and Ghatak (2005); Dewatripont, Jewitt, and Tirole (1999); Dixit (2002); Francois (2000); Laffont and Tirole (1993); North et al. (2008).

2. Khemani (2019, 2020) reviews the game theory view of how communication is necessary to shift norms and build trust when it is lacking.

3. For the case of Uganda, for example, see Matta (2003).

4. World Bank, Development Impact Evaluation, https://www.worldbank.org/en/research/dime.

5. An example is the impact evaluation of Progresa, Mexico's flagship poverty alleviation program, which was sustained through political party turnover because of the hard evidence on its impact.

6. This is the Shake, Pause, Engage, Envision, Deploy (SPEED) method described in Lombana Cordoba, Saltiel, and Perez Penalosa (2022).

7. World Bank (2016) and Khemani (2019) provide reviews of the evidence on the role of politics in the performance of public sector organizations.

8. For example, Dinar (2000), written two decades ago, remains relevant today.

9. See Andrés et al. (2021) for a general discussion. The practices of water supply and sanitation utilities in MENA were presented in chapter 3 and 4 of this report.

10. For an in-depth discussion of these approaches, see Laffont and Tirole (1993). For a policy appraisal of these regulatory models within the experience of the United Kingdom (which pioneered the shift toward the adoption of incentive-based and competition-driven regulation), see Lodge and Stern (2014).

REFERENCES

Alesina, A., and G. Tabellini. 2007. "Bureaucrats or Politicians? Part I: A Single Policy Task." *American Economic Review* 97 (1): 169–79. https://www.jstor.org/stable/30034389.

Alesina, A., and G. Tabellini. 2008. "Bureaucrats or Politicians? Part II: Multiple Policy Tasks." *Journal of Public Economics* 92 (3–4): 426–47. https://doi.org/10.1016/j.jpubeco.2007.06.004.

Andrés, L. A., G. Saltiel, S. Misra, G. Joseph, C. Lombana Cordoba, M. Thibert, and C. Fenwick. 2021. "Troubled Tariffs: Revisiting Water Pricing for Affordable and Sustainable Water Services." World Bank, Washington, DC.

Ashraf, N., E. L. Glaeser, and G. A. M. Ponzetto. 2016. "Infrastructure, Incentives, and Institutions." *American Economic Review* 106 (5): 77–82. https://doi.org/10.1257/aer.p20161095.

Banerjee, A. V., E. Duflo, and R. Glennerster. 2008. "Putting a Band-Aid on a Corpse: Incentives for Nurses in the Indian Public Health Care System." *Journal of the European Economic Association* 6 (2-3): 487–500.

Besley, T., and M. Ghatak. 2005. "Competition and Incentives with Motivated Agents." *American Economic Review* 95 (3): 616–36. https://doi.org/10.1257/0002828054201413.

Besley, T., and M. Ghatak. 2017. "The Evolution of Motivation." London School of Economics, London. https://personal.lse.ac.uk/GHATAK/Evolution_of_Motivation.pdf.

Besley, T., and M. Ghatak. 2018. "Prosocial Motivation and Incentives." *Annual Review of Economics* 10: 411–38. https://doi.org/10.1146/annurev-economics-063016-103739.

Bloom, N., E. Brynjolfsson, L. Foster, R. Jarmin, M. Patnaik, I. Saporta-Eksten, and J. Van Reenen. 2019. "What Drives Differences in Management Practices?" *American Economic Review* 109 (5): 1648–83. https://www.jstor.org/stable/26636973.

Bloom, N., A. Mahajan, D. McKenzie, and J. Roberts. 2010. "Why Do Firms in Developing Countries Have Low Productivity?" *American Economic Review* 100 (2): 619–23. http://www.jstor.org/stable/27805069

Bukenya. 2020. "The Politics of Building Effective Water Utilities in the Global South: A Case of NWSC Uganda." ESID Working Paper 152, Effective States and Inclusive Development Research Centre, University of Manchester, U.K. https://www.effective-states.org/wp-content/uploads/2020/08/esid_wp_152_bukenya.pdf.

Chaudhury, N., J. Hammer, M. Kremer, K. Muralidharan, and F. H. Rogers. 2006. "Missing in Action: Teacher and Health Worker Absence in Developing Countries." *Journal of Economic Perspectives* 20 (1): 91–116.

Das, J., A. Holla, A. Mohpal, and K. Muralidharan. 2015. "Quality and Accountability in Healthcare Delivery: Audit Evidence from Primary Care Providers in India." Policy Research Working Paper 7334, World Bank, Washington, DC.

Dewatripont, M., I. Jewitt, and J. Tirole. 1999. "The Economics of Career Concerns, Part I: Comparing Information Structures." *Review of Economic Studies* 66 (1): 183–98. https://doi.org/10.1111/1467-937X.00084.

Dhaliwal, I., and R. Hanna. 2014. "Deal with the Devil: The Successes and Limitations of Bureaucratic Reform in India." NBER Working Paper 20482, National Bureau of Economic Research, Cambridge, MA.

Dhaliwal, I., and R. Hanna. 2017. "The Devil Is in the Details: The Successes and Limitations of Bureaucratic Reform in India." *Journal of Development Economics* 124: 1–21. https://doi.org/10.1016/j.jdeveco.2016.08.008.

Dinar, A., ed. 2000. *The Political Economy of Water Pricing Reforms.* New York: Oxford University Press for the World Bank.

Dixit, A. 2002. "Incentives and Organizations in the Public Sector: An Interpretative Review." *Journal of Human Resources* 37 (4): 696–727. https://doi.org/10.2307/3069614.

Finan, F., B. Olken, and R. Pande. 2015. "The Personnel Economics of the State." NBER Working Paper 21825, National Bureau of Economic Research, Cambridge, MA. https://EconPapers.repec.org/RePEc:nbr:nberwo:21825.

Francois, P. 2000. "'Public Service Motivation' as an Argument for Government Provision." *Journal of Public Economics* 78 (3): 275–99. https://doi.org/10.1016/S0047-2727(00)00075-X.

Habyarimana, J. P., S. Khemani, and T. Scot. 2018. "Political Selection and Bureaucratic Productivity." Policy Research Working Paper 8673, World Bank, Washington, DC. http://documents.worldbank.org/curated/en/573111544644789517/Political-Selection-and-Bureaucratic-Productivity.

Hall, D. C. 2000. "Public Choice and Water Rate Design." In *The Political Economy of Water Pricing Reforms,* edited by A. Dinar, 189–212. New York: Oxford University Press.

Hanna, R., and S.-Y. Wang. 2013. "Dishonesty and Selection into Public Service: Evidence from India." NBER Working Paper 19649, National Bureau of Economic Research, Cambridge, MA.

Johnson, R. N., and G. D. Libecap. 1994. *The Federal Civil Service System and the Problem of Bureaucracy,* first edition. University of Chicago Press. https://EconPapers.repec.org/RePEc:ucp:bknber:9780226401713.

Kala, N. 2020. "The Impacts of Managerial Autonomy on Firm Outcomes." NBER Working Paper W26304, National Bureau of Economic Research, Cambridge, MA. https://mitsloan.mit.edu/shared/ods/documents?PublicationDocumentID=7583.

Kandel, E., and E. P. Lazear. 1992. "Peer Pressure and Partnerships." *Journal of Political Economy* 100 (4): 801–17. http://dx.doi.org/10.1086/261840.

Khemani, S. 2019. "What Is State Capacity?" Policy Research Working Paper 8734, World Bank, Washington, DC. https://openknowledge.worldbank.org/handle/10986/31266.

Khemani, S. 2020. "An Opportunity to Build Legitimacy and Trust in Public Institutions in the Time of COVID-19." Research and Policy Brief 32, World Bank, Washington, DC. https://openknowledge.worldbank.org/handle/10986/33715.

Laffont, J.-J., and J. Tirole. 1993. *A Theory of Incentives in Procurement and Regulation.* Cambridge, MA: MIT Press.

Lodge, M., and J. Stern. 2014. "British Utility Regulation: Consolidation, Existential Angst, or Fiasco?" *Utilities Policy* 31: 146–51. https://doi.org/10.1016/j.jup.2014.08.002.

Lombana Cordoba, C., G. Saltiel, and F. Perez Penalosa. 2022. "Utility of the Future: Taking Water and Sanitation Utilities Beyond the Next Level 2.0 – A Methodology to Ignite Transformation in Water and Sanitation Utilities." World Bank, Washington, DC. http://documents.worldbank.org/curated/en/099325005112246075/P1655860d146090dc097dc0165740604044.

Matta, N. 2003. "Uganda: Turn-Around of the National Water and Sewerage Corporation." Africa Region Findings & Good Practice Infobriefs 228, World Bank, Washington, DC. https://openknowledge.worldbank.org/bitstream/handle/10986/9729/310470ENGLISH0find228.pdf?sequence=1.

Mohanan, M., K. Hay, and N. Mor. 2016. "Quality of Health Care In India: Challenges, Priorities, and the Road Ahead." *Health Affairs* 35: 1753–58. https://www.healthaffairs.org/doi/10.1377/hlthaff.2016.0676.

Muralidharan, K., and V. Sundararaman. 2011. "Teacher Performance Pay: Experimental Evidence from India." *Journal of Political Economy* 119 (1): 39–77.

North, D., D. Acemoglu, F. Fukuyama, and D. Rodrik. 2008. "Governance, Growth and Development Decision-Making." World Bank Group, Washington, DC. http://documents.worldbank.org/curated/en/373891468314694298/Governance-growth-and-development-decision-making.

Rasul, I., D. Rogger, and M. J. Williams. 2017. "Management and Bureaucratic Effectiveness: A Scientific Replication." Final Report S-33301-GHA-1. International Growth Centre, London School of Economic and Political Science, London.

Rauch, J., and P. B. Evans. 1999. "Bureaucratic Structure and Bureaucratic Performance in Less Developed Countries." Economics Working Paper Series, Department of Economics, University of California at San Diego. https://EconPapers.repec.org/RePEc:cdl:ucsdec:qt0sb0w38d.

Singh, P., and W. A. Masters. 2017. "Impact of Caregiver Incentives on Child Health: Evidence from an Experiment with Anganwadi Workers in India," *Journal of Health Economics* 55: 219–31. https://doi.org/10.1016/j.jhealeco.2017.07.005.

Wilson, J. Q. 1989. *Bureaucracy: What Government Agencies Do and Why They Do It*. New York: Basic Books.

World Bank. 2016. *Making Politics Work for Development: Harnessing Transparency and Citizen Engagement*. Washington, DC: World Bank. https://openknowledge.worldbank.org/handle/10986/24461.

World Bank. 2018. *World Development Report 2018: Learning to Realize Education's Promise*. Washington, DC: World Bank.

World Bank. 2020. "Field Level Leadership: Motivation to Serve—A Guide to FLL and Implementation (English)." World Bank, Washington, DC. http://documents.worldbank.org/curated/en/099925001162311748/P16984800f367f0000aa310d9a294f5cb46.

CHAPTER 11

Approach to Institutional Reforms in Water Management and Allocation

INTRODUCTION

States in the Middle East and North Africa (MENA) have been responding to demand for water from various constituencies and in effect deciding how to allocate water through highly centralized national government agencies. This system of allocation, however, appears unable to cope with the increasing competition for water from the constituents, alongside declining water resources and the increasing cost of augmenting the resource, such as through desalination.

Over much of the past half century, water resource professionals, including in MENA, have engaged in preparing integrated, multipurpose "master" development plans. Professionals have dominated this top-down approach with limited active participation of stakeholders. In parallel, governments and their development partners have invested in grassroots water user associations (Loucks and van Beek 2017). In the case of MENA, these associations have mainly been linked to the management of irrigation water (Ghazouani, Molle, and Rap 2012). There has been not only a disconnect between the top-down and bottom-up approaches to water management but also a lack of coordination across water-consuming subsectors, particularly water for agriculture and urban domestic supply. The result has been overexploitation of groundwater and surface water (Molle 2008; Molle and Closas 2016) in diverse situations and scales. In the Sahel of Doukkala in Morocco, an export boom drove groundwater withdrawals to the point at which saline intrusion was irreversible (World Bank, forthcoming). In Basra, Iraq, upstream abstraction and pollution of the Euphrates and Tigris have led to summer tidal surges of seawater in the Shatt al Arab and a recurrent summer domestic water supply crisis (World Bank 2020). The combined limitations of these top-down and bottom-up approaches to water management are repeatedly put down to the "lack of political will" to limit abstractions or prevent pollution (Molle and Closas 2020). Yet the alternative approaches that have been put forward—co-management and water auditing[1]—shy away from directly engaging with political economy or harnessing local political institutions and local political contestability. They instead expect bureaucracies to make changes in water management once presented with sound technical analysis.

This chapter proposes an approach to water allocation decisions that would enhance the following:

- Their legitimacy and citizen compliance with water regulations, by directly tapping into public political sentiment on water management
- The potential for economic efficiency or reallocation of water across competing uses to increase overall welfare (of both those trading away the water and those receiving it)

This approach adapts the principle of "cap and trade," which has been used in energy markets to address the negative externality of carbon emissions for the ambient environment, to the common pool problem of water. However, the specifics of a "cap-and-trade" policy framework for water, proposed here, have distinct institutional features, chief among which is that property rights for the purpose of trading or transferring water across different uses would remain with government agencies rather than private firms as is the case in carbon trading. It is important to emphasize up front that the idea being proposed *involves not the allocation of individual private water rights, but rather decentralization to tiers of government* that would make decisions over the allocation of water across competing uses. This idea is consistent with incremental change in the institutional context of MENA countries where decision-making over the allocation of water is generally concentrated in national government agencies (see chapter 3).

This type of arrangement has emerged organically within the extreme water scarce context of the United Arab Emirates. Each of the federated emirates has jurisdiction over its own water resources and long-term financing of the water sector. This arrangement was originally related to their federated structure, with the "cap" being the requirement to manage water within their own means, which today is overseen by the Federal Ministry of Energy and Infrastructure. The requirement for each emirate to resolve the problem of reconciling the competing claims on water by agriculture and cities led to diversity in the long-term water sector financing models as well as cooperation among the emirates. Despite some degree of unsustainable use of groundwater, withdrawals have been falling as more has been invested in reusing treated wastewater for agriculture—a sector that has been growing since 2010.[2] The diversity in long-term water sector financing models is seen by comparing Dubai with Abu Dhabi. Whereas the Dubai Electricity and Water Authority pursues full cost recovery and is one of the few utilities borrowing from international financial markets, the utility in Abu Dhabi is financed through a combination of tariffs and general taxation. Cooperation among the emirates, the "trade" element, is seen in the way Abu Dhabi imports water from the northern emirates and in a series of memorandums of understanding for strategic water connections enabling the exchange of water, in case of emergencies, between Dubai and Abu Dhabi as well as between Dubai and the northern emirates.[3]

The approach to institutional reforms in this chapter comes from thinking about water allocation decisions as tasks assigned to different government agents within the interdependent principal-agent framework laid out in chapter 6, as well as building and further developing the arrangements that have emerged organically in the United Arab Emirates. The key idea is to assign responsibility and authority over different aspects of water allocation on the basis of variation in informational advantages across agents. The principle is the same as the one being used in carbon emission abatement policies of cap and trade: to enable those agents with more information and expertise on how to reduce carbon emissions to do so in lowest-cost ways. However, the execution of the principle—of giving decision-making power to agents according to their information advantage—would be substantially different in the case of the water sector. In water, and especially in the institutional context of MENA, the proposed policy relies on agents within government as representatives of the people both to devise the caps using climate and water science and to decide whether and where to engage in trade/exchange of water.[4]

Local governments, as representatives of the communities they serve, would employ decentralized information about the relative value of water to farmers and urban residents within their jurisdictions to identify potential gains from trade. National government agencies would set the "caps" to which each local government would need to adhere. Aggregate "macro" calculations about the status of water resources in a country, and the science of its sustainability into the future, can be used to set limits, or caps, on the amounts of water that can be consumed, abstracted, and polluted by different local jurisdictions. These caps would be enshrined in a national water strategy, through which national ministries would hold local government authorities accountable for adhering to national regulations over water use. Local government authorities, in turn, would be empowered to enter into trade with each other, using their water entitlement under the national strategy as a starting point. Constituents would hold local governments accountable for their performance in managing these water entitlements, including identifying any opportunities for gains from trade in water between and within local government areas. This arrangement builds on the principle of subsidiarity, which has long been discussed in the water sector (UNEP and WMO 1992), in two explicit ways: (1) by putting the local political process at the center of decision-making on trade-offs in water allocation across different water-consuming sectors within a local jurisdiction (rather than focusing on users in a subsector, such as irrigation), and (2) by allowing amounts above/below the cap to be traded or exchanged with other local jurisdictions.[5]

Like the principle of "cap and trade" that is applied in carbon abatement policies, the idea proposed above is rooted in economic logic. Just as the application of cap and trade in energy markets has resulted in both successes and failures and depends on a variety of conditions in energy markets, so too is variation to be expected in the application of the logic to water. Outcomes of water management under the local government cap-and-trade framework proposed here would depend on the actual behavior and performance of local government agents. The key to whether good outcomes are obtained depends on the capacity of local government officials and the functioning of local politics. If local political contestation yielded leaders who protested the caps imposed, or who captured the water entitlements to benefit local elites while leaving their constituents impoverished and insecure, the state would remain in its existing predicament. Even with well-intentioned local leaders, local governments may lack the basic capacity to undertake the new tasks assigned to them.

The idea is for focused policy attention to harness the *potential* of local political markets, where forces of contestation are already at play, to yield high-quality local leaders who can employ local information to achieve legitimacy and economic efficiency. Focused policy attention would also be needed to build the capacity of local government organizations. The failure of conventional top-down approaches, the persistent and growing problem of water scarcity, and the rise in public protests and social unrest have created a need to engage with new ideas. This chapter offers such ideas and is cognizant of the pitfalls and challenges to taking up these ideas and the need for tailoring them to specific country contexts.

Before presenting ideas for how to harness the potential of local leaders, table 11.1 lays out the proposed cap-and-trade framework for water in MENA. The framework is organized along the lines of the required "tasks" in managing water allocation and arguments for which types of government agencies are likely to have an informational advantage to undertake the tasks successfully. The output expected of each agency is described from the perspective of managing water in sustainable and welfare-improving ways. As table 11.1 shows, there is a simultaneous need for strong, national-level agencies as well as decentralization of some parts of the water management tasks to representative local governments.

Table 11.1 Assigning tasks according to the informational advantages of different types of government agencies

Task	Information needed to the perform task	Type of government agency with informational advantage	Output expected
Understanding the "water balance" and the overall restrictions on water consumption that are needed to sustain the resource into the future	Highly specialized scientific information about climate, temperature, precipitation patterns, and other external conditions that shape the availability of water	Autonomous national technical agency	Credible information about the state of water resources. Credibility would be derived from the extent to which the agency functions according to technical expertise and is *not* tasked with allocation decisions (which are inherently political).
Developing a national water strategy—how much the country would invest in water infrastructure, how it would finance the infrastructure, where the infrastructure would be located, and how the country would negotiate transboundary water treaties	National information about internal budgets, ability to borrow in international markets and attract foreign assistance, and geopolitics of transboundary negotiations	National water ministry, drawing authority from the highest source of political power	Caps—water entitlement—available to each local government area within a country. Selection of the level of local government to be specific to country context. Selection on the principle of the lowest-level existing local government jurisdiction that encompasses at least one city and at least some agricultural areas. Selection matches local government with the infrastructure nodes through which water can reach the places and people they represent. Caps assigned in the context of those nodes. National ministries can design the water "market" tailored to their institutional context where local governments exist, where water infrastructure exists for local government caps to be established and monitored, and any trade between local governments to be effected. Delegation to the technical agency the task of monitoring and measuring local government compliance with caps. Delegation to local governments the tasks of managing the allocation of water within their caps. Communication of the strategy to the people through media and local government townhall meetings.

(table continues on next page)

Task	Information needed to the perform task	Type of government agency with informational advantage	Output expected
Deciding how the water from available sources (groundwater, surface water, and nonconventional water) is distributed across places and people in the reach of that node	Local information about the relative value of water across competing uses Local information about whether others are likely to comply with restrictions (information pertinent for legitimacy)	Local governments representing the places and people in the reach of that node	Local decisions about water allocation to farmers, industries, and cities through local political processes and town hall meetings. Local decisions about selling any part of water entitlement to another local government or buying additional water from another local government. Quantity restrictions (quotas) on water supply for irrigation and across farms devised by the ministry of agriculture—monitored and enforced by local government. Quantity restrictions on water supply to households devised by utilities—local government to win compliance of citizens.

Source: Original table for this publication.

Furthermore, the tasks of managing water as a resource and allocating it across competing uses are interdependent and thus also require coordination across multiple government agencies.

TENSION BETWEEN THE SCIENCE BEHIND THE WATER BALANCE AND THE POLITICAL PROCESS OF SETTING LIMITS

Overarching macro-level decisions on the availability of water resources in a country require highly specialized or scientific information about "the state of nature." In economics, this phrase is used to describe a variety of conditions that are exogenous to or outside the control of an agent and that are varying and uncertain. In the case of water, the phrase quite literally translates into the state of the climate, temperature, precipitation patterns, and other external conditions that shape the availability of water and the water needs of the environment. A crucial "task" in shaping water policies thus falls in the domain of agents who are technical experts—water scientists and engineers—and can work with global experts to provide information about the caps or limits being imposed on countries through forces outside their control—climate and nature. Empowering national-level technical agencies to perform this task—of ascertaining the characteristics of the water balance or how much water is likely to be available in different parts of the country, and how its consumption needs to be regulated to sustain the resource into the future—is the first step of the "cap-and-trade" idea proposed here.

To build legitimacy for water regulations at the local level, credible water accounting information is needed about the country's water resources. For credible information to be generated, the national agency tasked with assessing the state of water resources needs to be apolitical, with credibility derived from the extent to which the agency functions according to technical expertise—for example, with appointments and recruitment into the agency and promotions to leadership positions driven by technical peer reviews. With a few exceptions, such agencies appear to be missing in the MENA landscape. This report makes a case for their establishment as a crucial part of tackling the water crisis in the region.

As set out in chapter 7, experience from other parts of the world confirms that setting limits is the first step toward water allocation reform (Garrick and Hahn 2021; OECD 2015). Limits on abstraction refer to policies or practices that restrict water withdrawals. Three main types of limits can be identified:

1. Explicit caps with specifications for the volume and timing of withdrawals
2. Quotas that function as implicit caps for user groups
3. Moratoriums on building new withdrawal infrastructure

Although the limits are generally set at the basin or aquifer scale (a hydrological or hydrogeological unit), the role of enforcement and accountability for operating within that limit falls to jurisdictions (political/ administrative entities) rather than technical or administrative water institutions (see chapter 7).

This discrepancy brings to the fore the separate and distinct tasks of (1) providing independent scientific advice and information on what the limits are, and (2) recognizing the often highly politicized nature of water allocation decisions. For example, in Australia, the Murray-Darling Basin Authority's 2010 assessment of sustainable diversion limits was based on independent scientific advice (MDBA 2010). However, given the protests following the release of the 2010 Guide, there was a political response to secure a compromise across competing interests to ensure passage of the 2012 Basin Plan (Grafton 2019). Although determination of the sustainable diversion limit was based on scientific understanding, winning compliance from protesters forced a political decision to set environmental flows below the volume needed to sustain healthy freshwater ecosystems. Grafton enumerates a long list of governance failures leading to this decision, but he also offers insights about managing the trade-offs between water for irrigation and the environment. In this iterative process, past actions are scrutinized and modified on the basis of new evidence and a decision-making process that includes a genuine participatory process with all the relevant stakeholders, not just irrigators. The solution Grafton proposes is neither to vest political decisions with science nor to hand science to the political process, but rather to provide each with oxygen and make the tension transparent.

Credible information about the state of water resources is needed at all scales, from local to transboundary. Information is key for tackling new sources of transboundary tensions over water. Wheeler et al. (2020), for example, discuss how perceptions about water scarcity in a nation may be erroneously shaped by nationalistic media that distort the impact of neighboring countries' water infrastructure. To reach cooperative solutions for mutually beneficial outcomes, politically independent technical agencies in countries can play an important role in providing credible information. Striking water allocation agreements requires that trust be built among citizens about the sources of water problems. Whether at the subnational scale or at the transboundary scale, autonomous technical agencies that provide credible information about the status of water resources (in collaboration with relevant scientific communities) are a crucial signal for winning compliance and getting agreements to stick.

EMPOWERING LOCAL LEADERS TO MANAGE WATER ALLOCATION DECISIONS AND TRADE-OFFS

In contrast to the missing autonomous technical agency, chapter 3 outlined the rise in politically powerful national ministries to manage water and the fading role of local governments in the management of water. Chapter 7 described how the many competing demands on water are not fully under the control of these ministries, which forces them to focus on supply-side interventions. The chapter also showed that forming national-level, cross-government institutions for water allocation has the advantage that it acknowledges that various sectors influence water use and help align incentives and solve the principal-agent problems between political leaders and public officials. However, given the hydrological variability across countries, particularly larger countries, there may be advantages to delegating these politically difficult decisions to local governments.

Compared to top-down directives from national ministries, local decision-making by farmers and urban residents through their representatives in local governments is more likely to lend legitimacy to difficult trade-offs in the use of water between agriculture and the water supply and sanitation sector. Empowering local leaders in the policy area of managing their capped allocations of water, along with strengthening institutions of contestability for new leaders to emerge, can enable a shift in the equilibrium of low trust in society and government to a higher trust equilibrium. Such a shift is implied by available research on how contestation among local leaders on platforms of local public goods can serve to coordinate expectations for higher performance (Acemoglu and Jackson 2015; Bidner and Francois 2013; Ostrom 2000).

Jordan, a country that typifies the way centralized state ministries have been deciding how to allocate water, provides a useful illustration. The objective of Jordanian state policy in the 1960s was to develop the Highlands region and help settle Bedouins there, through irrigated agriculture. Molle and Closas (2016, 69–70) provide a striking description of how this overarching state policy, combined with traditional land rights, encouraged agriculture to grow in the Highlands, depleted groundwater resources, increased salinity, and destroyed wetlands. Without taking an economic stance on whether this water use has been efficient, or even on whether the depletion of resources and environmental damage represent a trade-off willingly made by society, the current policy on the table is to reduce the abstraction of groundwater in Azraq.

The illustration first assumes that the amount of reduction—the overall size of the quantity restriction on groundwater abstraction—is given by some combination of the science and physics of water and a trade-off that the centralized decision-maker is willing to make. Next, the illustration applies the logic of the interdependent principal-agent relationships to understand how any policy with the goal of reducing groundwater abstraction in Azraq would likely play out. Citizens—farmers in the Highlands—would need to comply with quantity restrictions on how much groundwater they can abstract. The notion of "legitimacy" comes into the analysis through citizens' attitudes toward these policies, and their behavior (whether to comply, abstract water illegally, protest, or other). National policy makers and their external partners can obtain ideas on how to build legitimacy—compliance with water abstraction restrictions, as opposed to protests and illegal flouting of rules—from the economics of institutions. Economic and game theoretic analysis of strategic interaction among large numbers of "players," grouped by level of formal and informal decision-making power, yields these ideas.

Legitimacy can be defined in a game theory framework as the ability of leaders to win compliance with new laws or public orders because of widespread beliefs among people that everyone is complying. Beliefs about how others are behaving are key in this view of legitimacy, making new laws and regulations easier to enforce. For example, Akerlof (2017) models how the legitimacy of an authority in any complex organization can enable the authority to get agents to follow rules simply by announcing them. It does so because agents incur costs—such as social sanctions from peers—if they do not comply with rules announced by legitimate authorities, whereas they face no such costs if they do not comply with rules announced by authorities who lack legitimacy. Akerlof (2017) links his economic modeling of legitimacy to insights in the sociology and political science literature. He cites Blau (1964) as arguing that, in the absence of legitimacy, rules will be disobeyed because coercive power alone can lead to resistance. He also quotes from Ostrom (1990) that "the legitimacy of rules...will reduce the costs of monitoring, and [its] absence will increase [the] costs" (Akerlof 2017, S158).

Legitimacy arising from beliefs about the behavior of others can also be specific to rules or laws. A view of legitimacy as a rule-specific attribute is consistent with legal scholarly and philosophical tradition examining compliance with laws (Basu and Cordella 2018; Hart 1961). Recent work on law and economics reexamines the puzzle of why developing countries have laws on paper that are not effectively implemented (Basu and Cordella 2018; World Bank 2017). Instead of relying on explanations about weak governance, low capacity, and perverse political incentives, Basu and Cordella (2018) argue that a conceptually clearer way of thinking about compliance with a new law is whether the new law changes beliefs about how others are behaving.

The role of decentralization in the policy framework for water offered here uses this game theoretic perspective on legitimacy. Legitimacy depends on beliefs, or *focal points* in the language of game theory, about how others are behaving in political and bureaucratic institutions (see chapter 6). Local politics is a crucial public theater in which people become aware of others' beliefs and behavior toward public good issues and where leaders can create new focal points for coordinated action for the public good.

Ideas that have been tried in the past to win legitimacy and economic efficiency in the water sector focused on the creation of farmer groups—water user associations (WUAs)—that were then tasked with managing themselves. To continue the Jordan case study from Molle and Closas (2016), a farmers' association called the Highland Forum was established through external support from development partners. The association was tasked with devising plans and actions that would both reduce abstraction and not cause hardships (such as by improving water use efficiency, switching crops, and so forth). Regarding the Forum, the paper states, "Most observers are pessimistic about the future of the Forum and farmers in particular have the feeling that a lot of time has been spent in vain" (Molle and Closas 2016, 71).

There are at least two rationales for moving away from the policies of WUAs, which are institutions imposed from outside by external partners[6] and include only farmers as members, and toward general purpose local governments that are homegrown institutions and selected by local citizens across rural farming households and urban nonfarming households:

1. Institutions of participation, such as the Highland Forum, have not evolved endogenously from prior institutions of water sharing and collective decision-making among farmers. Research has shown that trust and legitimacy are more likely to come from organic or homegrown institutions (Dal Bó, Foster, and Putterman 2010; World Bank 2016).
2. Farmer institutions are sector specific, representing only farmers, and thus are not suited to address larger resource allocation problems, which involve other sectors. For example, farmers cannot make policy decisions that spur the growth of nonfarm income-earning opportunities, but such decisions may be the most effective path to reducing the use of water in agriculture.

The direction of policy proposed in this chapter is to take the example of the Highland Forum, as a WUA, and apply its tasks to local government. The change is crucial and substantial because it would empower an institution that is broadly representative of local society, including farmers and nonfarmers, rather than an institution that represents only farmers, as has been the case with WUAs.[7] Furthermore, by design, local government agencies are supposed to be responsible for local "public goods," within a national policy framework, beyond any one area such as water. This general purpose role and the broadly representative structure of local government contains the potential for building legitimacy through local political processes. This potential could be harnessed through a national water strategy, including strategically designed local communication campaigns around current water allocations and water balance, and complementary social protection policies for distressed farmers. A large body of evidence has shown that communication can work to nourish forces of local political contestation to strengthen incentives and norms in government for public good policies.[8] The argument is that this direction can potentially be transformative, by shifting how the state functions not only in devising and implementing water policies, but also more broadly. Strengthening local political contestation using the critical water sector in MENA has the potential to address the three key mechanisms of state capacity for bringing about economic transformation (Khemani 2019):

1. Accountability (incentives)
2. Selection of leaders (intrinsic motivation)
3. Norms (legitimacy and trust)

Consultation and engagement with country officials, think tanks, citizens, survey-based evidence on local institutions, and policy experiments (if and where there is a window of opportunity) are needed to evaluate whether this idea can work by getting local governments to do what WUAs could not. The potential effect of these ideas may go beyond water sector agencies to other areas of service delivery that affect water use in agriculture, such as by creating opportunities for nonfarm income that move the next generation of households out of agriculture. The potential extends to the role of cities as drivers of "green growth," investing in urban infrastructure and building architecture to conserve water. It also extends to raising general revenues through urban property taxation, which builds state fiscal capacity to invest in national water infrastructure.

A powerful lesson also emerges for external partners. When it comes to the water sector, supply-side, project-based development assistance may simply delay finding sustainable demand-side solutions. Incentives in external partner organizations skewed toward financing supply-side capital expenditure projects mean that too much effort may go toward constructing water infrastructure rather than addressing policy frameworks and legitimacy to regulate water use. Correspondingly, too little effort may go toward other ways in which external partners can bring value to developing countries to manage water, such as investing in hydrological and financial data and transparency, strengthening the credibility of politically independent national technical agencies, building the capacity and accountability of local governments to make local decisions on water allocations, and understanding how local institutions can be designed to help the millions of agents (irrigators, firms, and frontline utility workers) facing the difficult trade-offs of allocating scarce water.

NOTES

1. Water auditing goes a step further than water accounting by placing trends in water supply, demand, accessibility, and use in the broader context of governance, institutions, public and private expenditure, laws, and the wider political economy of water in specified domains (Batchelor et al. 2017; FAO 2020).

2. The United Arab Emirates' agricultural gross value added was US$3.30 billion in 2020, 50 percent higher than that of Jordan (US$1.98 billion), a country of similar land area and population (World Development Indicators).

3. Dubai and Abu Dhabi Memorandum of Understanding (2017) and Dubai and United Arab Emirate's Federal National Council Memorandum of Understanding (2019), referenced in ITAC (2021).

4. Chapter 1 of the report explained how the economics of water leads to an inescapable role of the state, or government intervention, because of the challenges of establishing property rights, pricing externalities that are nonmarginal and global in nature, and accounting for the characteristics of a natural monopoly in water investments.

5. Any potential for gainful trade between or even within local government areas would depend on the availability of hydrological infrastructure to address flow constraints. Much more country context–specific work is needed to understand whether there are potential gains from trade (for example, by estimating whether the marginal productivity of water in agriculture varies substantially across a country's geography). This chapter lays out a framework for thinking about the role of local governments and focusing on the problem of legitimacy, while relegating the potential for trade in water for future work to examine.

6. Mustafa, Altz-Stamm, and Scott (2016) provide a case study of this "imposition" and its consequences for how WUAs function in Jordan.

7. These rationales can be further expanded by bringing in examples from the United States (California) of what not to do. Irrigation districts (akin to WUAs)—established in California at a time when water was abundant and promoting agriculture in the West was a policy goal—have become a constraint to welfare-enhancing trade of water in California from farmers to growing urban populations. The reason is the high transaction costs embedded in existing institutions of irrigation districts, where any one farmer can hold up a water transfer (Bretsen and Hill 2009). Leonard, Costello, and Libecap (2019, 47) write, "...irrigation districts were designed to solve allocation problems within, but not between, their memberships, further complicating the transaction costs of trading either out of basin or with urban and environmental users who are not members of irrigation organizations."

8. World Bank (2016) provides a review of the evidence. A powerful example comes from the impact of town hall meetings examined by Fujiwara and Wantchekon (2013) in Africa.

REFERENCES

Acemoglu, D., and M. O. Jackson. 2015. "History, Expectations, and Leadership in the Evolution of Social Norms." *Review of Economic Studies* 82 (1): 1–34.

Akerlof, R., 2017. "The Importance of Legitimacy." *World Bank Economic Review* 30 (Supplement_1): S157–S165.

Basu, K., and T. Cordella, 2018. *Institutions, Governance and the Control of Corruption.* Palgrave Macmillan.

Batchelor, C., J. Hoogeveen, J.-M. Faures, and L. Peiser. 2017. *Water Accounting and Auditing: A Sourcebook.* FAO Water Report 43. Rome: Food and Agriculture Organization of the United Nations. www.fao.org/3/a-i5923e .pdf.

Bidner, C., and P. Francois. 2013. "The Emergence of Political Accountability." *Quarterly Journal of Economics* 128 (3): 1397–1448.

Blau, P. M. 1964. "Justice in Social Exchange." *Sociological Inquiry*, 34: 193–206. https://doi.org/10.1111/j.1475 -682X.1964.tb00583.x.

Bretsen, S. N., and P. J. Hill. 2009. "Water Markets as Tragedy of the Anticommons." *William & Mary Environmental Law and Policy Review* 33 (3): 723–83. https://scholarship.law.wm.edu/wmelpr/vol33/iss3/3.

Dal Bó, P., A. Foster, and L. Putterman. 2010. "Institutions and Behavior: Experimental Evidence on the Effects of Democracy." *American Economic Review* 100 (5): 2205–29.

FAO (Food and Agriculture Organization of the United Nations). 2020. *The State of Food and Agriculture 2020: Overcoming Water Challenges in Agriculture.* Rome: FAO. https://doi.org/10.4060/cb1447en.

Fujiwara, T., and L. Wantchekon. 2013. "Can Informed Public Deliberation Overcome Clientelism? Experimental Evidence from Benin." *American Economic Journal: Applied Economics* 5 (4): 241–55. https://doi .org/10.1257/app.5.4.241.

Garrick, D. E., and R. W. Hahn. 2021. "An Economic Perspective on Water Security." *Review of Environmental Economics and Policy* 15 (1). https://doi.org/10.1086/713102.

Ghazouani, W., F. Molle, and E. Rap. 2012. "Water Users Associations in the Near-East Northern Africa Region: IFAD Interventions and Overall Dynamics." Project Report Submitted to the International Fund for Agricultural Development by the International Water Management Institute, Colombo, Sri Lanka.

Grafton, R. Q. 2019. "Policy Review of Water Reform in the Murray-Darling Basin, Australia: The 'Do's' and 'Do'nots.'" *Australian Journal of Agricultural and Resource Economics* 63 (1): 116–41. https://doi.org/10.1111/1467 -8489.12288.

Hart, H. L. A. 1961. *The Concept of Law*, second edition. London: Oxford University Press.

ITAC (International Technical Assistance Consultants). 2021. "A Description of the Institutional Setup of the Water Sector in the United Arab Emirates." Consultancy report, World Bank, Washington, DC.

Khemani, S. 2019. "What Is State Capacity?" Policy Research Working Paper 8734, World Bank, Washington, DC. https://openknowledge.worldbank.org/handle/10986/31266.

Leonard, B., C. Costello, and G. D. Libecap. 2019. "Expanding Water Markets in the Western United States: Barriers and Lessons from Other Natural Resource Markets." *Review of Environmental Economics and Policy* 13 (1): 43–61. https://www.journals.uchicago.edu/doi/10.1093/reep/rey014.

Loucks, D. P., and E. van Beek. 2017. "Water Resources Planning and Management: An Overview." In *Water Resource Systems Planning and Management*, 1–49. Cham, Switzerland: Springer. https://doi.org/10.1007/978-3 -319-44234-1_1.

MDBA (Murray-Darling Basin Authority). 2010. *Guide to the Proposed Basin Plan*, Technical Background Volume 1 Overview. Canberra, Australia: MDBA.

Molle, F. 2008. "Why Enough Is Never Enough: The Societal Determinants of River Basin Closure." *International Journal of Water Resource Development* 24 (2): 247–56. https://doi.org/10.1080/07900620701723646.

Molle, F., and A. Closas. 2016. *Groundwater Governance in the Middle East and North Africa*. IMWI Project Report No. 1. Colombo, Sri Lanka: International Water Management Institute.

Molle, F., and A. Closas. 2020. "Why Is State-Centered Groundwater Governance Largely Ineffective? A Review." *Wiley Interdisciplinary Reviews: Water* 7 (1): e1395. https://doi.org/10.1002/wat2.1395.

Mustafa, D., A. Altz-Stamm, and L. M. Scott. 2016. "Water User Associations and the Politics of Water in Jordan." *World Development* 79: 164–76. https://doi.org/10.1016/j.worlddev.2015.11.008.

OECD (Organisation for Economic Co-operation and Development). 2015. *Water Resources Allocation: Sharing Risks and Opportunities*. OECD Studies on Water. Paris: OECD Publishing. http://dx.doi.org /10.1787/9789264229631-en.

Ostrom, E. 1990. *Governing the Commons: The Evolution of Institutions for Collective Action*. Cambridge: Cambridge University Press.

Ostrom, E. 2000. "Collective Action and the Evolution of Social Norms." *Journal of Economic Perspectives* 14 (3): 137–58. https://www.aeaweb.org/articles?id=10.1257/jep.14.3.137.

UNEP and WMO (United Nations Environment Programme and World Meteorological Organization). 1992. *International Conference on Water and the Environment: Development Issues for the 21st Century*. Nairobi, Kenya: UNEP. https://wedocs.unep.org/20.500.11822/30961.

Wheeler, K. G., M. Jeuland, J. W. Hall, E. Zagona, and D. Whittington. 2020. "Understanding and Managing New Risks on the Nile with the Grand Ethiopian Renaissance Dam." *Nature Communications* 11: 5222. https:// doi.org/10.1038/s41467-020-19089-x.

World Bank. 2016. *Making Politics Work for Development: Harnessing Transparency and Citizen Engagement*. Washington, DC: World Bank Group. http://documents.worldbank.org/curated/en/268021467831470443 /Making-politics-work-for-development-harnessing-transparency-and-citizen-engagement.

World Bank. 2017. *World Development Report 2017: Governance and the Law*. Washington, DC: World Bank. https://openknowledge.worldbank.org/handle/10986/25880.

World Bank. 2020. "Iraq Water Resources Planning and Investments Analysis." World Bank, Washington, DC.

World Bank. Forthcoming. *The Dynamic of Groundwater Uses in Morocco*. Washington, DC: World Bank.

CHAPTER 12

Communication as a Necessary Complement to Water Policy Reforms

INTRODUCTION

Water played an important role in strengthening the legitimacy of political parties or systems in the Middle East and North Africa (MENA) in the 1960s and 1970s. During this period, governments reshaped the "water environment" as a symbol of the rise of the region. Nowadays, leaders still see assuring water availability—water security—as an important source of legitimacy; however, states have struggled to adapt to emerging and diffuse water issues, which require governance rather than infrastructure solutions (for example, managing pollution, environmental protection, private sector involvement, and nongovernmental stakeholder participation).

This report has shown how problems of water allocation can be explained as arising from the beliefs and expectations of a large number of actors—within utilities and ministries, and in society (citizens, whether urban dwellers or farmers). These beliefs and expectations can be summarized using the language of game theory:

- Lack of legitimacy for winning compliance with price and quantity regulations to address the negative externality in water consumption
- Lack of trust within public sector agencies that peers/others are motivated to find innovative ways of improving outcomes even within existing constraints

Strategic communication has been identified as the means to transition intentionally from situations of low trust in society to higher levels of trust. This chapter shows how purposefully designed communication campaigns are a necessary complement to other water policy reforms. It describes how countries might use communication, in the context of their political and bureaucratic institutions, to build trust—particularly in addressing the common pool resource problem—which is central to water management in MENA.

USING COMMUNICATION TO SHIFT BELIEFS AND EXPECTATIONS

The leaders and people of MENA know they are in a water crisis (Inglehart et al. 2014) or can expect to be in one in the near future, like their neighbors. Strategic communication is necessary to shift beliefs and expectations about how others are behaving, which in turn changes an individual's own behavior, moving society from a low-level equilibrium of lack of legitimacy and trust to a higher-level equilibrium in which individuals comply with water regulations (legitimacy) and public officials work together on solutions (with trust in each other).

The experience of the COVID-19 pandemic starting around March 2020 provides an example of how communication suddenly shifted, or "shocked," beliefs and expectations, leading to unexpected high levels of compliance with public health regulations in countries with low levels of trust to start (Khemani 2020). Although the specifics of what was being communicated were peculiar to COVID-19—new information about a new life-threatening disease—the initial ability of many countries with low levels of trust and legitimacy nevertheless to win compliance with new regulations is instructive and supportive of game theoretic insights (Padidar et al. 2021).[1]

In game theoretic models of how transition happens in public institutions, information and communication that shift expectations about how others are behaving are a necessary element (Khemani 2019). In some models, information is communicated through the types of leaders selected (Acemoglu and Jackson 2015). In others, information is gathered and shared over time among citizens through the experience of political participation (Bidner and Francois 2013). For any problem in which norms support a less than desirable outcome, shifting to a new norm requires information sharing and communication among the actors to update their beliefs about how others are behaving. The role of political leaders and processes of political participation as the channels for sharing information that shifts norms in public sector agencies is consistent with classical work on norms for collective action (Ostrom 2000).

Theoretical analysis of how changes in norms come about points to a triggering role for political contestation and the leaders selected through it. Leaders can play this role as "prominent agents" who signal a shift in beliefs among society at large (Acemoglu and Jackson 2015). Growing experience with political engagement and the learning that comes from it, such as through frustration and indignation with bad outcomes, can create fertile conditions for change in political norms (Bidner and Francois 2013). Recent theoretical developments on the management of complex organizations generally, both in the private and public sectors, also point to the role of leaders in shaping organizational culture. For example, Akerlof (2015, 2017) defines the concept of "legitimacy" as leaders getting lower-level personnel to follow the organization's objectives of their own accord, through peer-to-peer interaction, without incentive payments and monitoring from the top.

The following sections offer ideas for reform leaders in countries on how to design communication strategies to complement other reforms for managing the problem of water in MENA in the following areas:

- The role of local political leaders in winning legitimacy and public acceptance of water regulations and restrictions
- The use of the process of developing national water policies to reshape norms of water allocation and use

THE ROLE OF LOCAL POLITICAL LEADERS IN WINNING PUBLIC ACCEPTANCE AND LEGITIMACY FOR REDUCING WATER CONSUMPTION

As chapter 9 explained, local governments have a role in building legitimacy through the communication that happens in communities during the process of local political contestation for leadership positions. As the first mile of government—through which leaders such as local councilors and mayors are selected and sanctioned—local governments have strong incentives to address local concerns, including that of water. Using communication channels, such as town halls and community meetings complemented with social media, provides opportunities to share information on water scarcity; the costs of supply-side investments to increase water resources, such as through desalination; and the problem of unsustainable use.

In São Paulo, Brazil, South America's largest city and home to 20 million people, elevated temperatures and lack of rain in 2014 caused the worst water crisis in over 80 years. In tandem with various utility measures—water transfers from agriculture, pressure management, and leakage reduction—a communication campaign worked with communities and local leaders to explain the gravity of the situation and promote water savings. Across 39 municipal authorities, workshops on water saving were run with government entities and nongovernmental organizations. As part of the communication campaign, the utility promoted a bonus program that gave consumers who reduced consumption by over 20 percent a 30 percent discount on their water bill. As a result, over 70 percent of customers cut their water consumption by over 10 percent (Cathala, Núñez, and Rios 2018).

In South Africa, the "Day Zero" campaign in response to the 2016–18 drought that Cape Town experienced provides an example of local government action to win public acceptance of stringent restrictions on water use. Before the drought, average households in freestanding houses with a private water connection used 183 liters per person per day. As storage levels of the Big Six Western Cape Water Supply System dams fell, the city authority put in place a series of tariff increases, restrictions, and communication campaigns with the aim of reducing consumption to 50 liters per person per day. Together the measures more than halved the level of per capita water use, to 84 liters per person per day.

Using regression results, Brühl and Visser (2021) show how the various measures that were put in place correlate with reductions in water use. These results point to the significant contributions of the communication campaign in reducing consumption. The most effective "nudges" were those that officially recognized households' conservation efforts and those that asked households to save water because it was in the public interest. The city also used the threat of penalties, sending letters to households using more than 50 cubic meters per month; these letters showed their use compared to the average Cape Town household and warned them that continued use at this level would result in the installation of water-restricting devices.

Transparency and public trust were built by sharing detailed and timely information about the water crisis through the "Water Dashboard," which gave weekly updates about total water usage in Cape Town, the city's augmentation plans, the dam levels, and the approaching "Day Zero" date. It was considered a turning point in the campaign when the mayor predicted that April 21, 2018, would be "Day Zero." The international press coverage shocked residents with the imminence of the crisis, shifting responsibility from the city to the residents, who were asked to reduce usage still further. In the same month, the city launched the Water Map, a website showing all the freestanding residential households that were complying with the water restrictions. The aim was to show residents how well their neighborhood was complying and to motivate them to reduce usage even further (Brühl and Visser 2021).

In Israel, a 2008 public awareness campaign was used to promote water conservation among domestic households, public buildings, and government offices. It encouraged the installation of water-saving devices in bathrooms, toilets, and kitchens. The campaign used well-known people to promote the messages and solicited feedback from focus groups as well as polls to monitor the campaign's impact and continuously adjust its methods. The communication campaign proved to be cost effective. Although it cost US$7.5 million, it reduced consumption by 76 million cubic meters, and it was estimated to have freed up water for alternative uses at a cost of only US$0.10 per cubic meter. This campaign was run in parallel with a near doubling of water tariffs—helping to offset increases in the overall amount consumers would pay per month. Together these reform measures reduced urban water consumption per capita by 24 percent, to less than 100 liters per capita per day (Marin et al. 2017).

Turning to an irrigation-specific example, in Mozambique, experimental information campaigns on water use efficiency were shown to shift norms in water use patterns, reducing conflict among farmers. Management of common pool resources in the absence of individual pricing can lead to apparent water scarcity even when there is sufficient water to meet the total scheme requirements. In this specific context of Central Mozambique, farmers growing multiple rotations of horticultural crops throughout the year used surface irrigation water during the dry season. Before the experiment, a significant proportion of the farmers tended to overwater at earlier stages of the crop cycle, jeopardizing the amount of water available at later stages when water requirements are at their peak. When farmers were provided information to help them avoid overwatering crops in the early stages of the crop cycle, this additional knowledge shifted behaviors significantly, reducing the proportion of farmers across a scheme who self-reported having insufficient water. It also reduced the number of water-related conflicts in an irrigation scheme, compared to before the information campaign (Christian et al. 2018).

Winning legitimacy for water use restrictions might also involve creative and entertaining advertising and mass media communication (World Bank 2015). When a tunnel providing water to the city of Bogotá, Colombia, partially collapsed in 1997, triggering a water shortage, the city government declared a public emergency and initiated a communication program to invite inhabitants to use less water. The campaign relied on religious leaders and priests who were explicitly tasked with informing their communities about the need to save water. The campaign also involved a "name and blame" approach: people caught wasting water were forced to attend water conservation workshops and faced one-day punitive water cuts. Additionally, the city government launched entertaining campaigns to show how to reduce water consumption. For example, the mayor (Antanas Mockus) appeared in a television advertisement while taking a shower with his wife, explaining how the tap could be turned off while soaping, and suggesting taking showers in pairs.

Common to many of these examples is their reliance on local political leaders to play a key role in communicating water-related information to win public acceptance and legitimacy for reducing water consumption. This active use of hydrological information can also apply to excess water and to national-level political leaders who are "local" to a common river basin. In the Western Balkans, the five countries within the Sava River Basin jointly developed a river flood forecasting system (International Sava River Basin Commission 2019). The system acts as a communication platform for coordinated flood forecasting and early warning, which needs to be based on hydrological rather than national boundaries to be fully effective and informative. In this example, strategic communication through a flood forecasting and warning system helps countries' political leaders to enhance preparedness for water disasters and optimize flood mitigation measures.

The "local" nature of politicians can usefully be thought of as relative to hydrological planning units, which in MENA combine conventional water basins and nonconventional water systems.

USING NATIONAL WATER STRATEGIES TO RESHAPE NORMS OF WATER ALLOCATION AND USE

The importance of building a societal consensus on the importance of and priorities for water has been a recurring theme of this report. The process of developing national water laws, policies, and strategies presents an opportunity for an open and participatory communication process that can contribute toward building a social consensus by shifting norms even when deep divisions and difficult trade-offs exist.

In post-apartheid South Africa, the government initiated a review of the country's national water laws and strategy. At the start of the review, Minister Kader Asmal explained, "Our [new] Constitution demands this review, on the basis of fairness and equity, values which are enshrined as cornerstones of our new society" (De Coning 2006, 510). The review established a National Water Advisory Council to enable public involvement in the process of formulating water policy. In 1995, public comments were invited on a publication entitled "You and Your Water Rights." Public consultation followed, soliciting comments in workshops around the country, including in rural and poor communities. Establishment of a monitoring committee to consider the responses and recommend principles fed into a process of drafting new legislation, which included legal experts. The participatory and public nature of the process is credited with contributing to shifting norms that enabled the balancing of water allocations for basic human needs, environmental requirements, and international (transboundary) obligations without unfairly prejudicing existing users and user communities. This initiative is respected internationally, yet few such fundamental and far-reaching policy processes have been developed elsewhere in the world (De Coning 2006).

Communication and public outreach have been core elements of Singapore's national water strategy. Although the country is in a part of the world with high rainfall, Singapore's high population density means that renewable water resources per capita are about 100 cubic meters per capita per year—comparable to per capita resources Jordan. Development of the national water strategy involved the public at multiple stages, within Singapore's unique political structure. Public consultations were used, for example, during the preparation of Singapore's Green Plan and for subsequent water planning activities undertaken by the Public Utilities Board (Tortajada, Joshi, and Biswas 2013). Public engagement took place through apolitical civil society organizations that did not directly challenge the government's viewpoint. This process included successes in gaining public acceptance for wastewater reuse. Since the 1990s, Singapore has identified potable water reuse as key to its water security, and it has spent decades planning this scheme, now called NEWater. By the time the project was launched in 2003, comprehensive communication and education efforts on long-term safety and reliability issues, involving the government and other decision-makers, had already been established, contributing to high levels of public acceptance and ownership (Tortajada and van Rensburg 2019).

Conversely, developing national water strategies without public consultation and with only restricted access by senior political and technical personnel can lead to missed opportunities for drawing on the detailed local knowledge of subnational levels of government.

In Iraq, for example, water resources are centrally managed by the Ministry of Water Resources, whose role includes the management of water control structures (such as dams and barrages) along the Euphrates and the Tigris, as well as managing an intricate system of canals (and drains) connecting the two rivers to cities and irrigation systems. Faced with declining quantities of water availability, in 2015 the ministry developed a Strategy for Water and Land Resources of Iraq (the 2015 Strategy). The 2015 Strategy, based on detailed hydrological and engineering analysis,[2] recognized that, as a result of both upstream development in neighboring countries and climate change, the country would fall short of its minimum requirement by at least 10 billion cubic meters per year by 2035. The 2015 Strategy was led and financed by Ministry of Water Resources with external expert advice, but access to the process was restricted to a small number of political leaders and senior public officials. Because of the lack of communication in its final stages and following its development, the 2015 Strategy missed out on the detailed local knowledge of the (then active and influential) provincial councils. Involving governorate-level and other local actors who may have had a more detailed understanding of the benefits and consequences of water (re)allocations could have generated opportunities and synergies not considered by the central planners.

Greater communication with and among subnational entities, including presenting governorate-level water balances, would have facilitated dialogue on managing governorate water resource needs within national limits. It would have offered governorates the scope to reallocate water both within and among governorates. For example, within governorates possibilities might include (1) reallocating water that was originally designated for irrigation to support municipal and industrial uses; (2) leaving irrigated land fallow during droughts so that water could be diverted to cities; (3) using treated wastewater from cities to support irrigation close to cities, return flows to the environment, or irrigate greenbelts; and (4) investing in water substitution with oil companies to promote reusing drainage water pumped from the main agricultural drains for oil fields rather than surface or groundwater sources.

Water reallocation agreements among two or more governorates, potentially facilitated by an investment role for the central government to counterbalance perceived losses, could identify opportunities to reallocate water from relatively water rich governorates to relatively water poor governorates. Examples include (1) changing the operational rules for major dams in the governorates of Erbil, Ninawa, and Sulaymaniyah to provide downstream governorates greater flexibility in their water management; (2) upstream governorates agreeing to forgo building planned hydropower dams in exchange for capital investment in the capture and processing of natural gas for energy use; (3) agreements on the management of large irrigation canals spanning multiple governorates to achieve better balance between irrigation and urban water needs; and (4) federal government investment in nonrevenue water and wastewater treatment programs that would be conditional on reduced levels of future abstraction from groundwater or surface water sources.

Encouraging this type of decentralized stakeholder process can lead to win-win agreements—within or among governorates, the central government, and the private sector—that would both reduce the overall cost and expedite the implementation of an updated Strategy for Water and Land Resources in Iraq. For example, reallocating water that the 2015 Strategy had allocated for the reclamation of new irrigated land would reduce the capital expenditure of more than US$12.5 billion and decrease the water consumed in agriculture by nearly 8 billion cubic meters per year (World Bank 2020).

This chapter has shown how strategic communication, in tandem with other reforms, has been used successfully in a contexts as diverse as Brazil, Colombia, Israel, Mozambique, Singapore, and South Africa. Communication has been pivotal in shifting peoples' expectations of water availability and gaining their trust and cooperation to reduce consumption or reconsider priority uses of water at the societal level. Results such as halving water use in Cape Town, bringing domestic water use to less than 100 liters per capita per day in Israel, and reducing conflict among irrigators in Mozambique are significant demand-side outcomes. The chapter also set out opportunities that countries in MENA can purposely take to build the legitimacy of and trust in demand-side interventions in the water sector. These opportunities represent relatively low-cost options for reducing the pace at which supply-side interventions are needed and would greatly contribute to addressing the water scarcity and financial sustainability challenges of countries across MENA.

NOTES

1. The use of "shock" in community-led total sanitation approaches is familiar to water and health professionals. These approaches encourage local communities to analyze their sanitation conditions and internalize collectively the dire impact of open defecation on the public health of an entire neighborhood. Using participatory appraisal to analyze their practice shocks, disgusts, and shames people, triggering dialogue and collective action to eliminate open defecation by ensuring that everyone is able to build a toilet facility (Kar 2008). This participatory process establishes, the legitimacy of the objective—a healthier community—and trust that everyone in the community will act together. It includes community mechanisms to support the poorest to develop individual solutions to the collective public health problem. Through the community-led total sanitation process, natural leaders often emerge—women, men, youth, schoolchildren, and elderly people—facilitating dialogue and shaping community norms and rules.

2. The data were based on a combination of remote sensing technology, computer modeling, and extensive ground truthing. The Strategy for Water and Land Resources of Iraq field team walked along more than 25,000 kilometers of canals; surveyed 34,754 control structures, 3,733 bridges, and 494 pumps; and interviewed the managers of all of the major water control structures throughout the country.

REFERENCES

Acemoglu, D., and M. Jackson. 2015. "History, Expectations, and Leadership in the Evolution of Social Norms." *Review of Economic Studies* 82 (2): 423–56.

Akerlof, R. 2015. "A Theory of Authority." University of Warwick, United Kingdom.

Akerlof, R. 2017. "The Importance of Legitimacy." *World Bank Economic Review* 30 (Supplement_1): S157–S165.

Bidner, C., and P. Francois. 2013. "The Emergence of Political Accountability." *Quarterly Journal of Economics* 128 (3): 1397–1448.

Brühl, J., and M. Visser. 2021. "The Cape Town Drought: A Study of the Combined Effectiveness of Measures Implemented to Prevent 'Day Zero.'" *Water Resources and Economics* 34: 100177. https://doi.org/10.1016/j.wre.2021.100177.

Cathala, C., A. Núñez, and A. R. Rios. 2018. "Water in the Time of Drought: Lessons from Five Droughts around the World." Policy Brief IDB-PB-295, Inter-American Development Bank, Washington, DC. https://publications.iadb.org/publications/english/document/Water-in-the-time-of-drought-Lessons-from-five-droughts-around-the-world.pdf.

Christian, P., F. Kondylis, V. Mueller, A. Zwager, and T. Siegfried. 2018. "Water When It Counts: Reducing Scarcity through Irrigation Monitoring in Central Mozambique." Policy Research Working Paper 8345, World Bank, Washington, DC.

De Coning, C. 2006. "Overview of the Water Policy Process in South Africa." *Water Policy* 8 (6): 505–28. https://doi.org/10.2166/wp.2006.039.

Inglehart, R., C. Haerpfer, A. Moreno, C. Welzel, K. Kizilova, J. Diez-Medrano, M. Lagos, et al., eds. 2014. "World Values Survey Round Five—Country-Pooled Datafile." JD Systems Institute, Madrid. www.worldvaluessurvey.org/WVSDocumentationWV5.jsp.

International Sava River Basin Commission. 2019. "Flood Management Plan in the Sava River Basin." International Sava River Basin Commission, Zagreb, Croatia. https://www.savacommission.org/UserDocsImages/05_documents_publications/water_management/eng/SavaFRMPlan//sfrmp_eng_web.pdf.

Kar, K. 2008. *Handbook on Community-Led Total Sanitation.* London: Plan UK and Brighton, UK: Institute of Development Studies at the University of Sussex. https://opendocs.ids.ac.uk/opendocs/bitstream/handle/20.500.12413/872/rc314.pdf.

Khemani, S. 2019. "What Is State Capacity?" Policy Research Working Paper 8734, World Bank, Washington, DC. https://documents1.worldbank.org/curated/en/336421549909150048/pdf/WPS8734.pdf.

Khemani, S. 2020. "An Opportunity to Build Legitimacy and Trust in Public Institutions in the Time of COVID-19." Research and Policy Brief 32, World Bank, Washington, DC. https://openknowledge.worldbank.org /handle/10986/33715.

Marin, P., S. Tal, J. Yeres, and K. Ringskog. 2017. "Water Management in Israel: Key Innovations and Lessons Learned for Water-Scarce Countries." World Bank, Washington, DC. https://openknowledge.worldbank.org /handle/10986/2809.

Ostrom, E. 2000. "Collective Action and the Evolution of Social Norms." *Journal of Economic Perspectives* 14 (3): 137–58. https://www.aeaweb.org/articles?id=10.1257/jep.14.3.137.

Padidar, S., S.-M. Liao, S. Magagula, T. A. M. Mahlaba, N. M. Nhlabatsi, and S. Lukas. 2021. "Assessment of Early COVID-19 Compliance to and Challenges with Public Health and Social Prevention Measures in the Kingdom of Eswatini, Using an Online Survey." PLoS ONE 16 (6): e0253954. https://www.aeaweb.org /articles?id=10.1257/jep.14.3.137.

Tortajada, C., Y. K. Joshi, and A. K. Biswas. 2013. *The Singapore Water Story: Sustainable Development in an Urban City State.* Oxfordshire, UK: Routledge.

Tortajada, C., and P. van Rensburg. 2019. "Comment: Drink More Recycled Wastewater." *Nature* 577: 26–28. https://www.nature.com/articles/d41586-019-03913-6.

World Bank. 2015. "Spotlight 5: Promoting Water Conservation in Colombia." In *World Development Report 2015: Mind, Society, and Behavior*, 176–77. Washington, DC: World Bank. https://www.aeaweb.org /articles?id=10.1257/jep.14.3.137.

World Bank. 2020. "Learning Review: World Bank Water Sector Technical Assistance to Iraq FY19–21." Report AUS0002015, World Bank, Washington, DC.

Appendix: Institutions Involved in Developing Supply-Side Infrastructure Versus Institutions Operating and Maintaining Infrastructure

Country or territory	Policy oversight water resources	Policy oversight water supply and sanitation	Bulk infrastructure development	Operation and maintenance	Water supply and sanitation regulator	Subnational deconcentrated units (admin 2)	Municipal units elected councils
Algeria	Ministry of Water Resources (MRE)	Algerian Water Company (AdE), under MRE Centralized management through AdE the National Office of Sanitation, and contracts with the private sector	National Dams and Transfers Agency (ANBT)	AdE ONA Contracts with the private sector	Regulatory Authority of Public Water Services	58 provinces (wilaya) Governors (wali) appointed by the president Provincial assembly elected with some devolved powers, including over agriculture, water, and forestry	1,541 municipalities Council elected by citizens and mayor elected by council Devolved powers for management of hygiene and sanitation
Bahrain	Ministry of Works Ministry of Energy Ministry of Municipalities Affairs and Urban Planning	High Council for Water Resources	Public-private partnerships for desalination	Electricity and Water Authority (water supply) Ministry of Works, Municipalities Affairs and Urban Planning (sanitation)	High Council for Water Resources	4 governorates with governor appointed by the prime minister; each governorate has an elected council	n.a.
Djibouti	Ministry of Agriculture, Water, Fisheries, Livestock and Fish Resources	Ministry of Agriculture, Water, Fisheries, Livestock and Fish Resources	Djibouti National Office of Water and Sanitation (ONEAD)	ONEAD	Ministry of Agriculture, Water, Fisheries, Livestock and Fish Resources	5 regions and Djibouti City divided into 11 districts	20 municipalities

(table continues on next page)

Country or territory	Policy oversight water resources	Policy oversight water supply and sanitation	Bulk infrastructure development	Operation and maintenance	Water supply and sanitation regulator	Subnational deconcentrated units (admin 2)	Municipal units elected councils
Egypt, Arab Rep.	Ministry of Water Resources and Irrigation	Ministry of Housing Utilities & Urban Communities	National Organization for Potable Water & Sanitary Drainage Holding Company for Water and Wastewater	26 water services companies (state-owned enterprises) with 98,500 employees	Cabinet (for example, for tariff changes)	26 governorates; each governor is appointed by the president	Municipal councils closed in 2011; article 180 provides for municipal elections
Iran, Islamic Rep.	Ministry of Energy	Ministry of Energy	National Water and Wastewater Engineering Company	60 companies (state-owned enterprises) with 38,000 employees	National Economic Council	30 provinces; each governor is appointed by the president	1,000-plus urban and 68,000-plus rural municipalities; each mayor is jointly appointed by the Ministry of Interior and an elected council
Iraq	Ministry of Water Resources	Ministry of Public Housing, Municipalities, and Public Works	Ministry of Municipalities for water supply and sanitation (except Baghdad) Ministry of Water Resources (dams)	Ministry of Municipalities (except Baghdad) with 40,000 employees	Cabinet (for example, for tariff changes)	19 governorates, 4 of which are part of the Kurdistan Regional Government	15 elected provincial councils dissolved in 2019; new provincial elections announced to take place in November 2023
Israel	Israeli Water Authority	Israeli Water Authority	Mekorot Water Company Ltd (public)	52 regional water and sewer corporations that serve 132 local authorities	Ministry of Interior and Finance (for water tariffs)	6 administrative districts and 15 subdistricts; each district commissioner is appointed by the Minister of Interior	Local authorities are made up of 73 municipalities, 124 local councils, and 54 regional councils; elections held every 5 years

(table continues on next page)

Country or territory	Policy oversight water resources	Policy oversight water supply and sanitation	Bulk infrastructure development	Operation and maintenance	Water supply and sanitation regulator	Subnational deconcentrated units (admin 2)	Municipal units elected councils
Jordan	Ministry of Water and Irrigation	Ministry of Water and Irrigation	Water Authority of Jordan	Water Authority of Jordan 3 regional companies (state-owned enterprises) with 8,000 employees	Cabinet (for example, for tariff changes)	3 regions and 12 governorates	Municipal councils within governorates elected by local residents
Kuwait	Ministry of Electricity & Water & Renewable Energy	Ministry of Electricity & Water & Renewable Energy	Ministry of Electricity & Water & Renewable Energy	Ministry of Public Works (sanitation)	Ministry of Electricity & Water & Renewable Energy	6 governorates	n.a.
Lebanon	Ministry of Energy and Water	Ministry of Energy and Water	Council for Development and Reconstruction	4 regional Water Establishments (state-owned enterprises)	Cabinet (for example, for tariff changes)	26 districts	1,108 municipalities with elected councils; 75% of municipalities participate in 57 municipal unions with other municipalities
Libya	General Authority for Water Resources (GAWR)	GAWR	General Company for Water Supply and Wastewater (GCWW) Great Man-Made River Authority (GMRA) General Desalination Company (GDC)	CCWW GMRA GDC	GAWR	18 districts with 11 directorates per district	38 municipalities have elected councils

(table continues on next page)

Country or territory	Policy oversight water resources	Policy oversight water supply and sanitation	Bulk infrastructure development	Operation and maintenance	Water supply and sanitation regulator	Subnational deconcentrated units (admin 2)	Municipal units elected councils
Malta	Ministry for Environment, Energy and Enterprise	Energy & Water Agency	Water Services Corporation	Water Services Corporation with 1,149 employees	Regulator for Energy & Water Services	n.a.	68 local councils (54 in Malta and 14 in Gozo)
Morocco	Ministry of Equipment and Equipment and Water	Ministry of Equipment and Water	National Office of Electricity and Drinking Water (ONEE)	ONEE (state-owned enterprise), 13 public regional authorities; 4 private operators in Casablanca, Rabat, Tangiers, and Tetouan	Ministry of Equipment and Water	12 regions, each with an elected regional council	Elected representatives from 249 urban and 1,298 rural municipalities participate in municipal councils and are represented in provincial and regional councils
Oman	Ministry of Regional Municipalities, Environment and Water Resources	Ministry of Regional Municipalities, Environment and Water Resources	Oman Water and Wastewater Services Company; Some privately owned and operated desalination plants	Oman Water and Wastewater Services Company; Some privately owned and operated desalination plants	Public Authority for Electricity and Water	11 governorates and 60 provinces	11 municipal councils with elections
West Bank and Gaza	Palestinian Water Authority	Palestinian Water Authority	Palestinian Water Authority	300-plus utilities, service councils, municipalities, and village councils	Cabinet (for example, for tariff changes)	16 governorates; each governor is appointed by the president	119 municipalities; municipal mayor and council members are directly elected

(table continues on next page)

Country or territory	Policy oversight water resources	Policy oversight water supply and sanitation	Bulk infrastructure development	Operation and maintenance	Water supply and sanitation regulator	Subnational deconcentrated units (admin 2)	Municipal units elected councils
Qatar	Permanent Water Resources Committee	Permanent Water Resources Committee	Qatar General Electricity and Water Corporation (KAHRAMAA)	KAHRAMAA	Permanent Water Resources Committee	8 municipalities	Central Municipal Council with 29 elected members representing 29 constituencies from more than 242 regions
Saudi Arabia	Directorate of Water within the Ministry of Environment, Water & Agriculture (MEWA)	Directorate of Water within MEWA	Water Transmission and Technologies Company (WTTCO) Independent water and power projects	National Water Company (NWC) Private sector operates urban water and sanitation infrastructure MEWA operates and maintains irrigation and drainage projects, and distributes irrigation water	Electricity & Cogeneration Regulatory Authority (ECRA)	13 administrative regions and 118 governorates	285 municipal councils
Tunisia	Ministry of Agriculture, Water Resources and Fisheries General Directorate of Water Resources	National Water Council Hydraulic Public Domain Commission	National Office of Sanitation (ONAS) National Society of Water Distribution (SONEDE)	ONAS SONEDE	Ministry of Agriculture, Water Resources and Fisheries	24 governorates; each governor is appointed by the central government	262 municipalities governed by an elected council that elects its mayor from within its ranks

(table continues on next page)

Country or territory	Policy oversight water resources	Policy oversight water supply and sanitation	Bulk infrastructure development	Operation and maintenance	Water supply and sanitation regulator	Subnational deconcentrated units (admin 2)	Municipal units elected councils
United Arab Emirates	Ministry of Energy Ministry of Environment and Water	Water and Electricity Council	Emirates Water & Electricity Company (EWEC) Sharjah Electricity, Water & Gas Authority (SEWA) Etihad Water & Electricity (EtihadWE) Dubai Electricity & Water Authority (DEWA)	EtihadWE Abu Dhabi Water & Electricity Authority DEWA SEWA (water) Ministry of Environment and Water (sanitation)	Regulation and Supervision Bureau (Abu Dhabi), Abu Dhabi Department of Energy (DoE) Regulation and Supervision Bureau (Dubai) SEWA	7 emirates, in which water services are managed by public companies under 4 regions (Abu Dhabi, Dubai, Sharjah, and Northern Emirates)	n.a.
Yemen, Rep.	Ministry of Water and Environment National Water Resources Authority	Ministry of Water and Environment	Urban Water Project Management Unit	Local Water and Sanitation Corporations and their branches Autonomous utilities	Ministry of Water and Environment National Water	22 governorates; each governor is appointed by the president	n.a.

Source: World Bank.

Note: n.a. = not applicable; — = not available.

188 | The Economics of Water Scarcity in the Middle East and North Africa